Efficiency and Working of Regional Rural Banks in India

About the Authors

Jaynal Ud-din Ahmed (b. 1974) completed his Post Graduation (Accounting and Finance) with a first class and obtained Ph. D degree in Business Administration from Assam (Central) University, Silchar. He also achieved a Bachelor's degree in Law (LL.B.) and a Master's degree in Law (LL.M). He has completed successfully two projects—one UGC and the other from ICSSR, New Delhi. Dr. Ahmed has published research papers in international and referred journals besides ten books to his credit. He has presented research papers and has delivered lectures as resource person in various international, national and regional level seminars and conferences. He is devotedly involved in various socio-economic and research institutions. He is life member of various academic and professional bodies. He is the recipient of Best Thesis Award (2004) and Best Young Faculty Award (2005) for recognition of his teaching and research work. His areas of interest are finance, quantitative technique and north east economy, and he is actively engaged in teaching and research for over fourteen years. At present, he is holding the position of Professor and Head in the Department of Management at North-Eastern Hill University, Tura Campus, Meghalaya, India.

Govinda Prasad Bhandari (b. 1974) is currently working as an Assistant Professor in the School of Business, Kaziranga University, Jorhat, Assam. He has teaching experience of more than 12 years and taught in various reputed colleges and business schools of north-eastern region. He holds Master's degree in economics from Gauhati University, Guwahati and a Ph.D degree in Management from the North Eastern Hill University, Shillong, Meghalaya. He is a member of various academic and professional bodies. Dr. Bhandari has several publications in various national and international journals. He has also presented research papers in various international, national and regional level seminars, symposiums and conferences. His areas of interest are micro and macro economics, rural banking and north east economy. He is actively engaged in teaching post graduate students and research activities.

Efficiency and Working of Regional Rural Banks in India

An Implication

Jaynal Ud-din Ahmed
Govinda Prasad Bhandari

CONCEPT PUBLISHING COMPANY PVT. LTD.
NEW DELHI-110059

ISBN-13 : 978-93-5125-043-2

First Published 2015

Published and Printed by

Concept Since 1974

Concept Publishing Company Pvt. Ltd.
A/15-16, Commercial Block, Mohan Garden
New Delhi-110059 (India)
T: 25351460, 25351794, *F*: 091-11-25357109
E: publishing@conceptpub.com, W: www.conceptpub.com
Editorial Office: H-13, Bali Nagar, New Delhi-110 015, India.

Cataloging in Publication Data—*Courtesy:* D.K. Agencies (P) Ltd. <docinfo@dkagencies.com>

Ahmed, Jaynal Uddin, 1974-
Efficiency and working of regional rural banks in India : an implications / Jaynal Uddin Ahmed, Govind Prasad Bhandari.
p. cm.
Includes bibliographical references (p.) and index.
ISBN 9789351250432

1. Banks and banking—India—Meghalaya. 2. Rural credit—India—Meghalaya. 3. Regional economics—India—Meghalaya. 4. Meghalaya Rural Bank. I. Bhandari, Govind Prasad, 1974-, joint author. II. Title.

DDC 332.10954164 23

Dedicated

To

Prof. Sujit Sikidar

(*Gauhati University , Guwahati, Assam*)

Preface

The origin of the Regional Rural Banks (RRBs) can be traced to the need for a stronger institutional arrangement for providing rural credit. The various committees conceptualized the creation of RRBs in 1975 as a new set of regionally oriented rural banks with the professionalism and large resource base of commercial banks. Subsequently, the RRBs were set up through the promulgation of RRB Act of 1976. In the wake of introduction of financial sector reforms in 1991-92, the feasibility of RRBs emerged as the most crucial factor in deciding about the desired role due to their limited business flexibility with hardly any scope of diversification, smaller size of loans with higher exposure to risk-prone advances and professional inefficiency in financial deployment. To strengthen RRBs and to improve their performance many initiative have been taken by the Government of India (GoI) and Reserve Bank of India (RBI). As a part of comprehensive restructuring programme, recapitalization of RRBs was initiated, the branch licensing policy of RRBs has been liberalized. The branches of RRBs are allowed to undertake government business including foreign exchange business with prior approval. These banks have also been allowed to open extension counters and permitted to open off-site ATMs. As against the policy of opening a large number of branches in far flung rural areas, RRBs have been permitted to close down their unviable branches. In addition, RRBs were under compulsion to adhere to good governance practices and comply with prudential regulations.

At present, RRBs have a large branch network in the rural area forming around 43 per cent of the total rural branches of commercial banks. The rural orientation of RRBs is formidable with rural and semi-urban branches constituting over 97 per cent of their branch network. The growth in the branch network has enabled the RRBs to expand banking activities in the un-banked areas and mobilize rural savings. The mandate of promoting banking with a rural focus, however, would be an enduring phenomenon only when the financial health of the RRBs is sound. With built in restrictions on their operations, it is common to expect that fhe financial health of the RRBs itself would be a matter of concern.

In the light of the above, the present work is an attempt to diagnose the efficacy and working of RRBs in India. The book proposes to bring to light the efficiency and working of aspects Meghalaya Rural Bank (MRB) through comparative studies in Indian context. It is expected therefore that this book will provide intellectual motivation for many more studies on various aspects of working of RRBs and also serve as a basis for bank executives to frame guidelines for better performance of the banks in other RRBs similar to this.

The entire study has been displayed in seven chapters. The chapter breakup of the book includes *Introduction; Performance of Regional Rural Banks in India: Deposits, Advances and CD Ratios; Evaluation of Performance of Meghalaya Rural Bank; Profitability Analysis of Meghalaya Rural Bank; Productivity of Meghalaya Rural Bank: An Analysis; Loan Recovery and Asset Quality of Meghalaya Rural Bank: An Analytical Study and Findings and Suggestions*

On completion of the present work, we express our deep gratitude and indebtedness to Prof. E. D. Thomas, Pro-Vice-Chancellor, North Eastern Hill University, Tura Campus, Meghalaya, India and Prof. R. K. Raul, Department of Business Administration, Assam University for their inspiration in our academic hobby. We take this opportunity to offer our gratitude to Prof. S.S. Khanka, National Institute of Financial Management, Faridabad, Prof. Sujit Sikidar, Gauhati University, Guwahati, Prof. A.R.M. Rehman, Dibrugarh University and Prof Ranajit Chakraborty, University of Calcutta for their encouragement in our academic pursuit.

The work would not have been accomplished without the systematic support rendered by the officials of the Central Library, North Eastern Hill University, North Eastern Institute of Bank Management (NEIBM), NEC library, Shillong and many other libraries. We are particularly thankful to the branch managers and staffs of the banks for their generous help in procuring the needed data relating to the various aspects of bank's performance. We are also obliged to the family members of North Eastern Hill University and to our colleagues and students for encouraging us in our academic pursuit.

Finally, we are obliged to Mr. A. K. Mittal of Concept Publishing Company Pvt. Ltd. New Delhi for accepting the manuscript and bringing out this book in a well-designed manner.

Independence Day
The 15th August 2014

Jaynal U. Ahmed
Govinda P. Bhandari

Contents

List of Tables

1

Introduction

1. Introduction

Institutional credit system has been playing a vital role in the economic development of rural India specially to meet the need of the weaker sections viz, small and marginal farmers, agricultural labourers, rural artisans, small entrepreneurs. The history of rural credit in India dates back to 1904, when co-operative credit societies were established. These institutions, however, could not keep pace with the growing demand for rural credit. The establishment of the State Bank in 1955 and nationalization of major commercial banks in 1969 and 1980 made a significant impact on institutional rural finance. However, the high salary structure and urban orientation were supposed to be major hurdles in their efforts to accomplish the social objectives of rural financing. It was observed by the Banking Commission (1972)[1] that the co-operatives and commercial banks both were lacking in many ways and would not be able to fill the regional and functional gap in the rural credit system and that a more determined effort was needed in this direction. In such conditions, Banking Commission 1972 recommended the establishment of a chain of 'Rural Banks' in addition to rural branches of commercial banks.

Consequently on July (1975)[2], the Government of India appointed a Working Group on 'Rural Banks' under the Chairmanship of Mr. M. Narasimham to examine in depth the setting up of new rural banks as subsidiaries to public sector banks to cater the needs of the rural people. Considering the size and regional diversity, the Working Group viewed that no single pattern—be it commercial banks or co-operative credit institutions can be expected to meet all the emerging requirements in all areas. A degree of adaptation and improvisation is called for and the range of institutional alternative widened. It is in this context that the group recommended a new type of institution combined with the local feel and familiarity with the local problems which co-operatives poses, and the degree of business organization, ability to mobilize deposits, access to central markets and a modernize outlook which commercial banks have. The Government of India accepted the recommendations of the Working Group. Accordingly, RRB ordinance 1975 was promulgated which was later replaced by the Regional Rural Banks Act. On 2nd October 1975[3] five RRBs were established whose number has increased to as high as 196 and presently reduced to 82 numbers.

The main objectives of the establishment of RRBs were to boost up rural development, to provide credit facilities to small and marginal farmers, landless labourers and rural artisans, to inculcate banking habit in the rural masses; to help small entrepreneurs in the establishment of industries; to eradicate unemployment of rural areas. The authorized capital of RRBs was ₹ 1 crore and paid up capital was ₹ 25 crore which contributed by Central and State government and sponsor banks in the ratio of 50: 15: 35.

On June 23, (1977)[4], RBI appointed a committee under the Chairmanship of Prof M.L. Dantwala. The committee recommended that over a period of time the rural branches of commercial banks be totally replaced by the RRBs. Another Working Group known as Kelkar Committee (1984)[5] examined the basic problems of the RRBs and made recommendations to improve the viability, efficiency and managerial effectiveness of RRBs. For a general review of the agriculture credit delivery system with the objective of improving the quality of lending, the RBI in consultation with the Government and the World Bank constituted a senior expert group, under the Chairmanship of Prof A.M. Khusro in August (1986)[6]. The group analyzed the causes of the weaknesses of the RRBs and recommended the mergers of the RRBs with the sponsor's banks. However, the recommendations of the group were not accepted by the government Afterwards the Narasimham Committee (1991)[7] on financial sector reforms set up by the Government of India, gave recommendations on setting up of rural banking subsidiaries and mergers.

In 1994, Hon'ble Finance Minister in his budget speech remarked that out of 196 RRBs, 150 incurred losses during the last five years. The Committee on Restructuring of RRBs, 1994 (Bhandari Committee)[8] identified 49 RRBs for comprehensive restructuring. It recommended greater devolution of decision-making powers to the Boards of RRBs in the matter of business development and staffs. The option of liquidation again was mooted by the Committee on Revamping of RRBs, 1996 (Basu Committee)[9]. The Expert Group on RRBs in 1997 (Thingalaya Committee)[10] held that very weak RRBs should be viewed separately and possibility of their liquidation be recognized. They might be merged with neighbouring RRBs. The Expert Committee on Rural Credit, 2001 (Vyas Committee)[11] was of the view that the sponsor bank should ensure necessary autonomy for RRBs in their credit and other portfolio management system. Subsequently, another committee under the Chairmanship of Chalapathy Rao in 2002 (Chalapathy Rao Committee)[12] recommended that the entire system of RRBs may be consolidated while retaining the advantages of regional character of these institutions. As part of the process, some sponsor banks may be eased out. The sponsoring institutions may include other approved financial institutions as well, in addition to commercial banks. The Purwar Committee (2004)[13] recommended the amalgamation of RRBs on regional basis into six commercial banks one each for the Northern, Southern, Eastern, Western, Central and North-Eastern Region (NER). Thus one finds that a host of options have been suggested starting with vertical merger (with sponsor banks), horizontal merger (amongst RRBs operating in a particular region) to liquidation by different committees that have gone into the issue of financial viability and restructuring strategies for the RRBs.

Among the various official committees that were set up to review the situation and make policy recommendations on the future course of development of the RRBs, the Parliamentary Estimates Committee (2002-03)[14] suggested to undertake the shrinking credit delivery to the priority sector and the rural areas. From the year 2003-04, the RBI revised upwards the lending target for priority sector to 60 per cent of the total advances for the RRBs. The farm credit target for the RRBs at ₹ 11,900 crore for the fiscal year 2005-06 is 40 per cent higher than ₹ 8,500 crore target set during the fiscal year 2004-05. In reviewing the action taken by the RBI on the proposals of the

Estimates Committee (2002-03), the Estimates Committee in (2004-05)[15] found that no specific action has been taken on most of the major recommendations. RRBs have completely bypassed the subject while making policy recommendations. Instead attention is held by issues of ownership and capital requirements for the RRBs as necessary steps towards restructuring. As there was no capital to risk weighted asset ratio (CRAR) prescription for RRBs, the Internal Working Group on RRBs (RBI, 2005) has recommended that the RRBs be asked to maintain a CRAR of 5 per cent to begin with, and over time they may align themselves to the Basel I standards. The committee under the Chairmanship of A.V. Sardesai dealt with the issue of restructuring the RRBs (Sardesai Committee, 2005)[16]. The Sardesai Committee held that to improve the operational viability of RRBs and take advantage of the economies of scale, the route of merger/amalgamation of RRBs may be considered taking into account the views of the various stakeholders. Merger of RRBs with the sponsor bank is not provided in the RRB Act 1976. Mergers, even if allowed, would not be a desirable way of restructuring. The Committee was of the view that merging a RRB with its sponsor bank would go against the very spirit of setting up of RRBs as local entities and for providing credit primarily to weaker sections. Having discussed various options for restructuring, the Committee was of the view that a change in sponsor banks may, in some cases help in improving the performance of RRBs. A change in sponsorship may, *inter alia*; improve the competitiveness, work culture, management and efficiency of the concerned RRBs.

As per the financial statements of RRBs for the year 2006-07, 29 RRBs were having negative networth amounting to ₹ 1,857.05 crore. One of the budget proposals for 2007-08 was that RRBs having negative networth would be recapitalized in a phased manner. With a view to providing more business avenues and opportunities to RRBs for lending, RBI (2007)[17] has permitted them to participate in consortium lending, within the existing exposure limits, with their sponsor banks as also with other PSBs and Development Financial Institutions (DFIs). However, this is subject to the condition that the project to be financed is in the area of operation of the RRB concerned and guidance and appraisal of the project is provided by their sponsor bank. In order to review of the financial status of RRBs, a committee was constituted in September 2009 (Chakroborthy Committee)[18], under the Chairmanship of Dr. K.C. Chakrabarty, Deputy Governor, RBI to analyze the financials of the RRBs and to suggest measures including re-capitalization to bring the CRAR of RRBs to at least 9 per cent in a sustainable manner by 2012. The committee has *inter-alia* recommended the following.

- RRBs to have CRAR of atleast 7 per cent as on 31st March 2011 and at least 9 per cent from 31st March, 2012 onwards.
- The recapitalization requirement of ₹ 2200 crore for 40 RRBs out of the 82. This amount is to be released in two installments in 2010-11 and 2011-12. The remaining 42 RRBs will not require any capital and will be able to maintain CRAR at least 9 per cent as on 31st March, 2012.

Against this backdrop, a number of issues need empirical probing in the wake of aforesaid measures. Such as whether RRBs have been working efficiently? What changes have been undertaken in the focus and operation of banks? What factors drive the performance of RRBs? This situation calls for an investigation in the working of RRBs particularly at micro level. The present study is an attempt in this direction.

2. RRBs and Financial Sector Reforms

In the year 1989 for the first time, the conceptualization of the entire structure of Regional Rural Banks was challenged by the Agricultural Credit Review Committee (Khusro Committee)[19], which argued that banks have no justifiable cause for continuance and recommended their mergers with sponsor's banks. The Reserve Bank and Government of India quite prudently pushed the Khusro Committee Report under the sprinter without the public debate. With the onset of economic reform and liberalization of financial system, RRBs came under the scanner once again. The Committee on Financial System, (1991)[20] stressed the poor financial health of the RRBs to the exclusion of every other performance indicator. 172 of the 196 RRBs were recorded unprofitable with an aggregate loan recovery performance of 40.8 per cent (June 1993). The low equity base of these banks (paid up capital of ₹ 25 lakh) didn't cover for the loan losses of most RRBs. In the case of a few RRBs, there had also been an erosion of public deposits, besides capital. In order to impart viability to the operations of RRBs, the Narasimham Committee suggested that the RRBs should be permitted to engage in all types of banking business and should not be forced to restrict their operations to the target groups, a proposal which was readily accepted. This recommendation marked a major turning point in the functioning of RRBs. For the time being though, the suggestion of mergers of the RRBs with their sponsor bank, which the Committee on Financial Systems had put forth in a slightly modified form sponsor banks might decide whether to retain the identities of sponsored RRBs or to merge them with rural subsidiaries of commercial banks to be set up on the recommendation of the committee was put on hold.

In the ensuing years, reforms of the RRBs largely followed the same format as that of the commercial banks, irrespective of the fact that their very role in the society required a special status and a different set of policies. Since, the early 1990s, there was a complete freeze on recruitment of new staff in the RRBs. As a part of comprehensive restructuring programme, recapitalization of the RRBs was initiated in the year 1994-95, a process which continued till 1999-2000 and covered 187 RRBs with aggregate financial support of ₹ 2188.44 crore from the stakeholders. Simultaneously, prudential norms on income-recognition, asset classification and provisioning for loan-losses following customary banking benchmarks were introduced. From 1996-97 there has been a tendency to allow greater role and larger operational responsibilities to sponsor banks in the management of RRBs.

3. Review of Literature

A wide body of literature already exist dealing with the various aspects of working of RRBs both in India and abroad. A brief review of these studies is highlighted in the following paragraph to identify the significance of the present study.

RRBs though operate with a rural focus are primarily scheduled commercial banks with a commercial orientation. The literature probing into factors influencing performance of banks recognizes two broad sets of factors, i.e., internal factors and factors external to the bank. The internal determinants originate from the balance sheets and/or profit and loss accounts of the bank concerned and are often termed as micro or bank specific determinants of profitability. The external determinants are systemic forces that reflect the economic environment which conditions the operation and performance of financial institutions. A number of explanatory variables have been suggested in the literature for both the internal and external determinants. Given the nature of banking business, the need for risk management is of crucial importance for a bank's financial health. Risk management is a reflection of the quality of the assets with a bank and availability of liquidity with it. During periods of uncertainty and economic slow down, banks may prefer a more diversified portfolio to avoid adverse selection and may also raise their liquid holdings in order to reduce risk. In this context, both credit and liquidity risk assumes great importance.

The literature provides mixed evidence on the impact of liquidity on profitability. Bourke (1989)[21] in contrast, reports an opposite result. One possible reason for the conflicting findings may be the different elasticity of demand for loans in the samples used in the studies. Credit risk is found to have a negative impact on profitability (Miller and Noulas, 1997)[22]. This result may be explained by taking into account the fact that more the financial institutions are exposed to high risk loans; the higher is the accumulation of unpaid loans implying that these loan losses have produced lower returns to many commercial banks (Athanasoglou, Brissimis and Delis, 2005)[23]. Some of the other internal determinants found in the literature are funds source management and funds use management (Haslem, 1968)[24], capital and liquidity ratios, the credit-deposit ratio and loan loss expenses (Bell and Mushy, 1969)[25], (Kwast and Rose, 1982)[26]. Expense management, a correlate of efficient management is another very important determinant of bank's profitability. There has been an extensive literature based on the idea that an expenses-related variable should be included in the cost part of a standard microeconomic profit function. In this context, Molyneux and Thornton (1992)[27] found that better quality management and profitability go hand in hand. As far as (the external determinants of bank profitability are concerned the literature distinguishes between control variables that describe the macroeconomic environment, such as inflation, interest rates and cyclical output, and variables that represent market characteristics.

The most frequently used macroeconomic control variables are the inflation rate, the long-term interest rate and/or the growth rate of money supply. Revell (1979)[28] introduced the issue of the relationship between bank profitability and inflation. He notes that the effect of inflation on bank profitability depends on whether banks' wages and other operating expenses increase at a faster pace than inflation. Perry (1992)[29] in a similar vein contends that the extent to which inflation affects bank profitability depends on whether inflation expectations are fully anticipated. The influence arising from ownership status of a bank on its profitability is another much debated and frequently visited issue in the literature. The proposition that privately owned institutions are more profitable, however, has mixed empirical evidence in favour of it. For instance, while Short (1979)[30] provides cross-country evidence of a strong negative relationship between government ownership and bank profitability, Barth *et al.* (2004)[31] claimed that government ownership of banks is indeed negatively correlated with bank efficiency.

The literature on RRBs recognizes a host of reasons responsible for their poor financial health. According to the Narasimham Committee, RRBs have low earning capacity. They have not been able to earn much profit in view of their policy of restricting their operations to target groups. The recovery position of RRBs is not satisfactory. There are a large number of defaulters. Their cost of operation has been high on account of the increase in the salary scales of the employees in line with the salary structure of the employees of commercial banks. In most cases, these banks followed the same methods of operation and procedures as followed by commercial banks. Therefore, these procedures have not found favour with the rural masses. In many cases, banks have not been located at the right place. For instance, the sponsoring banks are also running their branches in the same areas where RRBs are operating. The issue whether location matters for the performance has been addressed in some detail by Malhotra (2002)[32]. Considering 22 different parameters that impact on the functioning of RRBs for the year 2000, Malhotra asserted that geographical location of RRBs is not the limiting factor for their performance. He further finds that 'it is the specific nourishment which each RRB receives from its sponsor bank, is cardinal to its performance'. In other words, the umbilical cord had its effect on the performance of RRBs. The limitation of the study is that the financial health of the sponsor bank was not considered directly to infer about the umbilical cord hypothesis. Banking Enquiry Commission (1972)[33] reviewed bank operating methods and procedures and made recommendations for improving and modernizing operating methods and procedures, particularly relating to customers service, credit procedures and internal control system. The commission further observed that present methods of working out branch profitability are not appropriate. Considering the need of an integrated cost and financial reporting system it suggested the use of certain ratios for the measurement of operational efficiency of branches.

Singh (1979)[34] examined the relationship between cost of bank credit and prices and concluded that high rates of interest produces in general a significant tender to the prices to raise more and the percentage spread of the difference between interest received and interest paid has been decreasing for the banks. Prasad (1985)[35] studied the role of SBI in rural development. He has covered various aspects of its functioning and recommended further simplification of security norms, improvement in reporting system and computerization of operation, etc. The decline in profitability has originated both from factors of income and of expenditure of banking industry. In this context, the Committee on Financial System (1991)[36] recommended that to impart viability of banks, they should be permitted to engage in all types of banking business and should not be forced to restrict their operations to the target groups. This recommendation marked a major turning point in the functioning of RRBs. Basu (1991)[37] studied on performance of the RRBs. He focused on financial viability, staff resources, asset management etc. He suggested for proper efficiency, management of resources and improvement of customer quality.

The Narasimham Committee (1998)[38] emphasized that 'while discharging their functions as purveyors of rural credit and mobilizes of rural savings, RRBs should not ignore the importance of financial viability and operational efficiency. The productivity, profitability and solvency of the RRBs must be maintained and sustained to enable them to function as an effective and efficient institution of rural credit.

Naidu ((2001)[39] viewed that until and unless the RRBs functionaries serve the rural poor with urge and devotion, mere cosmetic changes would pay little in revamping the present scenario. Sikidar (1992)[40] in his study on the rise of banking for rural development has critically evaluated one side of bank finance in the development of hill area in the north east. He has suggested for a practical approach towards recovery of bank outstanding from the tribal population in hill areas. Tarapore (1994)[41] observed that there is a reasonable spread between cost of raising fund and the return of development of funds. He suggested that rural financial agencies like RRBs should not hesitate to finance large projects in rural areas strictly on commercial basis. Rangarajan (1996)[42] in a study on role of rural credit highlighted that the drive of Indian public policy towards rural credit to ensure that sufficient and timely credit at reasonable rates of interest. The study suggested that credit should be made available to a large segment of rural population to the possible extent. Kaushik (1999)[43] in his study on credit productivity of RRB has found that an inverse relationship between credit assets and credit productivity has been establish due to low income generation, lack of appropriate skills and infrastructural facilities. He suggested that RRBs should supply adequate credit along with skill and training facilities to the beneficiaries. Sinha *et al.* (2003)[44] in a field study of 5 RRBs has found that non-priority sector advances increased sharply in the second-half of the 1990s for all the sample banks. The study recommended for priority sector advances by RRBs for the benefit of low income group clients. Uddin (2003)[45] in his study identified the problems like defective control, poor staffing, lack of trained staff, rigid policies, inefficient management etc. In the context of institutional dimension, Nitin and Throat (2004)[46] observed that efforts taken during the reform era have limited impact because the reform process change in institutional dimension has not been given adequate importance. Few efforts were made to redesign the perverse institutional arrangements that gave rise to incompatible incentive structures for key stakeholders, such as political leaders, policy makers, stockholders, bank staff, and clients and suggested to bring change further to increase productivity of the bank.

Das and Ghosh (2004-05)[47] in their examining study on excess capacity in RRBs focuses on regional rural banks because, if excess capacity exists in banking, it is in this setting where it is likely to be most prominently manifested. If the demand for traditional banking activities declines, commercial banks are likely to have greater flexibility to rationalize their operations and diversify their activities than RRBs with limited option to rationalize branches. The study develops indicators of potential excess capacity in the RRB segment and illustrates its application to individual banking firms. Bose (2005)[48] concluded that the inception and expansion phase (1976-1990) saw rapid growth of the RRBs activities; the reform phase (1991-2002/3) raised the profitability of these banks at the cost of massive rural disintermediation, particularly of the targeted borrower categories; and the most recent phase of stock taking and perhaps some repositioning to strike a balance in the conundrum of `viability versus outreach'. Batra and Dangwal (2005)[49] observed a better performance of RRBs after the introduction of prudential norms in 1996-97 and recommended for further improving the efficiency in the present competitive era. Rammohan and Roy (2004)[50] compared the performance of banks using revenue maximization efficiency approach and found that Indian banks did not have much freedom in trimming costs especially the cost of labour. Chatterjee and Sinha (2006)[51] estimated efficiency of banks taking net interest income, non-interest income and loan as output indicators and branches and borrowed capital as inputs. Their study observed an improvement of bank's performance in Indian context. Pati (2005)[52] studied the economic viability of RRBs in general and Subansiri Gaonlia Bank (SGB) of Assam in particular. He found that the banks are facing the problem of loan recovery and fresh accretion in NPAs, lower profitability and the management problem. His study suggested that proper management of spread and burden will improve the performance of the bank. Reddy (2006)[53] examined total factor productivity technical and scale efficiency changes in regional rural banks by using data from 192 banks for the period 1996 to 2002. It observed that total factor productivity growth of rural banks was higher than the service provision during liberalization. Banks located in economically developed as well as low banking density regions exhibited significantly higher productivity growth. It also observed that parent PSBs have no influence on the efficiency and productivity growth of rural banks.

Tasi (2006)[54] studied the role of RRBs in general and Arunachal Pradesh Rural Bank in particular. The study dealt with the performance evaluation of Arunachal Pradesh Rural Bank (APRB) for the economic development of the state. The study has ignored the technical parameters of banks rather it has assessed role of RRBs in economic development in general. The financial viability and possible restructuring of RRBs was studied by Misra (2006)[55]. He has categorized RRBs into profit making and loss making. He recommended sponsor bank for the loss making RRBs could be given time to improve the performance. The paper has also enquired the factors that influence the performance of RRBs. Hadi and Bagchi (2006)[56] assessed the performance of RRBs in India in general and in West Bengal in particular. The study reviewed the progress of the RRBs in West Bengal in terms of expansion of branches, credit expansion and deposit mobilization since inception till the end of June 2001. The analysis revealed that RRBs have been more or less successful in expanding outreach of institutional credit in rural areas. However, it has identified certain coherent causes of unsatisfactory state of recovery performance and loan repayment in the case of selected branches and beneficiaries of Murshidabad Gramin Bank. Shivappa (2007)[57] in a study examined the growth in advances, deposits and financial performance of the RRBs. The study covered the RRBs as a whole; discussed mostly theoretical issues rather than any analytical depth. Sadakkadulla (2007)[58] observed that with the passage of three decades, the RRBs are now looked upon with hope for rejuvenating the rural India. They have been empowered to make their operations viable. One of the recent policy interventions in this regard is the Constitution of Empowered Committees (EC) of RRBs to provide an institutionalized mechanism to resolve all operational and regulatory problems of RRBs then and there. The study looks at role of the Empowered Committees, particularly in making RRBs as a tool to fill the gap in rural development.

In a study, Banos (2007)[59] by using panel data for the period 1993 to 2005 from 16 regions of the Philippines investigated whether the resource allocation efficiency of Philippine rural banks resulting from the quantity and quality of banking intermediation activities affects regional economic growth. To explore this relationship, four measures of resource allocation efficiency were alternatively tested employing pooled generalized least squares (EGLS) estimation. The findings suggest that Philippine rural banks need to make allocative adjustments in the areas of branch presence, operational efficiency and credit participation. These results lend support to government efforts to strengthen the rural banking sector and to increase the volume of investments in the regions. The important policy implications of these findings include the need to enhance confidence in the Philippine rural banking system, to encourage savings in regional rural banks, and to ensure efficient transfer of resources from savers to investors. Khankhoje and Sathye (2008)[60] investigated the implication of restructuring strategies on the efficiency of RRBs with the help of DEA. The study considered the variables like interest income and non-interest income as outputs and interest expenses and non-interest expenses as inputs. The analysis found that efficiency of rural banks has significantly improved after restructuring and hence it recommended its continuance. Kumar (2008)[61] in a case study on the amalgamation of RRBs highlighted that amalgamation became a death blow to the credit starved rural poor, most of whom are small and marginal farmers, agricultural and landless labourers, and artisans. The paper recommended for an immediate de-amalgamation of RRBs in the interest of the vast majority of the rural poor. Dhaliwal, Kaur and Arora (2009)[62] in their study pointed out that Regional Rural Banks (RRBs) were established in India in 1975 essentially for taking banking to the doorstep of rural masses, particularly in areas without banking facilities. RRBs were expected to operate as State sponsored, region based and rural-oriented commercial banks. RRBs were expected to mobilize resources from rural areas and play a significant role in developing agriculture and rural economy by deploying mobilized resources in rural sectors for the needy not conversed by other formal credit institutions. Singh and Singh (2009)[63] in their paper examined the recovery performance of Manipur Rural Bank. The study observed that the repayment of loans mainly depends on proper utilization of the loan amount, supply of quality assets, generation of sufficient income from schemes, availability of infrastructural and marketing, facilities, willingness to repay, continuous supervision and follow-up visits etc. Ibrahim (2010)[64] made a study on the performance evaluation of Regional Rural Banks in India investigated whether the merger/amalgamation of Regional

Rural Banks in India, undertaken in 2005-06 has helped to improve their performance. Several committees have also emphasized the need to improve the performance of these banks which play an important role in the rural credit market in India. The study finds and concludes that performance of rural banks in India has significantly improved after amalgamation process which has been initiated by the Government of India.

Bhaskar (2011)[65] in his study concludes that distribution of RRBs is not same in India. RRBs have to be repositioned and carry out their entrusted responsibility of meeting the credit requirement in rural sector, their various constraining factor such as low credit off take, small ticket business, low recovery rate and high employee cost. In order to reposition RRBs loss making RRBs should take step for enhancing productive by improving the skill and performance of their employees by better and specialized training in the areas of banking and finance, IT, management, etc. Reddy and Prasad (2011)[66] in his evaluative study observed that these banks penetrate every corner of the country and have been extending a helping hand in the growth of the economy. Despite the RRBs journeyed over three decades, they have achieved performance to the expected level quantitatively but not turning towards sound financial management and productivity. He made an attempt to discuss the financial performance of selected regional rural banks during post reorganization period by using the technique of CAMEL Model. Again Kumar and Sharma (2011)[67] on the comparative study of Himachal Gramin Bank and Parvatiya Gramin Bank found that the Parvatiya Gramin Bank is more conservative as compared to the Himachal Gramin Bank with regard to NPAs' management. It is because NPAs to total assets ratio for the Parvatiya Gramin Bank has decreased during the last few years of the study. This may be due to better management of NPAs by the bank and the use of better methods of loan recovery.

Whatever, studies have emerged on the topic, they have primarily relied on exploratory analysis done for a particular year or on a group of RRBs to draw inferences. This kind of an approach has a serious limitation that the findings are guided by the choice of the year of analysis. To overcome this problem, one need to consider, as attempted in this proposal, reasonably long period for analysis where extreme observations would be evened out so that one may get results that are more dependable.

4. Research Problem

RRBs have been in existence for around three and half decades in the Indian financial scene. The inception of RRBs can be seen as a unique experiment as well as experience in improving the efficacy of rural credit delivery mechanism in India. With joint share holding by Central Government, the concerned State Government and the sponsoring bank, an effort was made to integrate commercial banking within the broad policy thrust towards social banking keeping in view the local peculiarities. The genesis of the RRBs can be traced to the need for a stronger institutional arrangement for providing rural credit. The Narasimham Committee conceptualized the creation of RRBs in 1975 as a new set of regionally oriented rural banks, which would combine the local feel and familiarity of rural problems characteristic of cooperatives with the professionalism and large resource base of commercial banks. Subsequently, the RRBs were set up through the promulgation of RRB Act of 1976.

RRBs were supposed to evolve as specialized rural financial institutions for developing the rural economy by providing credit to small and marginal farmers, agricultural labourers, artisans and small entrepreneurs. Over the years, the RRBs, which are often viewed as the small man's bank, have taken deep roots and have become a sort of inseparable part of the rural credit structure. They have played a key role in rural institutional financing in terms of geographical coverage, clientele outreach and business volume as also contribution to development of the rural economy. A remarkable feature of their performance over the past three decades has been the massive expansion of their retail network in rural areas. From a modest beginning of 6 RRBs with 17 branches covering 12 districts in December 1975, the numbers have grown into 196 RRBs with 14,446 branches working in 518 districts across the country in March 2004. Government of India initiated the process of structural consolidation of RRBs by amalgamating RRBs sponsored by the same bank within a State as per the recommendations of the Vyas Committee (2004)[68]. The amalgamated RRBs were expected to provide better customer service due to better infrastructure, computerization of branches, pooling of experienced work force, common publicity marketing efforts, etc. and also derive the benefits of at large area of operation, enhanced credit exposure limits and more diverse banking activities. As a result of the amalgamation, the number of RRBs was reduced from 196 to 133 as on March, 2006 and further to 82 RRBs with 15,658 branches operating in 621 districts as on March 2011. Thus, under the amalgamation process, a number of RRBs have been amalgamated but the branches have increased. The credit deposit ratio of RRBs has increased from 46.3 per cent in March 2004 to 59.6 per cent in March 2011 (RBI, 2010-11)[69].

RRBs have a large branch network in the rural area forming around 43 per cent of the total rural branches of commercial banks. The rural orientation of RRBs is formidable with rural and semi-urban branches constituting over 97 per cent of their branch network. The growth in the branch network has enabled the RRBs to expand banking activities in the un-banked areas and mobilize rural savings. The mandate of promoting banking with a rural focus, however, would be an enduring phenomenon only when the financial health of the RRBs is sound. With built in restrictions on their operations, it is common to expect that the financial health of the RRBs itself would be a matter of concern. As regards to their financial status, during the year 2003-04, 163 RRBs earned profits amounting to ₹ 953 crore while 33 RRBs incurred losses to the tune of ₹ 184 crore. The aggregate income of RRBs during 2007-08 grew by 20 per cent on account of higher interest as well as non-interest income. The growth in expenditure during the year was relatively subdued. As a result, profitability of RRBs improved significantly. RRBs earned a net profit of ₹ 1374 crore in March 2008 as compared to ₹ 625 crore in previous year. (Out of 90 RRBs, 82 RRBs earned a combined profit of ₹ 1429 crore whereas 8 RRBs incurred a combined loss of ₹ 55 crore during 2007-08). The branch productivity of RRBs has been increased from ₹ 7.71 crore in March 2006 to ₹ 10.7 crore in March 2008. Further more, non-performing assets (NPAs) of the RRBs in absolute terms stood at ₹ 3,299 crore as on March 2004. The percentage of net NPAs was 8.51 per cent during the year ending March 2004 reduced to 1.80 per cent in March 2010 (2010)[70].

Given the multi-agency share holding and various restructuring strategies of RRBs introduced from time to time, the bank under severe pressure to improve their foundation with a view to attain competitiveness. Given the attention at the policy level to restructure the RRBs, it is necessary that the functioning of RRBs be analyzed separately than the RRBs as a whole so that it helps in policy formulation. The present study is an attempt to enquire into such factors that influence the working of the RRBs in general and MRB in particular.

5. Meghalaya Rural Bank: A Profile

Meghalaya Rural Bank (MRB) is the only RRB (sponsored by State Bank of India) operating in 6 districts out of 7 districts of Meghalaya as on March 2010. The bank was established on 29th December 1981 under the RRBs Act 1976 as a joint undertaking of Government of India, the Government of Meghalaya and State Bank of India with the share capital at the ratio of 50: 15: 35. Prior to 1st May 2007 the name of this RRB was 'Ka Bank Nonkyndong Ri Khasi Jaintia'. As per power conferred by sub-section (1) Section (3) of the RRB Act 1976 (21 of 1976) Department of Economic Affairs (Banking Division), Ministry of Finance, Government of India, in its notification dated 1st May 2007 substituted the name "Ka Bank Nonkyndong Ri Khasi Jaintia" as "Meghalaya Rural Bank". The MRB is operating in 6 districts with 58 branches as on March 2011. It is the 2nd largest bank in Meghalaya in terms of branches. The network of MRB is presented in Table 1.1 and Table 1.2.

Table 1.1: Network of Meghalaya Rural Bank as on March 2011

Sl. No	*Districts*	*No. of Branches*
1.	East Khasi Hills District	25
2.	West Khasi Hills District	14
3.	Jaintia Hills District	13
4.	RiBhoi District	4
5.	East Garo Hills District	1
6.	West Garo Hills District	1
7.	South Garo Hills District	0
	Total	**58**

Table 1.1 depicts that as on 2010-11, the East Khasi Hill constituted 25 number of branches, West Khasi Hills 14 branches, Jaintia Hills 13, Ri Bhoi district 4, West Garo Hill and East Garo Hill districts are having 1 branches in each district. The branch expansion of MRB in Garo Hills district of Meghalaya is very negligible because the MRB has started functioning in West Garo Hill from 31.03.2008 and East Garo Hill district from 09.01.2009 with only one branch in each district.

Table 1.2: Population Group-wise Branch Network of Meghalaya Rural Bank

(Number of branches)

Year	Rural	Semi urban	Urban	Total
2000-01	43	3	5	51
2001-02	42	7	2	51
2002-03	42	7	2	51
2003-04	42	7	2	51
2004-05	42	7	2	51
2005-06	42	7	2	51
2006-07	42	7	2	51
2007-08	42	8	2	52
2008-09	42	9	3	54
2009-10	42	10	3	55
2010-11	43	12	3	58

Source: Annual Report of Meghalaya Rural Bank, Various Issues

It is also observed that more number of branches is expanded in rural areas than the semi-urban or urban areas except in East and West Garo Hill districts as revealed from Table 1.2.

As on March 2008, the total deposit mobilized ₹ 304 crore and advances channeled of ₹ 95 crore by MRB. Though credit deposit ratio of MRB has been increased i.e., from 24.7 per cent in March 2004 to 29.4 per cent in March 2007. The same is far lower than the ratio of RRBs as a whole. The bank has shown profit consistently for the last 15 years, the net figure posted ₹ 3.4 crore in March 2007. The productivity per branch has increased from 5.3 crore in March 2005 to ₹ 7.1 crore in March 2008. The percentage of net NPA to advances increased from 6.8 in March 2006 to 7.7 in March 2008. The aforesaid brief profile shows some disagreement in the performance of MRB with the RRBs of the country as a whole. Hence, there is the necessity of further enquiry on the working of the bank.

6. Need of the Study

In the wake of introduction of financial sector reforms in 1991-92, the feasibility of RRBs emerged as the most crucial factor in deciding about the desired role due to their limited business flexibility with hardly any scope of diversification, smaller size of loans with higher exposure to risk-prone advances and professional inefficiency in financial deployment. To strengthen RRBs and to improve their performance many initiative have been taken by the Government and Reserve Bank of India. As a part of comprehensive restructuring programme, recapitalization of RRBs was initiated in the year 1994-95. The process continued till 1999 and covered 187 RRBs with an aggregate financial support of ₹ 2,188.44 crore from the shareholders viz, Government of India, State Governments and sponsors banks. Further the branch licensing policy of RRBs has been liberalized. Under the new norms, empowered committees at the regional offices of RBI are clear about the RRB's application to open new branches. The branches of RRBs may undertake govt. business including conducting foreign exchange business with prior approval of the government authority and RBI. These banks have also been allowed to open extension counters and permitted to open off-site ATMs. As against the policy of opening a large number of branches in far flung rural areas, RRBs have been permitted to close down their unviable branches. As per Mid-Term Review of Annual Policy statement for 2004-05, RRBs have to adhere to good governance practices and comply with prudential regulations. In view of their importance as providers of rural credit, the union budget 2004-05, emphasized that the sponsor banks would be accountable for the performance of their RRBs. As per the financial statements of RRBs for the year 2006-07, 29 RRBs are having negative networth amounting to ₹ 1,857.05 crore. One of the budget proposals for 2007-08 was that RRBs having negative networth would be recapitalized in a phased manner. The process of recapitalization has already commenced and its completion would make all RRBs comply with the necessary prescribed minimum capital requirements. As a first step to bring RRBs to international capital adequacy standards, all RRBs have been advised to disclose their Capital to Risk Weighted Assets Ratio (CRAR) as on March 31, 2008 in their balance sheets.

It is, therefore, clear that RRBs have moved far away from the conditions and compulsions that were prevailing at the time of RRBs in 1975. Hence, an evaluation in respect of performance of RRBs is extremely relevant in the present scenario.

7. Objectives of the Study

The main objective of the proposed study is to evaluate the performance of RRBs in general and Meghalaya Rural Bank in particular over the period under consideration. The specific objectives of the study are:

1. To study the growth performance of MRB in terms of branch expansion, deposit mobilization, credit channelization, C/D ratio in the context of RRB as a whole.
2. To examine the efficiency in respect of profitability and productivity of MRB on the basis of selected parameters.
3. To study the asset quality and the level of NPAs of MRB over the years.

8. Hypotheses of the Study

The following hypotheses have been framed to meet the objectives of the proposed study.

1. MRB has made special dent in the banking operation in Meghalaya over the years.
2. Despite the onslaught of openness measures adopted in banking sector, MRB is performing efficiently.

9. Research Methodology

(a) Research Population and Data Collections

The RRBs operating in the State of Meghalaya has been considered as research population of the proposed study. As on March 2011, there is only one RRB i.e., Meghalaya Rural Bank with 58 numbers of branches is operating in six districts of Meghalaya (details are shown in Table 1.1 and Table 1.2). For the purpose of the proposed study, we have considered all the branches particularly for the analysis of working and efficiency of the bank. The sources of data collection are financial statements compiled by the head office of Meghalaya Rural Banks, RBI Bulletin, RBI Annual Reports, RBI Trend and Progress of Banking in India, Annual Reports of Meghalaya Rural Bank, Annual Reports of NABARD, Directorate of Economics and Statistics, various reports, surveys, published and unpublished research papers and dissertations.

(b) Variables Selected

To assess the growth performance of the bank, we have taken the variables like total deposits, total advances, and credit deposit ratio. The variables like net profit, paid up capital plus retained earnings, advances outstanding, loan recovered, etc. have been considered for measuring the efficiency of bank. The variables includes interest earned, interest paid, manpower expenses, non-interest income, spread, burden, cost responsiveness, return on working fund, volume of business (deposit plus advances), labour productivity and branch productivity for assessing the profitability and productivity of banks. To assess the nature of unbridled virus of NPAs of bank, the variables considered are net and gross NPA, total standard asset, doubtful and loss asset. The variables for identifying the determinants of NPAs includes priority sector lending, capital adequacy ratio, net NPA to net advances, branch expansion and credit deposit ratio.

(c) Research Tools and Techniques

A wide range of financial ratio and statistical techniques have been used to test the proposed hypotheses of the study. The statistical techniques viz, correlation co- efficient, regression analysis, skewness, measure of central tendency and dispersion have been used. The parametric test i.e., '*t*' test, has been considered to test significance level in appropriate cases. The most popularly used financial ratios has been used which include return on assets, return on equity, net profit per employee, liquid asset ratio, advances to total assets, interest income, non-interest income, spread, burden, slippage ratio (the ratio of fresh NPA added during the year to standard loan assets at the beginning of the year), NPA accretion ratio (the total NPA added during the year to total NPA reduce during the year) and so on.

The growth performance of banks has been tested with compound annual growth rate analysis. The correlation coefficient between incremental deposits and incremental advances has been used to find out the nature of growth of deposit as well as credit. Besides this, whether banks are deploying credit at the same rate what they have mobilized, researcher visited the branch managers of the bank for collecting necessary information and has discussed with them the present position, weaknesses, the problem being faced by them and future role of branch for the development of the operational area. The correlation matrix analysis has been employed to assess the relationship between advances and NPAs along-with its components viz, sub-standard assets, doubtful assets and loss assets. The regression models have also been fitted in appropriate places.

10. Period Coverage

The period coverage for the proposed study is 11 years from 2000-01 to 2010-11, to analyze the position of RRBs in the context of global financial sector recession in 2000-01. The impact of restructuring strategies adopted on RRBs performance has been studied for the aforesaid time period. The data prior to the period has also been considered in a few cases in order to make some sort of comparison and in the circumstances where historical information is required.

11. Chapter Plan

The entire study has been displayed as per the following chapter break up.

1. Chapter-I: Introduction.
2. Chapter-2: Performance of Regional Rural Banks in India: Deposits, Advances and CD Ratios.
3. Chapter-3: Evaluation of Performance of Meghalaya Rural Bank.
4. Chapter-4: Profitability Analysis of Meghalaya Rural Bank.
5. Chapter-5: Productivity of Meghalaya Rural Bank: An Analysis.

6. Chapter-6: Loan Recovery and Asset Quality of Meghalaya Rural bank: An Analytical Study.
7. Chapter-7: Findings and Suggestions.

12. Limitations of the Study

The data relating to the performance and working of rural banks is mostly based on secondary sources. The unavoidable limitations inherent with the data like year-wise inconsistent data are bound to exist. For the purpose of analysis of the data, some sort of uniformity and adjustments have been made.

Notes

1. Report of the Banking Enquiry Commission, New Delhi, 1972, NABARD, Annual Report.
2. Government of India (1975); "Report of the Committee on Rural Banks", New Delhi.
3. Originally established by an ordinance in September 1975, these banks are governed by the RRB Act which was passed in 1976, and amended in 1987.
4. RBI (1978); Report of the Committee on Rural Banks (Dantwala Committee, 1978).
5. RBI (1984); Report of the Working Group on Regional Rural Banks (Kelkar Committee, 1984).
6. RBI (1986); "Report of the Expert Group" (Khusro Committee).
7. Government of India (1991); "Report of the Committee on Financial System 1991 (Narasimham Committee)", Ministry of Finance, p. 54.
8. RBI Report of the Committee on Restructuring of RRBs (Bhandari Committee, 1994).
9. RBI (1996); Report of Committee on Revamping of RRBs (Basu Committee).
10. RBI, (1997); "Report of the Expert Group on Regional Rural Banks" (Thingalaya Committee).
11. RBI (2004); "Report of the Advisory Committee on Flow of Credit to Agriculture and Related Activities From the Banking System". (Vyas Committee II) URL: (www.rbi.org. in, date 20/6/2009).
12. Government of India, (June 2002); "Report of the Working Group to Suggest—Amendments in the Regional Rural Banks Act, 1976" (Chalapathy Rao Committee).

13. RBI (2004); "Group of CMDs of Select Public Sector Banks", 2004 (Purwar Committee).
14. The Estimates Committee, (2002-03); "Regional Rural Banks" Sixteenth Report on the Ministry of Finance and Company Affairs, Department of Economic Affairs, Banking Division. (Chairman: Prof. Umma Reddy Venkateswarlu).
15. GoI The Estimates Committee (2004-05); Report of the Review of Action taken by Government on the recommendations contained in the Sixteenth Report of Estimates Committee (Thirteenth Lok Sabha), the Ministry of Finance and Company Affairs (Department of Economic Affairs-Banking Division).
16. RBI (2005); "Report of the Internal Working Group on RRBs", Chairman: A.V. Sardesai, Mumbai. URL: (www.rbi.org.in), visited 24/5/2010.
17. RBI (2007); "Task Force on Empowering RRB Boards for Operational Efficiency".
18. Report of the Committee on Financials of RRBs (Chakroborthy Committee), May 2010, http://taxguru.in/rbi/recapitalization-of-regional-rural-banks-rrbs-to-improve-their-capital-to-risk - weighted-assets-ratio-crar.html
19. Khusro Committee (1989); "Report of Agricultural Credit Review Committee", RBI Publication, Mumbai.
20. Report of the Committee on Financial System (Narasimham Committee, 1991), Ministry of Finance.
21. Bourke, P. (1989); "Concentration and other Determinants of Bank Profitability in Europe, North America and Australia", *Journal of Banking and Finance*, Vol. 13, pp. 65-79.
22. Miller, S.M., Noulas, A.G. (1997); 'Portfolio Mix and Large-bank Profitability in the USA", *Applied Economics*, 29 (4), pp. 505-512.
23. Athanasoglou, P.P., Brissimis, S.N. and Delis, M.D. (2005); "Bank-Specific, Industry—Specific and Macroeconomic Determinants of Bank Profitability", *Bank of Greece Working Paper No. 25*.
24. Haslem, J. (1968); "A Statistical Analysis of the Relative Profitability of Commercial Banks", *Journal of Finance*, Vol. 23, pp. 167-176.
25. Bell, F.W. and Nell, Mushy (1969); "Impact of Market Structure on the Price of a Commercial Banking Service", *The Review of Economics and Statistics* (May).
26. Kwast, Myron L. and John T. Rose (1982); "Pricing, Operating Efficiency and Profitability Among Large Commercial Banks", *Journal of Banking and Finance*, Vol. 6.
27. Molyneux, P., Thornton, J. (1992); "Determinants of European Bank

profitability: A Note", *Journal of Banking and Finance,* Vol. 16, pp. 1173-1178.

28. Revell, J. (1979); "Inflation and Financial Institutions", *Financial Times*, London.
29. Perry, P., (1992); "Do Banks Gain or Lose from Inflation", *Journal of Retail Banking,* 14(2), pp. 25-30.
30. Short, B.K. (1979); "The Relation between Commercial Bank Profit Rates and Banking Concentration in Canada, Western Europe and Japan", *Journal of Banking and Finance*, Vol. 3, pp. 209-219.
31. Barth, J.R., Caprio, G., Levine, R. (2004); "Bank Supervision and Regulation: What Works Best?" *Journal of Financial Intermediation,* 13 (2), pp. 205-248.
32. Malhotra, Rakesh (2002); "Performance of India's Regional Rural Banks (RRBs): Effect of the Umbilical Cord". *URL: http:// www.alternativefinance. org. uk/rtf/, 7rrbsmalhotra.rtf.*(visited on 23/ 5/11).
33. Report of the Banking Enquiry Commission, New Delhi, 1972, NABARD, Annual Report.
34. Singh, S.P. (1979); "Cost of Bank Credit and Prices" *The Journal of Indian Institute of Bankers,* October-November.
35. Prasad, N. (1985); "The SBI and Rural Development" *Amar Prakasan,* New Delhi.
36. Government of India. (1991); "Report of the Committee on Financial System 1991 (Narasimham Committee)", *Ministry of Finance,* p. 54.
37. Basu, S.K. (1991); "Credit Worthiness of Purpose: A Study on RRBs", *Kurukshetra,* May, 1991.
38. Government of India (1998); "Report on Banking Sector Reforms" (Narasimham Committee - II) *Ministry of Finance.*
39. Naidu, M.C. (2001); "Regional Rural Banks: A Review", *Yojana,* Vol-45, March, pp. 40-50.
40. Sikidar, S. (1992); "*Rural Banking: An Infrastructural Input for Hill Area Development*", Anmol Publication, New Delhi.
41. Tarapore, S.S. (1994); "Rural Banking at Cross Roads", *RBI Bulletin,* September.
42. Rangarajan, C., (1996); "The Role of Rural Credit", *RBI Bulletin,* 1(5), May.
43. Kaushik, A.C., (1999); "Productivity of RRBs Credit in Haryana", *Productivity,* 40(3): October-December.
44. Sinha, S., Tanmay, C., Orlanda, R. and Pathak, N. (2003); "The Outreach/Viability Conundrum: Can India's Regional Rural Banks Really Serve Low-Income Clients'? *ODI Working Paper No. 229*, ODI, London.

45. Uddin, N. (2003); *Regional Rural Banks and Development*, Mittal Publications, New Delhi.
46. Nitin Bhatt and Thorat, Y.S.P. (2004); "India's Regional Rural Banks: The Institutional Dimension of Reforms", *National Bank News Review*, NABARD, April-September.
47. Das, A. and Ghosh, S. (2004-05); "Examining Excess Capacity in Regional Rural Banks: Some Empirical Insights for India", *Prajnan*, Vol. XXXIII, No. 4, 2004-05, NIBM, Pune.
48. Bose, Sukanya (2005); "Regional Rural Banks: The Past and the Present Debate", Macro Scan, *URL: http://www. macroscan. Com/ fet/jul05/fet200705RRB_Debate.htm*.(visited on 4-5-10).
49. Batra, G.S. and Dangwal, R.C. (2005); "Management of Non-Performing Assets in RRBs" in Jain S.C. (eds) *Management of Non-performing Assets in Banks*, RBSA Publishers, Jaipur, pp. 1-19.
50. Rammohan, T.T. and Roy, S.C. (2004); "Comparing Performances of Public and Privte Sector Banks: A Revenue Maximizing Approach", *Economic and Political Weekly*, March-20, pp. 1271-1276.
51. Chatterjee, B. and Sinha, R.P. (2006);"Intermediation Cost Efficiency: A Tale of two Bank Groups",*The IFAI Journal of Bank Management*, ICFAI University Press, Hyderabad.
52. Pati, A.P. (2005); *Regional Rural Banks in Liberalized Environment*, A Mittal Publication, New Delhi.
53. Reddy, A.A. (2006); "Productivity Growth in Regional Rural Banks", *Economic and Political Weekly*, March, 2006.
54. Tasi, K. (2006); *Role of Regional Rural Banks in Economic Development*, Eastern Book Corporation, New Delhi.
55. Misra, B.S. (2006); "The Performance of Regional Rural Banks (RRBs) in India: Has Past anything to Suggest for Future?" *RBI Occasional Paper*, 27 (1 & 2): 89-119.
56. Hadi, A. and Bagchi, K.K. (2006); *Performance of Regional Rural Banks in West Bengal: An Evaluation*, Serial Publications, New Delhi.
57. Shivappa, H. (2007); "Working of Regional Rural Banks in India," *Indian Journal of Agricultural Economics*, July 1, 2007.
58. Sadakkadulla, J. (2007); "Regional Rural Banks and the Role of Empowered Committees", *Cab-Calling*, (October-December).
59. Banos, J.A.L. (2007); "Rural Banks, Resource Allocation Efficiency and Regional Economic Performance," *Philippine Management Review*, Vol. 14, pp. 115-126.
60. Khankhoje, D. and Sathye, M. (2008); "Efficiency of Rural Banks; The Case of India" *International Business Research*, 1(2):140-149, (April).

61. Kumar, V.A. (2008); "Case for De-amalgamation of Regional Rural Banks" *Economic and Political Weekly*, 43(42):60-68, (October).
62. Dhaliwal, Kaur N. and Arora, R.S. (2009); "Profitability of Regional Rural Banks: A Study of Post Liberalization Period. (Report)", *Political Economy Journal of India*,(January).
63. Singh, N.T. and Singh T.J. (2009); "Recovery Performance of RRBs: A Case Study of Manipur Rural Bank" *Journal of Accounting and Finance*, 23((1): 66-74 (October 08- March 09).
64. Ibrahim, M.S. (2010); "Performance Evaluation of Regional Rural Banks in India, *International Business Research,* Vol. 3, No.4; (Nov).
65. Bhaskar, C.S. (2011); "Problems and Prospects of Regional Rural Banks in India", *Indian Streams Research Journal,* Vol. 1, Issue.X, pp. 1-4.
66. Reddy, D.M. and Prasad, K.V.N. (2011), "Evaluating Performance of Regional Rural Banks: An Application of Camel Model", *Research World, Journal of Arts, Science and Commerce*, Vol-II, Issue–4, Oct. 2011 [61].
67. Kumar, R. and Sharma, M. (2011); "Rural Banking in Himachal Pradesh: A Comparative Study of Himachal Gramin Bank and Parvatiya Gramin Bank", *Political Economy Journal of India,* (Jan-July, 2011).
68. RBI; Report of the Advisory Committee on Flow of Credit to Agriculture and Related Activities (Dr. Vyas Committee, 2004).
69. RBI (2010-11), Trend and Progress of Banking in India, Reserve Bank of India, Mumbai.
70. RRB Monitoring, Key Statistics of RRBs, 2009-10.

2

Performance of Regional Rural Banks in India

Deposits, Advances and Credit-Deposit Ratio

The previous episode has drawn the design of the entire study which has covered the conceptual framework and rationale of emergence of RRBs, the statement of the problem, review of related literature, need of the study, objectives set and hypothesis framed, methodology adopted, period coverage, etc. Having drawn the skeleton of the study, the present chapter is an overview on the performance of RRBs in India specifically assessed the deposit mobilization, credit channelization, credit deposit ratio, deployment of credit; agricultural and non-agricultural, priority sector and non-priority sector, etc. For this purpose, the analysis of data has been made with the statistical technique over a period of 11 years from 2000-01 to 2010-11.

1. Introduction

The bank nationalization witnessed an incredible achievement in the banking system through the expansion of bank branches in the country. The establishments of more rural branches undoubtedly have served the twin objective of mobilization of rural deposits and channelization of credit to the rural areas. However, the pace of acceleration of deposit mobilization depends on the economic and industrial infrastructure of higher magnitude as well as creating greater awareness among rural populace for effective use of bank credit. The credit absorption capacity in the rural areas largely depends on the availability of required infrastructure. The deposit mobilization and channelization of credit in social and productive units to meet the social objectives with profitability is the major motive of any financial institution. Regional Rural Banks (RRBs) as like any other Scheduled Commercial Banks (SCBs) in the country mobilizes the deposits of people and as a business institution it utilizes deposit in providing credit to needy people in rural and backward areas and thereby tries to earn certain profit for its survival. The RRB in India was established in the year 1975 and the prime objective behind its establishment was to provide banking facility to the rural people in the country and thereby accumulating the rural saving and out of it to give credit to the rural people like small and marginal farmers, small scale industries, village artisans and craftsmen etc (Ibrahim, 2010)[1] who failed to get credit from cooperative institutions.

The credit is a function of deposit. The higher amount of deposit, the higher can be the fund for credit to a financial institution to deploy in the economy. The deposit mobilization of a bank like RRB depends on the income of the surrounding environment where the bank exists and the number of branches spread by it. To make successful deposit accumulation, the RRBs need to bring the rural masses. Similarly, the deployment of credit depends upon the availability of funds, business condition in the economy and the recovery rate. Deposit mobilization is a significant indicator of bank's performance. The main idea is to tap deposit and culminate savings habit of the community. Further, tapping of potential savings and marshalling them especially for rural uses through small credit and to increase the village level income was the concern area for the RRBs of the country.

The RRBs followed usually the same methods of operation and procedures as followed by commercial banks which have not found favourable for the rural masses. In many cases, banks have not been located at the right place. For instance, the sponsoring banks are also running their branches in the same areas where RRBs are operating. The issue whether location matters for the performance has been addressed in detail by Malhotra (2002)[2]. The Narasimham Committee (1998)[3] emphasized that while discharging their functions as purveyors of rural credit and mobilisers of rural savings, RRBs should not ignore the importance of financial viability and operational efficiency. The productivity, profitability and solvency of the RRBS must be maintained and sustained to enable them to function as an effective and efficient institution of rural credit'. Hadi and Bagchi (2006)[4] assessed the performance of RRBs in India in general and in West Bengal in particular. The study reviewed the progress of the RRBs in West Bengal in terms of expansion of branches, credit expansion and deposit mobilization since inception till the end of June 2001. Shivappa (2007)[5] in a study examined the growth in advances, deposits and financial performance of the RRBs. The study covered the RRBs as a whole and discussed mostly theoretical issues rather than any analytical depth. Kumar (2008)[6] opined that amalgamation became a death blow to the credit starved rural poor, most of whom are small and marginal farmers, agricultural and landless labourers, and artisans. The study recommended for an immediate de-amalgamation of RRBs in the interest of the vast majority of the rural poor.

However, in the context of present day competition with other banking and non-banking institutions, improvement of performance level is essential for the survival of RRBs. Keeping in view the above facts in mind, the following paragraphs attempted to analyze the performance of RRBs in terms of deposit, credit and C/D ratio, etc. In order to examine the performance of RRBs at all India level, the data have been collected for the period 2000-01 to 2010-11 and interpreted the same with statistical method.

2. Branch Expansion of RRBs

The number of banks operating in India has undergone rapid changes as a result of the controlled expansion. There were 648 banks operating in India in 1947. A large number of them were very small non-scheduled banks with high mortality rates and poor capital base. The introduction of minimum capital base strengthened the financial base of banks for trimming their number. At the time of nationalization of banks, there were only 85 banks (Thingalaya, 1987)[7] in India. The establishment of RRBs in 1975 reversed the trend of healthy banking structure. Since then, 196 RRBs have joined the banking system. The Table 2.1 showed below exhibits that in the year 2000-01, the total numbers of RRBs in all India level were 196 which reduced to 82 in the year 2010-11. This decrease in number is due to restructuring strategies adopted and amalgamation of various RRBs in the country which started after the implementation of the Narasimham Committee recommendation by the Government of India. Although the numbers of RRBs have decreased over the years, the branch network has increased to 15,658 in 2010-11 from 14,301 branches in 2000-01. During the period of 11 years under consideration, 1357 number of branches has increased in order to cover more number of districts. This has been confirmed by the fact that the number of districts covered by the RRBs in the country has increased from 484 in 2000-01 to 621 districts in 2010-11. It indicates that an additional 137 numbers of districts were covered by setting up of new branches in the various uncovered and under-banked districts of the country. The population served per branch of RRBs is interestingly high i.e., roughly 84.6 thousand in 2000-01 which slightly improved and figured at 77.3 thousand populations served per branch in 2010-11. The scenario is extremely terrible while compared with the population per branch of commercial bank as a whole which covered 18 thousand populations by each branch during 2010-11 [Indian Banks' Association (IBA), 2011][8]. The number of employee per branch found to be very low i.e., around 4 to 5 persons throughout the period. In 2000-01, the average number of employee per office was 4.90 which has declined to 4.14 during the year 2010-11. This decrease in average number of employee per branch may be due to computerization of the in certain branches of RRBs.

Table 2.1: Branch Network of Regional Rural Banks in India

Year	*No. of RRBs*	*No. of Branches*	*No. of Employee per office*	*No. of Districts Covered*	*Population Per Branch**
2000-01	196	14,301	4.90	484	84622.99
2001-02	196	14,390	4.86	511	84099.61
2002-03	196	14,433	4.82	516	83849.06
2003-04	196	14,446	4.79	518	83773.60
2004-05	133	14,484	4.76	523	83553.81
2005-06	94	14,494	4.73	525	83496.17
2006-07	90	14,520	4.70	534	83346.65
2007-08	90	14,761	4.60	594	81985.87
2008-09	86	15,181	4.51	616	79717.64
2009-10	82	15,475	4.22	619	78203.13
2010-11	82	15,658	4.14	621	77289.14

* Population per branch of RRB is calculated with the total population as per 2011 census divided by the number of branches

Source: Reserve Bank of India, Basic Statistical Return of Scheduled Commercial Banks, Various Issues.

3. Deposit Mobilization of RRBs

The resource mobilization is an integral part of banking activity. The deposit mobilization is a significant indicator of bank's performance. The basic principle of branch expansion is to tap deposit and culminate savings habit of the community. Further, tapping of potential savings and marshalling them for strategic uses for productive purposes in particular is the main objective. As a result, various schemes were launched over the years. The Government has directed the banks to make all possible efforts to access to new deposits that can only expedite the pace of lending activities. There has been a substantial rise of deposits of RRBs during the period under consideration as depicted in Table 2.2. The total amount of deposit in the year 2000-01 was ₹ 37,027 crore and this figure has gone up to ₹ 1,63,928 crore in 2010-11 recording 4.43 times increase in total deposit over the years. Although there has been decrease in the total numbers of RRBs in the country, the quantum of deposit is increasing over the years. At the same time, deposit per branch has increased over the years. The average deposit per branch in 2000-01 was ₹ 2.59 crore which has gone up to ₹ 10.47 crore per office during the year 2010-11. The scenario of deposit per branch of Indian commercial banks is much higher than the RRB as a whole during the same span. The figures for commercial banks as a whole increased from ₹ 14.56 crore in 2000-01 to ₹ 44.65 crore in 2010-11 (IBA, 2011)[9]. The per capita deposit in RRBs is also very low; the figure for the same was ₹ 0.31 thousand in 2000-01, increased to ₹ 1.35 thousand in 2010-11. It could thus be inferred from the above analysis that the reform measures introduced following Narasimham Committee recommendations 1991 and 1998 have positive impact in mobilizing the rural deposits as reflected from the increase in deposit per branch of RRBs. But the fact remained that the RRBs failed to maintain the deposit performance of commercial banks of the country.

4. Credit Channelization of RRBs

The bank credit is an important input variable in the production functions of agriculture, industry, commerce and allied productive activities for the socio-economic development of the backward region of the country. In this connection, Pandey (1968)[10] suggested for the channelization of bank credit in proper direction, as otherwise, there will be adverse affect on the economy of the country. Raj Committee (1977)[11] recommended 40 per cent of lending to the priority sector. After nationalization, banks have attempted to steer the direction of change and strive towards achieving fundamental objectives of mitigation of regional disparities, dispersal of industries and reduction of concentration of economic wealth (Raul, 1997)[12]. Hartough (1994)[13] studied the implications of bankers action plan for profitable small business portfolio and suggested that customers payment track record and market condition, etc. Bank should make advances to most attractive and growth potential units. In order to review the efficacy of existing framework of money lending a technical group, was constituted under the chairmanship of S.C. Gupta, submitted its report on July 2007 and recommended alternative avenues of credit dispensation such as micro finance institutions (RBI, 2007)[14]. Kumar (2008)[15] opined that as a result of amalgamation of RRBs, quantum of credit allocation of bank has been under a severe concern mostly for small and marginal farmers, agricultural and landless labourers, and artisans. He recommended for an immediate de-amalgamation of RRBs in the interest of the vast majority of the rural poor. Hence, it is very interesting to know composition and direction of credit allocation of RRBs.

The loans and advances offered by the RRBs in the country are also increasing over the years in a continuous manner as observed from Table 2.2. The total amount of loans and advances of RRBs in the country was ₹ 15,794 crore in 2000-01; the amount has gone up to a total of ₹ 98,244 crore. It is clear that the total amount of loans and advances of RRBs in the country has increased by more than 5 times over the period. The per branch advances was ₹ 1.10 crore in 2000-01 which has increased to ₹ 6.27 crore in 2010-11. The RRBs are not in a position to deploy credit for socio-economic development alike commercial banks in India as the credit per office of RRBs is much lower while compared the figure for credit per commercial banks in India throughout the period. The credit per commercial banks increased to ₹ 41.55 crore in 2010-11 from ₹ 7.79 crore in 2000-01 (RBI, 2010-11)[16]. The per capita loans and advances of RRBs are also very low throughout the period under consideration.

5. Credit Deposit Ratio of RRBs

Credit deposit ratio is considered as dependable indicator of efficiency of bank's participation in the developmental process. It indicates the extent of bank deposits advanced to multifarious activities in the area. Nambiar (1980)[17] articulated that low credit absorption capacity due to low infrastructural facilities in the area particularly in 'no industrial region' is the main hurdle of increasing in C/D ratio. The banks along with developing and implementing authorities of the area can only take a challenge against the congenital impediments to sustain the economic development of that area. Sikidar (1990)[18] has aptly viewed that the C/D ratio should be looked into its segment and disaggregated forms and for extending advances, the sources of fund are deposits, refinance from higher financial institution, and accretion of profit. Nandal and Singh (2002)[19] viewed that due to larger quantum of deposits, banks have advanced credit to a large extent but C/D ratio has not been found satisfactory. They suggested that there should be proper recovery of loan amount from the loanee in order to have satisfactory C/D ratio, otherwise banks would suffer causing harm to the economy as a whole. Bhagawati (1999)[20] articulated that banks in north eastern region have not been able to increase their credit portfolio. As a result, bank's sensitiveness and effectiveness in planning of advances is required for bringing a paradigm change in the competitive environment.

The credit deposit of the RRBs in India has been increased over the years. The fact has been delineated in Table 2.2. In 2000-01, the credit deposit ratio of the RRBs in the country was 41.0 per cent which increased to 59.6 per cent in 2010-11. The trend of credit deposit ratio of commercial banks is much higher than that of the RRBs; the figure was 45.9 per cent in March 2001 which has reached to the level of 73.9 per cent in March 2008 (RBI, 2008)[21]. Hence, the apparent fact remains that the RRBs failed to maintain the C/D ratio of commercial banks of the country during the period. The reason of significantly low C/D ratio of RRBs may be attributed to nature of loans sanctioned, non-recovery of loans, stubborn cheaters, lack of direction of end use of bank credit, lack of implementation of bankable schemes and so on.

Table 2.2: Performance of Regional Rural Banks in All India Level

Year	Total Deposits (₹In Crore)	Deposit per branch (₹in Crore)	Per Capita Deposit (₹In thousand)	Total Loans and advances (₹in Crore)	Loans and advances per branch (₹in Crore)	Per Capita Loans and Advances (₹In Thousands)	Credit-Deposit Ratio (%)
2000-01	37,027	2.59	0.31	15,794	1.10	0.13	41.0
2001-02	43,220	3.00	0.36	18,629	1.29	0.15	41.8
2002-03	48,346	3.35	0.40	22,158	1.54	0.18	44.2
2003-04	57,010	3.94	0.47	26,115	1.81	0.22	46.3
2004-05	62,143	4.29	0.51	32,871	2.27	0.27	52.8
2005-06	71,329	4.92	0.59	38,520	2.66	0.32	55.6
2006-07	83,144	5.73	0.69	47,326	3.26	0.39	58.3
2007-08	99,093	6.71	0.82	57,568	3.90	0.48	59.5
2008-09	1,20,189	7.92	0.99	65,609	4.32	0.54	56.4
2009-10	1,45,035	9.37	1. 20	79,157	5.12	0.65	57.6
2010-11	1,63,928	10.47	1.35	98,244	6.27	0.81	59.6

Source: Reserve Bank of India, Basic Statistical Return of Scheduled Commercial Banks, Various Issues Consolidated RBI Report on Trend and Progress of Banking in India from 2000-01, 2010-11 RBI, Statistical Tables Relating to Banks in India 2003

In order to analyze the nature of relationship between growth of deposits and growth of advances, coefficient of correlation (r) analysis has been employed. For this purpose, 'r' value between deposit per office and advance per office have been calculated for the period of 11 years from 2000 to 2011. The result obtained is as under:

$$r = 0.99$$
$$t = 21.06 \text{ (cal.)}$$
$$t_{0.05} \text{ (9 df.)} = 1.833$$
$$t_{0.01} \text{ (9 df.)} = 2.821$$

The high positive correlation ($r = 0.997$) value between deposit per office and advances per office are statistically significant at 1 per cent and 5 per cent level of significance at 9 degree of freedom. The calculated value of 't' is much higher than the table value. It confirms that along with the increase of deposits, loans and advances has increased at the same proportion. This implies that the RRBs deploying credit at the same rate what they have mobilized for this purpose although they have not attained the stipulated C/D ratio of 60 per cent.

6. Deposit Mobilization of RRBs: Type-wise Analysis

The current deposit, saving deposit and term deposit are the major deposit types of RRBs like other commercial banks. The deposit is the amount of resource mobilization which helps the banking institutions to enhance the ability of the banks to deploy its credit for the socio-economic development. In order to make the banking business to perform better, a continuous increase in various types of deposits is imperative. In order to study the type-wise deposit of the RRBs in India, we have considered aforesaid three types of deposits i.e., current deposit, saving deposit and term deposit. Table 2.3 presents the type wise deposits of RRBs.

Table 2.3: Deposit of RRBs according to Type of Deposits (As on March)

(Amount ₹ in Crore)

Year	*Current Deposit*	*Saving Deposit*	*Term Deposit*	*Total Deposit*
2000	1,308.98 (4.1)	12,777.25 (39.9)	17,948.44 (56.0)	32,034.68 (100.0)
2001	1,502.35 (4.0)	14,731.77 (38.8)	21,719.12 (57.2)	37,953.23 (100.0)
2002	1,685.43 (3.8)	17,506.64 (39.7)	24,871.06 (56.5)	44,063.12 (100.0)
2003	1,873.46 (3.8)	20,814.16 (42.0)	26,881.52 (54.2)	49,558.14 (100.0)
2004	2,292.60 (4.1)	25,670.45 (45.9)	27,945.97 (50.0)	55,909.02 (100.0)
2005	2,807.48 (4.6)	30,389.67 (49.5)	28,249.75 (46.0)	61,446.90 (100.0)
2006	3,449.38 (4.9)	37,559.48 (53.3)	29,425.38 (41.8)	70,434.24 (100.0)
2007	4,185.45 (5.1)	45,014.18 (55.1)	32,430.87 (39.7)	81,630.50 (100.0)
2008	5,054.61 (5.2)	52,834.24 (54.2)	39,620.56 (40.6)	97,509.41 (100.0)
2009	5,664.45 (4.8)	63,383.18 (53.5)	49,522.63 (41.8)	1,18,570.27 (100.0)
2010	8,065.00 (5.6)	75,906.00 (52.3)	61,064.00 (42.1)	1,45,035.00 (100.0)
b	**1.196**	**1.250**	**1.107**	**1.153**
CAGR	**17.97**	**17.58**	**11.77**	**14.72**

Note: (Figures in the parenthesis indicate percentage to total deposit).

Sources: 1. Basic Statistical Returns of Scheduled Commercial Banks in India, Various issues

2. RBI Report on Trend and Progress of Banking in India from 2000-01, 2001-02, 2010-11.

It is observed that the term deposit plays a prominent role as it appeared as one of the major component of total deposit. The total amount of term deposit in the year 2000 was ₹ 17,948.44 crore which has increased to ₹ 61,064.00 crore in 2010. The percentage share of term deposit to total deposit was 56.0 per cent in 2000 which decreased to 42.1 per cent in the year 2010. The total amount of saving deposit mobilized was ₹12,777.25 crore (39.9% of total deposits) in 2000 which increased to ₹ 75,906.00 crore (52.3% of total deposits) in 2010. The share of both saving deposit and term deposit together was 94.4 per cent in 2010. A negligible fraction of deposit composed of current deposit (ranging from 4 to 6% of total deposit mobilizations) during the period under consideration.

The Compound Annual Growth Rate (CAGR) analysis for various types of deposit of RRBs in India shows that saving deposit is mobilizing more amount as the CAGR for saving deposit (17.58%) as compared to 11.77 per cent for term deposit and 14.72 per cent for total deposit throughout the period.

7. Population Group-wise Deposits of RRBs

The population group-wise deposits and credit of RRBs viz, rural, semi-urban, urban and metropolitan area is presented in Table 2.4. It is clear from table that there is a quantum jump of rural deposit from ₹ 22,307.06 crore in March 2000 to ₹ 84,115.62 crore in March 2010 recording an increase 3.8 fold during 2000-2010. But the percentage share of rural deposit declined from 69.63 to 59.23 per cent during the same period. The semi-urban deposit was ₹ 7,268.64 crore in March 2000 which increased to ₹ 36,625.67 crore in March 2010. The percentage share of semi-urban deposit increased from 22.69 to 25.79 per cent. It shows positive growth of semi-urban deposits both in quantum and percentage term over the years. The urban and metropolitan deposits also increased both in quantitative and percentage term.

The above analysis found that deposits of all the population groups and their percentage share to total deposits of RRBs have increased except percentage share of rural deposit which has declined during the period under consideration. This indicates that in respect of deposit mobilization, the RRBs in rural areas are not performing

Table 2.4: Population Group-wise Deposits of Regional Rural Banks in India (As on March)

(Amount ₹ in Crores)

Year/Population Group	Rural	Semi-Urban	Urban	Metropolitan	Total
2000	22,307.06	7,268.64	2,393.70	65.28	32,034.68
	(69.63)	(22.69)	(7.47)	(0.20)	(100)
2001	26,312.89	8,568.89	2,994.39	77.08	37,953.23
	(69.33)	(22.58)	(7.89)	(0.20)	(100.0)
2002	30,154.59	10,218.22	3,589.09	101.23	44,063.12
	(68.43)	(23.19)	(8.14)	(0.22)	(100.0)
2003	33,745.05	11,664.81	4,039.04	109.25	49,558.14
	(68.09)	(23.54)	(8.15)	(0.22)	(100.0)
2004	37,711.63	13,433.77	4,619.74	143.88	55,909.02
	(67.45)	(24.03)	(8.26)	(0.26)	(100.0)
2005	40,957.13	15,154.59	5,160.81	174.37	61,446.90
	(66.65)	(24.66)	(8.40)	(0.28)	(100.0)
2006	44,359.98	17,978.85	7,403.50	691.91	70,434.24
	(62.98)	(25.53)	(10.51)	(0.98)	(100.0)
2007	50,913.97	21,361.13	8,489.90	865.50	81,630.50
	(62.37)	(26.17)	(10.40)	(1.06)	(100.0)
2008	59,661.45	25,883.31	10,883.46	1,081.20	97,509.41
	(61.19)	(26.54)	(11.16)	(1.11)	(100.0)
2009	71,646.76	31,651.27	13,862.90	1,409.34	1,18,570.27
	(60.43)	(26.69)	(11.69)	(1.19)	(100.0)
2010	84,115.62	36625.67	19,271.04	1,998.52	1,42,010.85
	(59.23)	(25.79)	(13.57)	(1.41)	(100)
CV	**42.54**	**53.38**	**70.24**	**108.10**	**48.62**

Note: Figures in the Parentheses Indicate per cent to Total Deposit.
Source: Statistical Returns of Scheduled Commercial Banks in India, Various Issues.

at par with others groups. The coefficient of variations results, however, gives contradictory results indicating that there have been a less variations of rural deposits. This has called for a further enquiry on the degree of relationship among the population group-wise deposits.

In order to study the extent of deposit mobilization in the rural areas, the correlation matrix analysis is employed among the population group-wise deposit during 2000-2010. The result obtained is presented in Table 2.5

It is observed that the '*t*' values (calculated) of the highly positive correlations are higher than the tabulated values. It means that '*r*' values are statistically significant. It indicates that with the increase

Table 2.5: Matrix of Correlation among the Population Group-wise Deposits

Variable	Total Deposit	Rural Deposit	Semi-Urban Deposit	Urban Deposit	Metropolitan Deposit
Total Deposit	1				
Rural Deposit	0.99* (21.06)	1			
Semi-Urban Deposit	0.99* (21.06)	0.99* (21.06)	1		
Urban Deposit	0.99* (21.06)	0.99* (21.06)	0.99* (21.06)	1	
Metropolitan Deposit	0.98* (14.7)	0.97* (12.13)	0.98* (14.7)	0.99* (21.06)	1

t0.05 (9 df.) = 1.833 & t 0.01 (9 df.)=2.821

Note. Figures in parentheses indicate the respective '*t*' values.
*Significant both at 5 per cent and 1 per cent level of significance.
Source: Calculated by the researchers on the basis of Table 2.4.

in total deposits, the population group-wise deposits increased in the same proportion.

8. Population Group-wise Credit Channelization of RRBs

There has been a quantum increase of population group-wise credits of RRBs during the period 2000-2010. But the percentage share of credit to total credit has declined in case of rural credit. The Table 2.6 presents the facts relating to population group-wise credit of RRBs.

From the analyses, it is observed that over the years, coefficient of variation of metropolitan credit is on fluctuating trend than that of other population groups i.e., rural, semi-urban and urban. As the percentage share of credit in rural areas has declined, it may be observed that a negative attitude of banks to fulfil the socio-economic objectives and thereby the motto of rural development although RRBs were created basically to serve weaker sections, village farmers, artisans etc.

An attempt has been made here under to find out the extent of credit utilization among the population group wise credit of RRBs in India. In this respect, the correlation matrix analysis is employed among the variables during 2000-2010. Table 2.7 presents the results of correlations.

Table 2.6: Population Group-wise Credit of Regional Rural Banks in India (As on March)

(Amount ₹ in Crore)

Year/Population Group (March)	Rural	Semi-Urban	Urban	Metro-politan	Total
2000	9,644.22 (73.47)	2,683.83 (20.45)	777.98 (5.93)	20.06 (0.15)	13,126.10 (100.0)
2001	11,826.11 (73.17)	3,491.50 (21.60)	1,009.43 (6.25)	24.57 (0.15)	16,163.51 (100.0)
2002	13,509.02 (71.59)	4,105.31 (21.75)	1,212.87 (6.43)	41.56 (0.22)	18,868.76 (100.0)
2003	16,177.11 (71.51)	4,921.71 (21.76)	1,470.67 (6.50)	53.44 (0.24)	22,622.92 (100.0)
2004	18,265.45 (70.19)	5,917.39 (22.74)	1,771.62 (6.81)	65.88 (0.25)	26,020.34 (100.0)
2005	23,017.35 (70.41)	7,529.16 (23.09)	2,072.83 (6.34)	69.49 (0.21)	32,688.83 (100.0)
2006	24,453.53 (66.73)	9,124.13 (24.90)	2,825.82 (7.71)	240.03 (0.65)	36,643.51 (100.0)
2007	32,226.20 (67.34)	11,759.79 (24.57)	3,581.75 (7.48)	287.38 (0.60)	47,855.11 (100.0)
2008	38,736.20 (66.91)	14,434.77 (24.94)	4,340.15 (7.50)	375.44 (0.65)	57,886.56 (100.0)
2009	44,247.18 (66.21)	16,693.32 (24.98)	5,429.25 (8.12)	459.16 (0.69)	66,828.91 (100.0)
2010	53623.12 (64.79)	20,970.86 (25.34)	7,529.29 (9.10)	638.50 (0.77)	82,761.76 (100)
CV	**55.64**	**65.08**	**73.11**	**101.83**	**59.50**

Note: Figures in the Parentheses Indicate per cent to total credit.
Source: Statistical Returns of Scheduled Commercial Banks in India, Various Issues.

From the correlation matrix table, it is observed that the highly positive '*r*' values are significant as the calculated values of '*t*' are higher than the table value at 5 per cent and 1 per cent level of significance at 9 *df*. It shows that there is high relationship exist among the variables. It can further be interpreted that along with the increase in total credit, the credit of rural, semi urban and urban areas have also been increasing proportionately.

9. Deployment of Credit of RRBs in India

The RRBs provide credit support for the development of rural and backward areas. It provides loans to various purposes like agriculture, industry, transport operators, professional and personal loans, etc. The credit extension of the RRBs in India during the last ten years is presented in Table 2.8.

Table 2.7: Matrix of Correlation Analysis of Population Group-wise Credit

Variables	*Total Credit*	*Rural Credit*	*Semi-Urban Credit*	*Urban Credit*	*Metropolitan Credit*
Total Credit	1				
Rural Credit	0.99* (21.06)	1			
Semi Urban Credit	0.99* (21.06)	0.99* (21.06)	1		
Urban Credit	0.99* (21.06)	0.99* (21.06)	0.99* (21.06)	1	
Metropolitan Credit	0.98* (14.7)	0.98* (14.7)	0.99* (21.06)	0.99* (21.06)	1

$t_{0.05}$ (9 df.) = 1.833 & $t_{0.01}$ (9 df.) = 2.821

Note: Figures in parentheses indicate the respective '*t*' values.
*Significant both at 5 per cent and 1 per cent level of significance.
Source: Calculated by the researchers on the basis of Table 2.6.

The amount of agricultural credit and the percentage share of total credit of RRBs have increased during 2000-2010. The agricultural credit was ₹ 6316.56 crore in March 2000 (which was 48.12% of total credit), has increased to the tune of ₹ 34063.23 crore in March 2010 (i.e., 61.47% of total credit). In case of industrial credit the total loan extended by the RRBs in India in March 2000 was ₹ 919.67 crore (7.01% of total credit) and in March 2010, amount of industrial loan has increased to ₹ 1707.76 crore (3.08% of the total credit extended). Although, there has been a quantum increase of industrial credit, the percentage shares of industrial credit to total credit of RRBs declined. In case of transport operators, the total amount of credit provided in March 2000 was ₹ 626.82 crore but the contribution to transport operator increased to ₹ 777.47 crore in March 2010. However, the share of credit for transport operators has been declining continuously. The transport operator received a meagre amount of loan during the period. The share of personal loan to the total amount although declined, its share remained around 13.42 per

Table 2.8: Credit Allocation of RRBs in India (As on March)

(Amount ₹ in Crore)

Sl. No	Occupation	2000	2001	2002	2003	2004	2005	2006	2007	2008	2009	2010
1	Agriculture	6316.56 (48.12)	7665.04 (46.88)	8741.08 (46.33)	10642.00 (47.04)	12237.51 (47.03)	16463.32 (50.36)	18820.42 (51.36)	26184.93 (54.72)	32139.74 (55.52)	36437.64 (54.52)	34063.23 (61.47)
2	Industry	919.67 (7.01)	1207.29 (7.38)	1349.95 (7.15)	1489.64 (6.58)	1536.34 (5.90)	1826.65 (5.59)	1871.99 (5.11)	2476.53 (5.18)	2336.59 (4.04)	2600.32 (3.89)	1707.76 (3.08)
3	Transport Operators	626.82 (4.77)	688.57 (4.21)	567.95 (3.01)	529.02 (2.34)	542.49 (2.08)	548.26 (1.68)	503.81 (1.37)	625.35 (1.31)	609.75 (1.05)	755.14 (1.13)	777.47 (1.40)
4	Professional and other services	384.47 (2.93)	469.47 (2.87)	534.14 (2.83)	659.31 (2.91)	706.26 (2.71)	726.39 (2.22)	808.13 (2.21)	1079.46 (2.26)	1610.07 (2.78)	1919.18 (2.87)	1266.70 (2.29)
5	Personal Loans	2469.22 (18.81)	3449.21 (21.09)	4440.28 (23.53)	5583.02 (24.68)	6680.56 (25.67)	7782.71 (23.81)	8240.91 (22.49)	9804.40 (20.49)	10395.51 (17.96)	12328.16 (18.45)	7435.16 (13.42)
6	Trade	1900.87 (14.48)	2234.41 (13.66)	2216.78 (11.75)	2462.73 (10.89)	2718.49 (10.45)	3196.11 (9.78)	3400.68 (9.28)	4322.24 (9.03)	4877.08 (8.43)	5866.81 (8.78)	4072.18 (7.35)
7	Finance	2.88 (0.02)	5.24 (0.03)	16.97 (0.09)	29.02 (0.13)	50.82 (0.20)	59.82 (0.18)	82.55 (0.23)	91.17 (0.19)	446.96 (0.77)	2738.81 (4.10)	2426.13 (4.38)
8	All Others	505.60 (3.85)	632.39 (3.87)	1001.62 (5.31)	1227.59 (5.43)	1547.85 (5.95)	2085.57 (6.38)	2915.03 (7.96)	327.104 (6.84)	5470.86 (9.45)	4182.86 (6.26)	3668.07 (6.62)
	Total Bank Credit	13126.1 (100)	16351.61 (100)	18868.76 (100)	22622.93 (100)	26020.32 (100)	32688.83 (100)	36643.52 (100)	47855.12 (100)	57886.56 (100)	66828.92 (100)	55416.70 (100)

Note: Figures in the Parentheses Indicate per cent to Total Credit.
Source: Statistical Returns of Scheduled Commercial Banks in India, Various Issues.

cent in 2010. The trade and finance together constitute approximately 12 per cent of total credit of RRBs in the year 2010.

In order to understand the extent of credit allocation of RRBs into various occupations, correlation analysis is employed. The correlation of total bank credit: (a) with agriculture, (b) industry credit, (c) transport operators, (d) professional and other services, (e) personal loans, (f) trade, (g) finance, (h) all others, and (i) during 2000-2010 is shown in Table 2.9.

It is found that almost all the '*r*' values are statistically significant both at 5 per cent and 1 per cent level of significance at 9 df. except the total bank credit with transport operators. It indicates that except the transport operators all other occupational groups are getting adequate credit along with the increase of total bank credit of the RRBs in the country. The correlation between total bank credit and transport operator is 0.51 which is not statically significant at 5 per cent and 1 per cent level of significance. This clearly designated that transport operator is getting comparatively less amount of loans for developmental purpose which might perhaps resultant the severe infrastructural backwardness that persist in rural areas of the country. Hence, an immediate step is necessary to enhance the adequate amount of credit to the transport operators.

Table 2.9: Correlation Analysis of Total Credit with Credit to Various Occupations of RRBs

Variables	*Correlation value*	*Calculated 't' value*
r_{ab}	0.99	21.06
r_{ac}	0.89	5.80
r_{ad}	0.51	1.78
r_{ae}	0.97	12.13
r_{af}	0.92	7.08
r_{ag}	0.98	14.70
r_{ah}	0.75	3.41
r_{ai}	0.79	3.82

$t_{0.05}$ (9 df.) =1.833 & $t_{0.01}$ (9 df.) = 2.821

Source: Self-calculated by the researchers.

10. Deployment of Agricultural Credit of RRBs in India

The objective of RRBs is to provide financial support to the needy in

Table 2.10: Agricultural Credit Advances of RRBs in India (As on March)

(Amount ₹ in Crore)

Year	2000	2001	2002	2003	2004	2005	2006	2007	2008	2009	2010
Short-Term Credit (Crop Loans)	2,865 (21.86)	3,095 (35.08)	3,812 (36.06)	6,495 (29.31)	7,664 (29.35)	10,980 (33.40)	13,877 (34.94)	18,707 (38.58)	22,748 (38.57)	26,652 (39.31)	33,663 (40.65)
Term Credit (for agriculture and allied activities)	3,339 (25.47)	871 (9.87)	782 (7.40)	3,766 (16.10)	4,058 (15.54)	5,730 (17.43)	7,632 (19.22)	3,745 (7.72)	10,468 (17.75)	10,715 (15.80)	12,619 (15.24)
Indirect Advances	23 (0.18)	—	—	—	—	—	—	—	—	—	—
Total Agricultural Credit	6,227 (47.50)	3,966 (44.9)	4,594 (43.46)	10,261 (46.3)	11,722 (44.9)	16,710 (50.8)	21,509 (54.2)	27,452 (56.6)	33,216 (56.3)	37,365 (55.1)	46,282 (55.89)
Total Credit Advances	13,109 (100)	8,823 (100)	10,571 (100)	22,158 (100)	26,115 (100)	32,871 (100)	39,712 (100)	48,493 (100)	58,984 (100)	67,802 (100)	82,819 (100)

Note: Figures in the Parentheses Indicate per cent to Total Credit.
Source: Report on Trend and Progress of Banking in India, various years.

the field of agriculture and other village and backward area development. Therefore, it is important to know the credit provided by the RRBs in agricultural sector. Table 2.10 shows that in agriculture, the various areas of credit advances by the RRBs are short-term credit or crops loans, term credit for agriculture and allied activities and indirect advances. Farmers require short-term, medium-term and long-term credit. The short-term credit for purchasing seeds, cattle's and equipments, etc. and they take medium and long-term credit for the purposes of land development, irrigation development and making of warehouse, fencing, etc.

From Table 2.10, it is observed that in the year 2000 the total amount of loans provided for short-term credit by the RRBs at the national level was ₹ 2865.00 crore which is 21.86 per cent of the total credit advances of the RRBs in the country. In 2010 the aggregate amount has increased to ₹ 33,663 crore which is 40.65 per cent of the total credit advanced by the RRBs. In case of term credit, the cumulative amount extended in 2000 was ₹ 3,339 crore which was 25.47 per cent of the total credit extended for agricultural sector. By 2010 the aggregate amount has increased to the extent of ₹ 12,691 crore which is 15.24 per cent. Furthermore, the table exhibited that the total amount of agricultural credit was ₹ 6,227 crore in 2000 which increased to the extent of ₹ 46,282 crore in 2010. The share of agricultural credit was 47.50 per cent in 2000, increased to 55.89 per cent in 2010 indicating an improvement in the credit scenario.

11. Deployment of Non-Agricultural Credit of RRBs in India

The various areas of the non-agricultural credit of RRBs are credit to rural artisans, industries in the village level, retail trade and credit for certain other purposes. The credit deployment of the RRBs in the non-agricultural sector during the period 2000-2010 may be had from Table 2.11.

It reveals from Table 2.1 that the total amount of credit provided by the RRBs for rural artisans etc. was ₹ 773 crore in March 2000 (5.90% of the total credit), increased to ₹ 810 crore (0.98% of the total credit) in March 2010. It is also observed that there has been continuous decline in the percentage share of credit among the sub-sectors of non-agricultural credit, except credit provided for 'other

Table 2.11: Non-Agricultural Credit Advances of RRBs in India (As on March)

(Amount ₹ in Crore)

Year	2000	2001	2002	2003	2004	2005	2006	2007	2008	2009	2010
Rural Artisans etc	773 (5.90)	181 (2.05)	198 (1.87)	695 (3.14)	715 (2.74)	713 (2.17)	748 (1.88)	736 (1.52)	671 (1.14)	772 (1.14)	810 (0.98)
Other industries	664 (5.07)	70 (0.79)	107 (1.01)	330 (1.49)	433 (1.66)	580 (1.76)	757 (1.91)	880 (1.81)	1,227 (2.08)	1,656 (2.44)	1598 (1.93)
Retail Trade etc.	2073 (15.81)	1,123 (12.73)	1,279 (12.10)	3,264 (14.73)	3,607 (13.81)	4,364 (13.28)	3,452 (8.69)	3,677 (7.58)	4,531 (7.68)	4,690 6.92)	5,234 (6.32)
Other purpose	3,372 (25.72)	3,483 (39.48)	4,393 (41.56)	7,608 (34.34)	9,638 (36.91)	10,504 (31.96)	13,246 (33.36)	15,748 (32.47)	19,339 (32.79)	23,317 (34.39)	28,895 (34.89)
Total Non-agricultural Credit	6,882 (52.50)	4,857 (55.05)	5,997 (56.73)	11,897 (53.7)	14,393 (55.1)	16,161 (49.2)	18,204 (45.8)	21,041 (43.4)	25,768 (43.9)	30,435 (44.8)	36,537 (44.1)
Total Credit	13,109	8,823	10,571	22,158	26,115	32,871	39,712	48,493	58,984	67,802	82,819

Note: Figures in the Parentheses Indicate per cent to Total Credit.
Source: RBI, Report on Trend and Progress of Banking in India, Various Issues.

purposes' over the years. The quantum of credit provided for other purposes was ₹ 3,372 crore in March 2000 which experienced a quantum jump to ₹ 28,895 crore in March 2010. The percentage share of other purpose also experienced a soaring from 25.72 to 34.89 per cent during the same period. The credit for retail trade was ₹ 2,073 crore but this amount has increased to ₹ 5, 234 crore.

12. Priority and Non-Priority Sector Lending of RRBs in India

The concept of priority sector lending is mainly intended to ensure that assistance from the banking system in an increasing manner to those sectors of the economy which has not received adequate support of the institutional finance in the past. Priority sector lending implies providing financial support to those important sectors which are vital for the economy like agriculture, small and tiny industries, rural artisans, transport operators, etc. Financial institutions are hesitant to provide credit to such specific areas because of collateral insecurity and high risk of becoming non-performing or loss assets. The Narasimham Committee (1991)[22] has drawn attention to the problem and stated that there is need for gradual phasing out of the directed credit programme, i.e. the stipulations that 40 per cent of all credit should go to the priority sector should be scrapped. The priority sector should be redefined and the proportion shall be fixed at 10 per cent of the aggregate credit. The Committee (1998)[23] indicated that timely and adequate availability of credit rather than its costs is very indispensable for intended beneficiaries. The impact of Narasimham Committee recommendations with regard to lending to priority sector has not been encouraging (Majumdar, 2001)[24]. It appears that there is a growing anxiety that the process of financial sector reforms has by-passed the priority sector. In this respect Dr. Y.V. Reddy (February 3, 2001)[25], Deputy Governor of RBI, remarked that the flow of credit to priority sector/rural areas has not been up to the mark owing to accumulation of losses in banks on account of mounting Non-Performing Assets (NPAs). The internal working group was set up by the RBI under the chairmanship of C.S. Murthy to examine the need of continuance of priority sector lending prescriptions. On the basis of the recommendations of the working group, the guideline for priority sector lending were revised on April 30, 2007 and overall priority sector lending target was fixed at 40 per cent for domestic banks. The share of priority sector advances to total advances of commercial banks in India declined from 35.4 per cent in 1999 to 31.2 per cent in 2009-10 (RBI, 2009-10)[26].

With this backdrop, an analysis of priority sector and non-priority sector lending of RRBs has been made in the following paragraphs. Table 2.12 presents the priority sector and non-priority sector advances of RRBs in India.

Table 2.12: Priority and Non-Priority Sector Lending of RRBs in India (As on March)

(Amount ₹ in Crore)

Year	Sector-wise Advances			Percentage Share of Priority Sector Advances	Percentage Share of Non-Priority Sector Advances	Priority sector advances per branch	Non-Priority sector advances per branch	Advances per branch
	Priority Sector	Non-Priority Sector	Total					
2001	7,143	3,428	10,571	67.6	32.4	0.50	0.24	1.29
2002	8,847	3,794	12,641	70.0	30.0	0.61	0.26	1.54
2003	11,722	3,857	15,579	75.2	24.8	0.81	0.27	1.81
2004	16,568	4,514	21,082	78.6	21.4	1.14	0.31	2.27
2005	26,077	6,794	32,871	79.3	20.7	1.80	0.47	2.66
2006	32,177	7,535	39,712	81.0	19.0	2.22	0.52	3.26
2007	39,852	8,641	48,493	82.2	17.8	2.70	0.59	3.90
2008	48,894	10,090	58,984	82.9	17.1	3.22	0.66	4.32
2009	56,555	11,247	67,802	83.4	16.6	3.65	0.73	5.11
2010	68,823	13,956	82,779	83.1	16.9	4.40	0.89	6.27

Source: Calculated by the researchers.

Table 2.12 shows that priority sector advances was ₹ 7,143 crore in 2001 which has increased to the total amount of ₹ 68,823 crore in 2010. In terms of the percentage also, the priority sector lending raised from 67.6 per cent to 83.1 per cent. This indicates a promising trend of Indian RRBs in lending the priority sector. In the non-priority sector lending of RRBs, the total amount of fund provided was ₹ 3,428 crore in 2001 which increased to ₹ 13,956 crore in 2010. Although non-priority sector evidenced a quantum increase of lending of RRBs, the percentage share has declined. The percentage share of non-priority sector lending decreased to the level of 16.9 per cent from 32.4 per cent during the period.

The correlation coefficient has been calculated to examine the relationship between– (a) priority sector lending, (b) non-priority sector lending, and (c) the total advances. For the purpose, the incremental advances of priority sector per branch (x^1), non-priority sector per branch (X^2) and the advances per branch (X^3) are considered for the period 2001 to 2010. The result obtained as under:

Table 2.13: Correlation Matrix of Analysis

Variables	x^1	X^2	X^3
x^1	1		
X^2	0.93 (7.54)	1	
X^3	0.69* (2.88)	0.58* (2.15)	1

$t_{0.05}$ (7 df.) = 1.895
$t_{0.01}$ (7 df.) = 2.998

Note: Figures in the parentheses indicate calculated '*t*' values.
*Significant at 5 per cent but not 1 per cent level of significance.
Source: Calculated by the researchers based on Table 2.12.

The analyses explores that the correlation between the incremental advances of priority sector per branch and the non-priority sector per branch is highly positive (r = 0.93) and significant both at 5 per cent and 1 per cent level of significance. This indicates that there is no difference in non-priority sector lending and priority sector lending of RRBs. Again the correlation of incremental advances per branch with incremental advances of priority sector per branch (r = 0.69) and with the non-priority sector lending (r = 0.58) which are statistically significant at 5 per cent level but not 1 per cent level of significance. This indicates that along with the increase in advances the priority sector and non-priority sector lending of the RRBs in the country is not increasing in the same rate. It may further be inferred that there are some disparity in lending practices of RRBs.

Notes

1. Ibrahim, M.S. (2010); "Performance Evaluation of Regional Rural Banks in India", *International Business Research,* 3(4), (November).
2. Malhotra, R. (2002); "Performance of India's Regional Rural Banks (RRBs): Effect of the Umbilical Cord", Retrived from URL: http://

www.alternativefinance. org.uk/rtf/;rrbsmalhotra.rtf. (Date of visit: 10/09/10)

3. Government of India (1998); "Report on Banking Sector Reforms" (Narasimham Committee-II) Ministry of Finance.
4. Hadi, A. and Bagchi, K.K. (2006); *Performance of Regional Rural Banks in West Bengal: An Evaluation*, Serial Publications, New Delhi.
5. Shivappa, H. (2007); "Working of Regional Rural Banks in India", *Indian Journal of Agricultural Economics,* July 1, 2007.
6. Kumar, V.A. (2008); "Case for De-amalgamation of Regional Rural Banks", *Economic and Political Weekly*, 43(42):60-68, October.
7. Thingalaya, N.K. (1987); "Banking Development in India Since Independence", *Pigmy Economic Review,* (August), 33 (1):1.
8. Indian Banks' Association, Indian Banking at a Glance, 2011.
9. IBA (2011); Performance Highlight of Banks.
10. Pandey, K.L. (1968); *Development of Banking in India Since 1949*, Calcutta Scientific Book Agency. p. 80.
11. Reserve Bank of India (1977); "Committee's Report on Financing of Public Sector Banks", RBI (Raj, J. as Chairman).
12. Raul, R.K., (1997); *Industrial Finance in India*, Anmol Publications, New Delhi.
13. Hartough, K.J. (1994); *Entrepreneurial Bankers; The Banker's Personal Action Plan for Building a Profitable Small Business Portfolio*, Probus Publishing, Chicago.
14. RBI (2007); "Report of the Technical Group to Review Efficacy of Existing Legislative Framework Governing Money Lending and its Enforcement Machinery".
15. Kumar, V.A (2008); "Case for De-amalgamation of Regional Rural Banks", *Economic and Political Weekly*, 43(42):60-68, (October).
16. RBI (2010-11); Trend and Progress of Banking in India.
17. Nambiar, P.C.D. (1980); "Banking Policy; Which Direction", *Commerce*, September 20), Vol. 13.
18. Sikidar, S. (1990); *Economic Development of Tribal India*, Ashish Publishing House, New Delhi, p. 160.
19. Nandal, R.S. and Singh, A. (2002); *Banking Infrastructure in Haryana"*, Banking and Financial Sector Reform in India, Deep and Deep Publication Pvt. Ltd. pp. 457.
20. Bhagawati, S.K. (1999); "Credit Deposit Ratio of Commercial Banks; A Case Study of North Eastern Region", *Journal of North Eastern Council,* (April, June) 19 (2): 14-19.
21. Reserve Bank of India (2008); "Basic Statistical Return of Scheduled Commercial Banks", p. 1.

22. Government of India. (1991a); "Report of the Committee on Financial System, Ministry of Finance", (Narasimham Committee), December.
23. Government of India (1998); "Report of the Committee on Financial System, Ministry of Finance", (Narasimham Committee-II), April.
24. Majumder, N.A. (2001); "The New Architecture of Rural Credit System" Prof. M.L. Dantwala Monograph Series, Department of Economics, University of Mumbai, August 2001.
25. Reddy, Y.V. (2001); "Address at the Conference of Indian Society of Agricultural Marketing at Vizag", (A.P) February.
26. RBI, "Trend and Progress of Banking In India", 2009-10.

3

Evaluation of Performance of Meghalaya Rural Bank

The previous chapter has examined the performance of Rural Regional Banks (RRBs) in terms of deposits, advances, priority sector lending and CD ratio at the national context. The analysis indicated that RRBs are doing well for socio-economic development of backward regions of the country. Conceived with the framework of the study, the present chapter is an attempt to analyze the performance of operational activities in terms of branch expansions, deposit mobilizations, credit channelization, credit deposit ratios, population served per branch of MRB in the study area over a period of 11 years i.e., 2000-01 to 2010-11 on the basis of some specific financial indicators.

1. Introduction

The North-Eastern Region (NER) comprised of seven sister states of India. These seven sisters are—Assam, Arunachal Pradesh, Meghalaya, Manipur, Mizoram, Nagaland and Tripura. The region constitutes 8 per cent of the geographical area which covers 3.73 per cent of the population and credit flow to the region for agriculture and allied sectors comprised of less than 0.50 per cent of the country as a whole (RBI, 2007)[1]. In the region, the network of commercial bank is not widely spread. The concentration of commercial banks branches are mostly in the State of Assam in comparison to other states of the region. Thus rural banking institutions have a greater responsibility for the development of the region.

In NER, there are eight number of RRBs with two in Assam and one each in other six states[2]. Out of eight RRBs in the region, five number of RRBs are sponsored by the State Bank of India while three number of RRBs in the region are sponsored by United Bank of India. At present, there are 675 number of RRB branches in the region which covers 62 districts out of 79 districts. The state of Assam is having the largest network of 401 number of RRB branches, followed by Tripura (104), Mizoram (59), Meghalaya (55), Manipur (28), Arunachal Pradesh (18) and Nagaland (10) as on March 2010 (RBI, 2010)[3].

The following paragraphs have highlighted the working of RRBs in north eastern region on the basis of operational parameters of banks like branch expansion, deposit mobilizations, credit channelization and credit deposit ratio, etc.

2. Branch Expansion, Deposit Mobilization and Credit Channelization of RRBs in North Eastern Region

The branch expansion, deposit mobilization and credit extended of RRBs are presented in Table 3.1. It is revealed from the table that in March 2000, there were 661 number of branches of RRBs functioning in the region. The number of branches have increased to 675 in March 2010. It shows that over the period of 11 years only 14 additional branches of RRBs were established in the region. The deposit mobilization of RRBs in the NER was ₹ 1,31,578 lakh in March 2000 which has increased to ₹ 6,74,572 lakh in March 2010 recording a 5.13 fold increases. The deposit growth scenario of RRBs of NER is better than the growth of deposit in RRB as a whole in India which recorded 4.43 times during the same span. Similarly, the deposit per branch in the region increased from ₹ 199.06 lakh to ₹ 999.36 lakh during the same period.

In case of credit channelization, the total amount of credit provided by RRBs in NER was ₹ 39,937 lakh in March 2000 increased to ₹ 3,03,162 lakh in March 2010. Over the years, there has been 7.59 fold of increase in the credit of the RRBs in the region while the same recorded 5 fold increases in RRBs at national level.

It is also observed that the Compound Annual Growth Rate (CAGR) for total deposit 16.02 per cent and for deposit per branch 15.80 per cent is lower than the growth of total credit (CAGR = 20.23%) and for growth of credit per branch (CAGR = 20.0%). This indicates that RRBs are doing better in NER.

Table 3.1: Branch Network, Deposits and Credit of RRBs in North East Region (As on March)

(Amount ₹ in Lakh)

Year	No. of Branches	Total Deposits	Deposit per Branch	Total Credit	Credit per Branch
2000	661	1,31,578	199.06	39,937	60.42
2001	663	1,50,454	226.93	46,879	70.71
2002	655	2,02,676	309.43	62,114	94.83
2003	654	2,27,619	348.04	76,627	117.17
2004	657	2,66,208	405.19	96,568	146.98
2005	659	2,95,009	447.66	1,21,826	184.86
2006	656	3,24,812	495.14	1,50,710	229.74
2007	655	3,76,121	574.23	1,86,150	284.20
2008	672	4,29,170	638.65	2,16,865	322.72
2009	684	5,52,462	807.69	2,47,772	362.24
2010	675	6,74,572	999.36	3,03,162	449.13
CAGR	—	16.02	15.80	20.23	20.0

Source: RBI, Basic Statistical Return of Scheduled Commercial Banks, Various Issues.

To know the nature of relationship between growth of deposits and growth of advances in the RRBs of NER, coefficient of correlation has been calculated. For this purpose, deposit per office and advance per office have been considered for the period of 11 years from 2000-2011. The result obtained as under:

$$r = 0.986$$
$$t = 17.40 \text{ (cal.)}$$
$$t_{0.05} \text{ (9 df.)} = 1.833$$
$$t_{0.01} \text{ (9 df.)} = 2.821$$

The analysis indicates that there is high correlation (0.98) between deposit and advances in the RRBs of the NER. At the same time it is also significant at 5 per cent and 1 per cent level of significance. It signifies that along with the increase in deposits there is an equivalent increase in the advances of the RRBs in the region. Hence, the RRBs in north east are channelizing exactly the proportionate amount in the region what they mobilized from the region.

3. Credit Delivery of RRBs in NER

In order to study the credit allocation scenario of the RRBs in NER, the occupation-wise data relating to credit schedule of RRB in the region is presented in Table 3.2.

The amount of credit provided for agriculture was ₹ 9,984 lakh in March 2000 which has increased to the total of ₹ 46,743 lakh. The percentage share to total credit has decreased from 24.99 per cent to 15.42 per cent over the years. The amount of industrial credit of RRBs and its percentage share in NER have been increased. Similarly, the total bank credit for transport operators in the region was ₹ 4,638 lakh in March 2000 which increased to ₹ 8,346 lakh in March 2000. It is observed that over the years there has been almost continuous decrease in the percentage share of credit for transport operators and reached to a negligible fraction i.e., 2.75. Similarly the credit allocation of the RRBs for professional and other services has increased although their percentage share is very low. The total credit provided for personal loans and their percentage share has increased. It is observed that RRBs in NER is following the same trend of deploying credit by the RRBs at national level. The total amount of loans provided to finance is very much less in comparison to other sectors. In March 2001, the credit available for finance was ₹ 11 lakh (0.02% of total credit) has increased to ₹ 10,911 lakh in March 2010 (3.60% of total credit). As a result, the total amount of outstanding credit of RRBs in NER was ₹ 39,957 lakh in March 2000, increased remarkably and reached to ₹ 3,03,162 lakh in March 2010.

With the aforesaid background of the performance of RRBs in NER on the basis of parameters viz., branch network, deposit mobilization and credit channelization, etc. in the context of RRB as a whole, an attempt is made in the consequent part of this chapter to assess the performance of Meghalaya Rural Bank (MRB) (i.e., RRB at Meghalaya) on the basis of commonly used performance indicators. The statistical techniques have been used to examine the variables considered.

4. The Glimpse of the Meghalaya Rural Bank

The Meghalaya Rural Bank was established in the year 1981 under the Regional Rural Banks Act, 1976 with its Head Office at Shillong,

Table 3.2: Credit Channelization of Regional Rural Banks in North East Region (As on March)

(Amount ₹ in Lakh)

Sl. No	Occupations	2000	2001	2002	2003	2004	2005	2006	2007	2008	2009	2010
1.	Agriculture	9,984 (24.99)	10,204 (21.73)	11,170 (17.98)	11,697 (15.25)	13,173 (13.75)	18,423 (15.10)	22,936 (15.20)	29,861 (16.0)	35,897 (16.54)	36,059 (14.53)	46,743 (15.42)
2.	Industry	4,018 (10.06)	5,293 (11.27)	5,988 (9.64)	6,513 (8.49)	7,355 (7.68)	12,380 (10.14)	11,351 (7.52)	17,601 (9.43)	26,002 (11.98)	25,811 (10.40)	33,582 (11.08)
3.	Transport Operators	4,638 (11.61)	5,129 (10.92)	5,100 (8.21)	3,884 (5.07)	4,506 (4.70)	4,236 (3.47)	4,115 (2.73)	4,168 (2.23)	3,914 (1.80)	4,590 (1.85)	8,346 (2.75)
4.	Professional and other services	1,616 (4.04)	1,397 (2.98)	1,628 (2.62)	2,443 (3.19)	2,819 (2.94)	2,820 (2.31)	4,244 (2.81)	5,882 (3.15)	7,091 (3.27)	7,855 (3.16)	9,128 (3.01)
5.	Personal Loans	8,988 (22.49)	13,278 (28.28)	24,575 (39.57)	37,274 (48.61)	51,065 (53.31)	62,770 (51.43)	81,894 (54.27)	98,001 (52.52)	98,256 (45.27)	1,19,552 (48.16)	13,1579 (43.40)
6.	Trade	10,111 (25.30)	10,747 (22.89)	11,732 (18.89)	11,722 (15.29)	13,062 (13.64)	13,946 (11.43)	16,500 (10.93)	19,225 (10.30)	24,374 (11.23)	28,212 (11.36)	39,786 (13.12)
7.	Finance	—	11 (0.02)	20 (0.03)	85 (0.11)	99 (0.10)	173 (0.14)	265 (0.18)	384 (0.21)	2,246 (1.03)	9,662 (3.89)	10,911 (3.60)
8.	All Others	6,02 (1.51)	889 (1.89)	1,899 (3.06)	3,062 (3.99)	3,709 (3.87)	7,294 (5.98)	9,601 (0.36)	11,460 (6.14)	19,246 (8.87)	16,509 (6.65)	23,087 (7.62)
Total Bank Credit		39,957 (100)	46,948 (100)	62,112 (100)	76,680 (100)	95,788 (100)	1,22,042 (100)	1,50,906 (100)	1,86,582 (100)	2,17,026 (100)	2,48,250 (100)	30,3162 (100)

Note: Figures in the brackets indicates share of total bank credit.
Source: RBI, Basic Statistical Return of Scheduled Commercial Banks, Various Issues

the state of Meghalaya. Previously this Bank was known as "*Ka Bank Nongkyndong Ri Khasi Jaintia*" but in December 2007, it is renamed as Meghalaya Rural Bank (MRB). As per power conferred by sub-section (1) section (3) of the RRB Act 1976 (21 of 1976), Department of Economic Affairs (Banking Division), Ministry of Finance, Government of India, in its notification dated 1st May 2007 substituted the name "*Ka Bank Nongkyndong Ri Khasi Jaintia*" as "Meghalaya Rural Bank". MRB is the only Regional Rural Bank in the state operating in six districts of Meghalaya out of seven districts having total number of 58 branches as on March 2011 and it is sponsored by the State Bank of India. As like any other RRBs, the proportion of share capital of Meghalaya Rural Bank is also 50:35:15. It means 50 per cent of the paid up capital is subscribed by the Government of India and 35 per cent is subscribed by the State Bank of India and remaining 15 per cent by the Govt. of Meghalaya.

The basic features of the Bank are the following:

(1) It is exclusively meant for weaker sections.
(2) It is basically for promotion of local employment.
(3) It is for combining the local experience and familiarity with rural problems.

5. Performance of Meghalaya Rural Bank

In order to measure the general performance of the MRB in the State of Meghalaya various operational indicators like expansion of branches, employee per office, deposits and advances, population served per branch, occupation-wise distribution of credit, priority sector lending, etc. are taken into consideration during the period 2000-2001 to 2010-11.

5.1. Branch Network of MRB

Meghalaya Rural Bank has an extensive network of 58 branches spread across the 6 districts of East Khasi Hills, West Khasi Hills, Jaintia Hills, Ri Bhoi, West Garo Hills and East Garo Hills. The bank has the distinction of accounting for over 50 per cent of the total number of rural bank branches in its area of operation. However, it has not set up any satellite branch or extension counter. The initiatives have taken in the area of renovation of branches with a view to improve the public image of the banks. It is revealed from the following Table 3.3 that in 2000-01, there were only 51 branches of MRB functioning in 4 districts out of seven districts of the state. In 2010-11, the total number of branches of the MRB has increased to 58 in 6 districts of Meghalaya.

Table 3.3: Branch Network of MRBs

Year	*No. of Branches*	*No. of employee per office*	*No. of Districts Covered*	*Population per Branch**
2000-01	51	3.6	4	58,118
2001-02	51	3.5	4	58,118
2002-03	51	3.6	4	58,118
2003-04	51	3.6	4	58,118
2004-05	51	3.6	4	58,118
2005-06	51	3.5	4	58,118
2006-07	51	3.5	4	58,118
2007-08	52	4.1	5	57,000
2008-09	54	3.8	6	54,889
2009-10	55	3.9	6	53,891
2010-11	58	4.4	6	51,104

* Population per branch of MRB is calculated with the total population of Meghalaya as per 2011 census divided by the number of branches.

Source: Annual Report of Meghalaya Rural Bank, Various issues.

It may be observed that during the period of 11 years, the MRB has able to expand seven more additional branches in the state. The population served per branch of MRB is 58.1 thousand in 2000-01 which slightly improved and figured at 51.1 thousand population served per branch in 2010-11. The scenario is relatively better while compared with the population per branch of RRBs as a whole.which covered 77.3 thousand populations by each branch during 2010-11. The number of employee per branch found to be very low i.e., around 3 to 4 persons throughout the period. This may be due to the abolition of clerical cadre over a period of time by converting the staff into multipurpose workers. The staff norms i.e., 4.2 number of staff per branch as recommended by Agarwal Committee in 2000[4], has not achieved by MRB till 2009-10. In 2000-01, the average number of employee per office was 3.6 which have risen to 3.9 in 2009-10 and a further increase of 4.4 during the year 2010-11.

The district-wise expansion of bank branches indicates that the East Khasi Hills district is having the highest number of branches. As on 2010-11, the East Khasi Hill constituted 25 number of branches, West Khasi Hills 14 branches, Jaintia Hills 13, Ri Bhoi district 4, West Garo Hill and East Garo Hill districts are having 1 branch in each district. The branch expansion of MRB in Garo Hills district of Meghalaya is very negligible because the MRB has started functioning in West Garo Hill w.e.f. 31.03.2008 and East Garo Hill district w.e.f. 09.01.2009 with only one branch in each district. It is also observed that more number of branches are expanded in rural areas than the semi-urban or urban areas except in East and West Garo Hill districts. Table 3.4 presents the district-wise and rural-urban area-wise expansion of MRB in Meghalaya.

5.2 Deposit Mobilization of MRB

The total amount of deposit mobilized by the MRB in 2000-01 was ₹ 12,26,293 thousand and the amount has increased to ₹ 67,74,188 thousand in 2010-11. It indicates, the increase in total deposit mobilization of the MRB is 5.52 fold during 2000-01 to 2010-11. The amount of deposit per branch for MRB was ₹ 2.4 crore in 2000-2001 which has increased to ₹ 11.6 crore in 2010-11. The average deposit per branch of RRBs was ₹ 2.59 crore in 2000-01 which has gone up to ₹ 10.47 crore per office during the year 2010-11. The MRB have been doing at par with the RRBs in terms of mobilization of deposits. However, scenario of per capita deposits indicates that MRB is performing much better than the RRBs as a whole. The per capita deposit of MRB increased from ₹ 0.41 thousand in 2000-01 to ₹ 2.28 thousand in 2010-11; the corresponding figure for RRBs increased from ₹ 0.31 thousand to ₹ 1.35 thousand. The data relating to deposit mobilization of MRB may be had from Table 3.5.

5.3 Credit Allocation of MRB

Similarly, the total loans and advances outstanding of the MRB in 2000-01 was ₹ 3,03,392 thousand. In 2010-11 the quantum of total loans and advances outstanding has increased to ₹ 21,61,545 thousand. The loans and advances per branch of the MRB was ₹ 0.59 crore in

Table 3.4: District-wise Branch Expansion of Meghalaya Rural Bank

(Figures in number)

Year	East Khasi Hills			West Khasi Hills			Jaintia Hills			Ri-bhoi			West Garo-Hills			East Garo Hills			Grand Total
	Rural	Semi urban & Urban	Total	Rural	Semi urban & Urban	Total	Rural	Semi urban & Urban	Total	Rural	Semi urban & Urban	Total	Rural	Semi urban & Urban	Total	Rural	Semi urban & Urban	Total	
2000-01	16	5	21	14	1	15	12	1	13	1	1	2							51
2001-02	15	6	21	14	1	15	12	1	13	1	1	2							51
2002-03	15	6	21	14	1	15	12	1	13	1	1	2							51
2003-04	15	6	21	14	1	15	12	1	13	1	1	2							51
2004-05	15	6	21	14	1	15	12	1	13	1	1	2							51
2005-06	15	6	21	14	1	15	12	1	13	1	1	2							51
2006-07	15	6	21	14	1	15	12	1	13	1	1	2							51
2007-08	15	6	21	13	1	14	12	1	13	2	1	3	—	1	1				52
2008-09	15	7	22	13	1	14	12	1	13	2	1	3	—	1	1	—	1	1	54
2009-10	15	8	23	13	1	14	12	1	13	2	1	3	—	1	1	—	1	1	55
2010-11	15	10	25	13	1	14	12	1	13	3	1	4	—	1	1	—	1	1	58

Source: Annual Report of Meghalaya Rural Bank, Various Issues.

2000-01 which increased to ₹ 3.72 crore in 2010-11; the corresponding figures for RRBs was ₹ 1.1 crore in 2000-01, increased to ₹ 6.27 crore in 2010-11. The information relating to loans and advances per branch indicate that MRB is lagging behind the RRB's loan performance. It is also observed that in terms of per capita loans and advances, the MRB has been maintaining the same rate at which RRBs of the country are deploying loans and advances. Table 3.5 presents the data relating to credit channelization of MRB.

Table 3.5: Performance of MRB: Deposit, Advances and CD Ratio

(Amount ₹ in thousand)

Year	Total Deposits	Deposit per branch	Per Capita Deposit	Total Loans and advances	Loans and advances per branch	Per Capita Loans and Advances	C/D Ratio
2000-01	12,26,293	24,044.91	0.414	3,03,392	5,948.86	0.102	30.00
2001-02	14,32,184	28,082.02	0.483	3,52,205	6,905.98	0.119	25.00
2002-03	15,53,924	30,470.00	0.524	4,06,167	7,964.06	0.137	26.00
2003-04	17,58,127	34,473.08	0.593	4,62,522	9,069.06	0.156	26.31
2004-05	21,99,196	43,121.49	0.742	5,42,438	10,636.04	0.183	24.67
2005-06	25,04,085	49,099.71	0.845	6,66,700	13,072.55	0.225	26.63
2006-07	28,01,385	54,929.12	0.945	8,25,357	16,183.47	0.279	29.36
2007-08	31,59,848	61,957.80	1.066	9,73,316	19,084.63	0.328	30.80
2008-09	40,39,445	74,804.54	1.363	11,86,477	23,264.26	0.400	29.37
2009-10	53,23,070	96,783.09	1.796	16,04,869	29,179.44	0.542	30.15
2010-11	67,74,188	1,16,796.34	2.286	21,61,545	37,268.02	0.729	31.91

Source: Annual Reports of Meghalaya Rural Bank, Various issues.

5.4 Credit Deposit Ratio of MRB

The credit deposit ratio of the Meghalaya Rural Bank was 30 per cent in 2000-01 which increased to 31.91 per cent in 2010-11 as displayed in Table 3.5. The C/D ratio of MRB is not up to the mark while compared with RRB as a whole. The same for RRBs was 41.0 per cent in 2000-01 which augmented to 59.6 per cent in 2010-11. The reason of significant low ratio of MRB may be attributed to non-recovery of loans, willful defaulters, lack of supervision of end use of bank credit, lack of implementation of bankable schemes. This exhibited poor credit absorption capacity of the entire area along with lack of entrepreneurial zeal to undertake viable projects.

5.5 Relationship between Growth of Deposit and Growth of Advances

In order to examine the degree of relationship between growth of deposits and growth of advances of MRB, coefficient of correlation analysis has been employed. For this purpose, deposit per office and advance per office have been considered for the period of 11 years from 2000-2001 to 2010-11. The result obtained as under:

$$r = 0.997$$
$$t = 21.06 \text{ (cal.)}$$
$$t_{0.05} \text{ (9 df.)} = 1.833 \text{ (tab)}$$
$$t_{0.01} \text{ (9 df.)} = 2.821 \text{ (tab)}$$

The high correlation ($r = 0.997$) value between deposit per office and advances per office are statistically significant at 1 per cent and 5 per cent level of significance. The calculated value of 't' is significantly higher than the table value at (5% and 1% level). It confirms that over the years deposit per office and advance per office of the Meghalaya Rural Bank are increasing in the same proportion. The high correlation coefficient will undoubtedly indicate more savings habit of the people as well as higher volume of credit deployment of MRB in the area. Hence, the hypothesis "There is no difference in the growth of deposit as well as the growth of credit of MRB" is found correct. It is also found that the relationship between deposits and advances per branch of MRB is exactly same as RRB as a whole.

Further, an attempt has been made to assess the relationship between growth of deposits of banks both RRB as a whole and MRB. We employ in this respect the analysis of correlation co-efficient between incremental deposits per branch of RRB and incremental deposits per branch of MRB during 2000-01 to 2010-11. The result of correlations is as follows

$$r = 0.83$$
$$t = 4.19 \text{ (cal.)}$$
$$t_{0.05} \text{ (8df.)} = 1.860$$
$$t_{0.01} \text{ (8df.)} = 2.896$$

The result shows high correlation ($r = 0.83$) between the

incremental deposit per office of RRBs and the MRB is statistically significant. This indicates that the MRB is mobilizing the deposits at the same rate what the RRB at the national level does. Hence, the hypothesis, "The MRB is mobilizing the deposits at par with RRB over the years" found valid.

In order to assess the extent of credit channelization by the MRB in the context of RRBs at the national level, we have calculated correlation coefficient between incremental advances per branch of MRB and RRB. The result obtained as under-

$$r = 0.93$$
$$t = 7.11 \text{ (cal.)}$$
$$t_{0.05} \text{ (8df.)} = 1.860$$
$$t_{0.01} \text{ (8df.)} = 2.896$$

The highly positive correlation ($r = 0.93$) between the incremental loans and advances per branch in the RRBs of India and the per branch loans and advances of MRB is significant both at 1 per cent and 5 per cent level of significance. It indicates that along with the increase in incremental credit in the national level RRBs, the incremental credit in the MRB is also increasing at the same pace. Hence, our hypothesis, "There exists a close relationship between the extent of credit channelization of MRB as well as RRBs" found to be correct. This implies that MRB maintained the national tempo of credit channelization rural banks. In other words, MRB are deploying credit for the economic growth of the area from which they have mobilized funds.

5.6 District-wise Performance of MRB

The district-wise data relating to deposits and loans shows that there is a quantum increase of both deposits and advances of MRB in almost all the districts of the State—Meghalaya. The CD ratio in East Khasi Hills and West Khasi Hills district is comparatively better than Jaintia Hills and Ri Bhoi districts indicated a better clientele of thc districts. Hence, MRB is able to culminate the saving habit amongst the rural people and also able to utilize them for the development of the region. The amount of deposit mobilization and credit channelization is not available in Garo Hills till 2008-09 because the MRB has started

functioning in West Garo Hills on 31.03.2008 and East Garo Hills district on 09.01.2009 with only one branch in each district. The CD ratio of two districts of Garo Hills is extremely high indicating that the extent of bank deposits advanced to multifarious activities in the area. The high CD ratio in these two districts may be due to only and urban/semi-urban located MRB branch operating in the districts (as displayed in district-wise branch expansion in Table 3.4). Table 3.6 depicts the position of district-wise deposits, advances and CD ratio of MRB.

5.7 Type of Deposit Mobilization of MRB

The MRB mobilizes various types of deposit viz, current deposit, saving deposit, term deposit, sundries, special term deposit and recurring deposit. Table 3.7 presents the data relating to type-wise Deposit in Meghalaya Rural Bank.

The total amount of current account deposit was ₹ 96,475 thousand in March 2000 (9.75% of total deposit) which has increased to ₹ 4,81,256 thousand in March 2010 (9.04% of total deposit). The amount of saving bank deposit constitutes lions share i.e., around 50 per cent of total deposit throughout the period. The figure increased from ₹ 4,11,383 thousand to ₹ 30,31,083 thousand during March 2000 an amount of ₹ 71 thousand mobilized under sundry which increased to ₹ 314 in March 2010. The term deposit of ₹ 1,13,286 thousand in March 2000 has increased to the quantum of ₹ 6,19,898 thousand in March 2010. Other than the term deposit the MRB has special term deposit. In March 2000, the amount mobilized under special term deposit was ₹ 3,59,362 thousand which has increased to ₹ 11,62,957 thousand in 2010-11. Likewise the amount of recurring deposits has also increased during the period under study.

The compound annual growth analysis shows that the saving account has the highest rate of growth i.e., 19.91 per cent which is followed by term deposit (16.71), current deposit (15.73), sundries (14.47), special term deposit (11.27) and recurring deposit (10.54). The result of growth rate analysis is contradicting with RRB as a whole where the growth rate in case of current deposit is higher than any other type of deposits.

Table 3.6: District-wise Deposit and Loans of Meghalaya Rural Bank

(Amount ₹ in Thousand)

Year	East Khasi Hills			West Khasi Hills			Jaintia Hills			Ri-Bhoi			West Garo-Hills			East Garo Hills		
	Credit	Deposit	CD Ratio	Credit	Deposit	CD Ratio	Credit	Deposit	CD Ratio	Credit	Deposit	CD Ratio	Credit	Deposit	CD Ratio	Credit	Deposit	CD Ratio
2001-02	1,78,795	6,25,457	28.59	72,560	2,42,192	29.96	80,695	5,00,657	16.12	20,155	63,878	31.55	—	—	—	—	—	—
2002-03	2,18,428	6,34,480	34.43	78,164	2,74,753	28.45	84,202	5,48,315	15.36	25,373	96,376	26.33	—	—	—	—	—	—
2003-04	2,49,712	7,10,308	35.16	88,553	3,07,556	28.79	92,502	6,22,158	14.87	31,755	1,18,105	26.84	—	—	—	—	—	—
2004-05	2,98,613	8,88,720	33.60	1,03,132	3,60,822	28.58	1,01,494	7,89,565	12.85	39,200	1,60,089	24.49	—	—	—	—	—	—
2005-06	3,49,210	1,00,9450	34.59	1,53,815	4,12,910	37.25	1,09,394	8,98,228	12.18	54,281	1,83,186	29.63	—	—	—	—	—	—
2006-07	4,22,691	11,44,464	36.98	2,07,608	5,02,360	41.32	1,34,441	9,99,219	13.45	60,617	1,55,342	39.02	—	—	—	—	—	—
2007-08	5,11,359	11,00,870	46.45	2,37,339	5,70,142	41.63	1,52,475	12,68,867	12.02	72,143	2,19,389	32.88	—	—	—	—	—	—
2008-09	6,06,131	14,43,978	41.98	2,57,259	6,82,538	37.69	2,21,900	16,39,893	13.53	80,771	2,66,826	30.27	20,416	6,021	39.08	0	189	0
2009-10	18,95,297	7,80,150	41.16	9,06,121	3,72,146	41.07	21,12,366	3,06,414	14.51	3,66,126	95,366	26.05	34,085	43,396	127.32	9,074	7,397	81.52
2010-11	10,30,040	26,05,027	39.54	5,03,128	12,24,761	41.07	4,33,507	23,91,942	18.12	1,28,628	4,87,980	26.36	50,555	48,571	104.08	15,687	15,406	101.82

(–) The MRB has started functioning in West Garo Hills on 31.03.2008 and East Garo Hills district on 09.01.2009. Hence, the figures for deposits credit and CD ratios is not available in Garo Hills till 2008-09).

Source: Annual Report of Meghalaya Rural Bank, Various Issues.

Table 3.7: Type-wise Deposit in Meghalaya Rural Bank (As on March)

(Amount ₹ in thousand)

Year	Current Account Deposit	Saving Bank Deposit	Sundries	Term Deposit	Special Term Deposit	Recurring Deposit	Total Deposit
2000	96,475 (9.75)	4,11,383 (41.57)	71 (0.007)	1,13,286 (11.45)	3,59,362 (36.31)	9,156 (0.93)	98,97,33 (100)
2001	1,87,642 (15.30)	4,80,688 (39.20)	16 (0.001)	1,22,870 (10.02)	4,23,304 (34.52)	11,773 (0.96)	12,26,293 (100)
2002	1,47,869 (10.32)	6,21,465 (43.39)	7 (0.0005)	1,45,285 (10.14)	5,02,400 (35.08)	15,158 (1.06)	14,32,184 (100)
2003	1,15,674 (7.44)	7,14,506 (45.98)	740 (0.05)	1,77,620 (11.43)	5,27,012 (33.91)	18,373 (1.18)	15,53,924 (100)
2004	2,00,773 (11.42)	7,56,964 (43.05)	350 (0.02)	2,14,165 (12.18)	5,65,791 (32.18)	20,084 (1.14)	17,58,127 (100)
2005	3,03,357 (13.79)	10,00,441 (45.49)	1074 (0.05)	2,55,302 (11.61)	6,18,337 (28.12)	20,685 (0.94)	21,99,196 (100)
2006	3,73,706 (14.92)	11,39,503 (45.51)	336 (0.01)	2,14,759 (8.58)	7,42,559 (29.65)	23,222 (0.93)	25,04,085 (100)
2007	3,83,981 (13.71)	13,62,052 (48.62)	779 (0.03)	2,96,836 (10.60)	7,37,388 (26.32)	20,349 (0.73)	28,01,385 (100)
2008	2,78,311 (8.81)	16,85,299 (53.33)	1540 (0.05)	3,59,967 (11.39)	8,14,177 (25.77)	20,555 (0.65)	31,59,848 (100)
2009	3,80,039 (9.41)	21,85,104 (54.09)	932 (0.02)	3,82,486 (9.47)	10,67,692 (26.43)	23,192 (0.57)	40,39,445 (100)
2010	4,81,256 (9.04)	30,31,083 (56.94)	314 (0.006)	6,19,898 (11.65)	11,62,957 (21.85)	27,562 (0.52)	53,23,070 (100)
b	**1.15**	**1.21**	**1.44**	**1.16**	**1.11**	**1.09**	**1.17**
CAGR	**15.73**	**19.91**	**14.47**	**16.71**	**11.27**	**10.54**	**16.53**

Note: Figures in brackets indicate percentage to total deposit.
Source: Annual Report of Meghalaya Rural Bank, Various Issues.

5.8 Credit Deployment of Meghalaya Rural Bank

The credit deployment of MRB under different heads like agriculture, industry, and transport operators, professional and other services, personal loans, etc., may be had from Table 3.8. From table, it is observed that the credit amount outstanding in agriculture sector was ₹ 1,164 lakh in March 2000 which has increased to the quantum of ₹ 3,485 lakh in March 2010. Although the quantum of credit has increased in agricultural sector during the period under consideration, the percentage share of total credit has declined from 43.34 to 22.20 per cent. This trend has contradicted with the credit allocation by RRBs as a whole. The percentage share of RRBs total credit to agricultural sector increased from 48.12 to 61.41 per cent during the same period. Hence, a reverse situation in respect of credit allocation of MRB is observed particularly for agricultural sector. This may be due to complicated nature of clientele in the region where MRB has been operating. In case of Industry, total bank credit was ₹ 192 lakh in March 2000 which increased to ₹ 843 lakh in March 2010. The same also declined in percentage term from 7.15 to 5.37 per cent. In the same manner the amount of credit outstanding for transport operators increased but as per cent to total credit, it has declined. However, the amount of credit for professional and other services was ₹ 14 lakh in March 2000 which increased to ₹ 196 lakh in March 2010. In percentage term also, there is little improvement from 0.52 to 1.25 per cent over the years. The personal loans of MRB have increased both in quantum and percentage term. It indicates that the MRB is deploying more for personal purpose as reflected from percentage share of total credit. This may be due to easy recovery of such loans.

The deployment of credit to trade purposes, the total amount of credit outstanding was ₹ 444 lakh in March 2000 (16.53% of total credit), which increased to ₹ 1,902 lakh in March 2010 (12.12% of total credit). In case of finance there was no allocation of fund during the year 2000 and 2001. In March 2002, the credit allocation for finance was ₹ 2 lakh (which was 0.05% of total credit) and this has increased to 99 lakh in March 2010 (which was 0.63%). The amount of credit and its percentage share in case of other purposes have also increased over the years.

In order to understand the extent of credit deployment to various occupation groups, correlation coefficient analysis has been employed. The correlation of total bank credit– (a) with agriculture, (b) industry, (c) transport operators, (d) professional and other services, (e) personal loans, (f) trade, (g) finance, (h) all others, (i) has been calculated during 11 years from 2000-01 to 2010-11 and results are presented in Table 3.9.

Table 3.8: Credit Deployment of MRB (As on March)

(Amount ₹ in Lakh)

Sl. No	*Occupation*	2000	2001	2002	2003	2004	2005	2006	2007	2008	2009	2010
1	Agriculture	1,164 (43.34)	1,262 (42.19)	1,247 (33.46)	1,243 (30.28)	1,289 (27.83)	1,406 (25.86)	1,856 (28.17)	2,302 (27.82)	2,488 (25.32)	2,297 (19.28)	3,485 (22.20)
2	Industry	192 (7.15)	265 (8.86)	524 (14.06)	496 (12.08)	395 (8.53)	480 (8.83)	500 (7.59)	564 (6.81)	939 (9.55)	574 (4.82)	843 (5.37)
3	Transport Operators	415 (15.45)	472 (15.78)	385 (10.33)	427 (10.40)	506 (10.92)	588 (10.81)	597 (9.06)	562 (6.79)	522 (5.31)	731 (6.13)	1349 (8.59)
4	Professional and other services	14 (0.52)	14 (0.47)	48 (1.29)	35 (0.85)	29 (0.63)	26 (0.48)	44 (0.67)	63 (0.76)	155 (1.58)	105 (0.88)	196 (1.25)
5	Personal Loans	374 (13.92)	472 (15.78)	1,009 (27.07)	1,296 (31.57)	1,746 (37.69)	2,175 (40.0)	2,735 (41.51)	3,563 (43.05)	4,193 (42.67)	6,060 (50.86)	7,189 (45.80)
6	Trade	444 (16.53)	451 (15.08)	428 (11.48)	509 (12.40)	543 (11.72)	620 (11.40)	662 (10.05)	904 (10.92)	1,039 (10.57)	1,391 (11.67)	1,902 (12.12)
7	Finance	0	0	2 (0.05)	23 (0.56)	14 (0.30)	0	24 (0.36)	5 (0.06)	83 (0.84)	104 (0.87)	99 (0.63)
8	All Others	82 (3.05)	56 (1.87)	83 (2.23)	76 (1.85)	110 (2.37)	142 (2.61)	171 (2.60)	313 (3.78)	409 (4.16)	654 (5.49)	635 (4.05)
	Total Bank Credit	2,686 (100)	2,991 (100)	3,727 (100)	4,105 (100)	4,632 (100)	5,437 (100)	6,589 (100)	8,276 (100)	9,828 (100)	11,916 (100)	15,697 (100)

Note: Figures in the parentheses percentage to total bank credit.
Source: RBI, Basic Statistical Return of Scheduled Commercial Banks, Various Issues.

Table 3.9: Correlation Analysis of Credit to Various Occupations

Variables	*Correlation value*	*Calculated 't' value*
r_{ab}	0.97	12.12
r_{ac}	0.80	4.00
r_{ad}	0.87	5.33
r_{ae}	0.92	7.08
r_{af}	0.99	21.06
r_{ag}	0.99	21.06
r_{ah}	0.87	5.33
r_{ai}	0.96	10.29

$t_{0.05}$ (9 df.) = 1.833 & $t_{0.01}$ (9 df.) = 2.821 (tabulated)

Source: Self-calculated by the researchers on the basis of Table 3.8.

The correlation analysis shows that '*r*' values are statistically significant at their respective degree of freedom indicating that there is close relationship between the variables considered. Thus, it can be inferred that all the sectors are getting proportionate amount of bank credit along with the rise of total credit of the MRB during the study years. Hence, the MRB are performing a logical and genuine credit deployment practices in the present situation considering socio economic development of the area from where they mobilized the fund.

5.9. Priority and Non-Priority Sector Lending of MRB

The lending practices of MRB may be divided into priority sector lending and non-priority sector lending. Table 3.10 presents the facts relating to priority and non-priority sector lending of MRB.

The total amount of priority sector lending was ₹ 60,800 thousand in 2000, the amount however, has increased to ₹ 5,39,552 thousand in 2010. The share of priority sector lending declined from 61.97 to 58.79 per cent. In case of non-priority sector lending the aggregate amount in 2000 was ₹ 37,311 thousand. In 2010, the amount has increased to the quantum of ₹ 3,78,190 thousand. The percentage share of priority sector lending to total lending is declining over the years but the percentage share of non-priority sector has increased over the years. In the year 2000, the share of non-priority sector lending was 38.03 per cent, increased to 41.2 per cent in 2010. This indicates that a positive attitude of MRB in lending the non-priority

Table 3.10: Priority and Non-Priority Sector Lending of Meghalaya Rural Bank (As on March)

(Amount ₹ in Thousand)

Year	Sector-wise Advances			Percentage Share of Priority Sector Advances	Percentage Share of Non-Priority Sector Advances	Priority Sector Advances per Branch	Non-Priority Sector Advances per Branch	Advances per Branch
	Priority Sector	Non-Priority Sector	Total					
2000	60,800	37,311	98,111	61.97	38.03	1,192.16	731.59	5,948.86
2001	71,450	52,166	1,23,616	57.80	42.20	1,400.98	1,022.86	6,905.98
2002	78,646	73,515	1,52,161	51.69	48.31	1,542.08	1,441.47	7,964.06
2003	77,281	94,367	1,71,648	45.02	54.98	1,515.31	1,850.33	9,069.06
2004	97,531	92,580	1,90,111	51.30	48.70	1,912.37	1,815.29	10,636.04
2005	1,20,051	1,28,543	2,48,594	48.29	51.71	2,353.94	2,520.45	13,072.55
2006	2,01,848	1,34,775	3,36,623	40.04	40.04	3,957.80	2,642.65	16,183.47
2007	2,58,688	1,54,011	4,12,699	62.68	37.32	4,974.77	2,961.75	18,717.62
2008	2,73,253	1,94,927	4,68,180	58.36	41.64	5,060.24	3,609.76	21,971.80
2009	3,92,945	3,30,195	7,23,140	54.34	45.66	7,144.46	6,003.55	29,179.44
2010	5,39,552	3,78,190	9,17,742	58.79	41.21	9,302.62	6,520.52	37,268.02

Source: Calculated by the Researcher based on Annual Reports of MRB, Various Issues.

sector. Similarly, the priority sector advances per branch was ₹ 1,192.16 thousand in 2000 and it increased to ₹ 9,302.62 thousand in 2010. In the same manner, the non-priority sector advances per branch was ₹ 731.59 thousand in 2000 which increased to ₹ 6,520.52 thousand in 2010. However, the declining share of priority sector lending of MRB over the years has a direct contradiction with the RRBs. The share of priority sector lending of RRBs as a whole has been improved from 67.6 to 83.1 per cent. This necessitates a further enquiry on the relationship of total advances with priority and non-priority sector advances.

An attempt has been made in the following paragraph to ascertain the relationship among priority sector advances, non-priority sector advances and the total advances. For this purpose, correlation coefficient analysis is employed among the variables i.e., incremental priority sector advances per branch, incremental non-priority sector advances per branch and incremental advances per branch for the period of 2001 to 2010. The results are shown in Table 3.11.

It reveals that the coefficient of correlation between priority sector and non-priority sector advances ($r = 0.46$) is neither significant at 5 per cent level nor at 1 per cent level of significance. This indicates that the increase in non-priority sector lending is not followed the growth of priority sector lending of MRB. In other words, there exist a difference in lending practices of MRB for priority and non-priority sector. The MRB shows a reverse trend in lending to priority and non-priority sector while compared with RRBs as a whole. In case of RRB, there is no difference lending practices in priority and non-priority sector (as observed in chapter 2). Similarly, the coefficient of correlation between advances and priority sector lending ($r = 0.88$) is statistically significant both at 5 per cent level and at 1 per cent level of significance. It indicates that along with the increase in advances, the priority sector lending is also increasing at the same pace.

The coefficient of correlation between the advances and non-priority sector lending ($r = 0.61$) is statistically significant at 5 per cent but not at 1 per cent level of significance. It also suggests that along with the increase in advances of the MRB, the non-priority sector lending is also increasing but not in the same rate. By and large, it inferred that the MRB is giving more weightage to the priority

Table 3.11: Correlation Matrix

Variables	*PSAPB*	*NPSAPB*	*APB*
PSAPB	1		
NPSAPB	0.46NS (1.46)	1	
APB	0.88* (5.19)	0.61** (2.19)	1

$t_{0.05}$ (8 df.) = 1.860 and $t_{0.01}$ (8df.) = 2.896
*significant at both 5 pc and 1 pc level
**significant at 5 pc level only
NS — not significant
PSAB = Priority Sector Advances Per Branch
NPSAB = Non-Priority Sector Advances Per Branch
APB = Advances Per Branch
Source: Calculated by the researchers based on Table 3.10.

sector than the non-priority sector by providing proportionately more advances to fulfill the motto of rural economic development of the region.

5.10 Deployment of Priority Sector Lending by MRB

The RRBs were established to serve the rural poor and backward areas. The MRB as a regional bank has an enormous role to strengthen the backward economy of the state by way of lending to the priority sector like agricultural loan, SHGs loan, retail trade, small industries and business loan etc. Table 3.12 presents the position of priority sector lending by MRB. The MRB provides crop loans to the farmers. The crop loan is required to farmers for buying seeds, manure and in harvesting time, etc. Under priority sector lending, the total amount of crop loans provided was ₹ 8,357 thousand in March 2000 increased to ₹ 1,48,237 thousand in March 2010. During the period under consideration, there has been increased in percentage share of crop loan from 22.40 to 27.47 per cent. For long-term purposes like land development, irrigation, etc. the bank gives loan as agricultural term loans. The agricultural term loans increased from ₹ 2,341 thousand to ₹ 22,771 thousand but its percentage share declined from 6.27 to 4.22 per cent over the years. Similarly for other agro allied activities the aggregate amount of credit increased from ₹ 8,371 thousand to

Table 3.12: Priority Sector Lending of the MRB (As on March)

(Amount ₹ in Thousand)

Category/ Year	2000	2001	2002	2003	2004	2005	2006	2007	2008	2009	2010
Crop Loans	8,357 (22.40)	11,572 (16.20)	13,133 (16.70)	16,531 (21.39)	18,023 (18.48)	30,744 (25.61)	45,336 (22.46)	64,707 (25.01)	85,951 (31.45)	1,17,005 (29.78)	1,48,237 (27.47)
Agricultural Term Loans	2,341 (6.27)	794 (1.11)	798 (1.01)	857 (1.11)	603 (0.62)	3,441 (2.87)	26,905 (13.33)	19,182 (7.42)	19,425 (7.11)	20,336 (5.18)	22,771 (4.22)
Allied Agriculture Term Loans	8,371 (22.44)	3,391 (4.75)	2,326 (2.96)	3,582 (4.64)	3 357 (3.44)	3,624 (3.02)	10,565 (5.23)	5,579 (2.16)	4,996 (1.83)	7,556 (1.92)	20,589 (3.82)
Self Help Groups	15 (0.04)	627 (0.88)	1,047 (1.33)	2,493 (3.23)	3 762 (3.86)	3,351 (2.79)	4 866 (2.41)	15,388 (5.95)	9,149 (3.35)	9,749 (2.48)	14,505 (2.69)
Retail Trade/ Small Business	12,052 (32.30)	15,024 (21.03)	18,437 (23.44)	14,499 (18.76)	22,429 (23.00)	22,169 (18.47)	37,508 (13.58)	49,492 (19.13)	46,334 (16.96)	82,727 (21.05)	1,08,254 (20.06)
Transport Operators	17,627 (47.24)	21,699 (30.37)	21,823 (27.75))	23,463 (30.36)	31,560 (32.36)	34,387 (28.64)	31,433 (15.57)	25,751 (9.95)	22,264 (8.15)	44,015 (11.20)	1,11,406 (20.65)
Small Scale Industries	9,259 (24.82)	13,765 (19.27)	15,753 (20.03)	7,336 (9.49)	10,608 (10.88)	12,587 (10.48)	14,440 (7.15)	17,786 (6.88)	33,134 (12.13)	34,303 (8.73)	37,788 (7.00)
Housing	2,772 (7.43)	4,578 (6.41)	108 (0.14)	8,329 (10.78)	6 770 (6.94)	5,911 (4.92)	21,021 (10.41)	48,971 (18.93)	43,250 (15.83)	37,820 (9.62)	55,777 (10.33)
Education Loan	0	0	5,221 (6.64)	191 (0.25)	191 (0.20)	150 (0.12)	314 (0.16)	1,663 (0.64)	1,871 (0.68)	2,194 (0.56)	3,534 (0.65)
Others	0	0	0	0	228 (0.23)	3,687 (3.07)	9,460 (4.69)	10,169 (3.93)	6,879 (2.52)	7,236 (1.84)	16,691 (3.09)
Total of Priority Sector Lending	37,311 (100)	71,450 (100)	78,646 (100)	77,281 (100)	97,531 (100)	1,20,051 (100)	2,01,848 (100)	2,58,688 (100)	2,73,253 (100)	3,92,945 (100)	5,39,552 (100)

Note: Figures in the parentheses indicate percentage to total priority sector advances.
Source: Annual Reports of Meghalaya Rural Bank, Various Issues.

₹ 20,589 thousand but its share to total priority sector lending declined sharply. In similar manner, the MRB's loans for self-help groups swelled from ₹ 15 thousand to ₹ 14,505 thousand. The share of the same also increased notably from a very negligible fraction i.e., from 0.04 to 2.69 per cent of priority sector lending over the years. This really brings the message of MRBs commitment for the development of rural and backward region. Similarly the aggregate amount of MRB priority sector lending for retail trade/small business was ₹ 12,052 thousand which increased to ₹ 1,08,254 thousand.

The total amount of credit provided to small scale industries although increased, it share has fallen down indicating a negligible attitude of MRB in sanctioning the loans to small sector. Similarly, in case of housing loan the credit amount was ₹ 2,772 thousand has increased to the aggregate of ₹ 55,777 thousand. It is observed that in first two years of the study period no education loan was provided by the MRB. In 2003, the MRB's credit amount as educational loan was ₹ 5,221 thousand which declined to ₹ 3,534 thousand. There has been decrease in the percentage share from 6.64 per cent in 2002 to 0.65 per cent in 2010. This indicates that MRB has not been giving much importance to the educational loans.

The correlation analysis is employed to check the relationship between the priority sectors lending and with various categories of such lending during the period covered. The result of correlations is displayed in Table 3.13.

Taking total priority sector lending into consideration, it is observed that the highest correlation is between total priority sector lending and self-help group loans ($r = 0.88$). It indicates that along with the increase in total credit, self-help group loan is also increasing highly in comparison to other sub-sectors. Similarly, the next high correlation figure with total lending is transport operators ($r = 0.81$) indicated a close nexus between priority sector lending and transport operators. The lowest correlation value observed with total lending is between priority sector lending and housing ($r = 0.62$). It indicates that housing loan is not increasing as speedily as other variables along with the increase of total priority sector lending of MRB. However, highly positive correlations among the variables have signified that MRB has made special dent in the banking operation in Meghalaya over the years.

Table 3.13: Correlation Matrix on Priority Sector Lending

	Row 1	Row 2	Row 3	Row 4	Raw 5	Rcw 6	Row 7	Row 8	Row 9	Row 10	Row 11
1.	1										
2.	0.990628	1									
3.	0.608236	0.632382	1								
4.	0.795227	0.742752	0.603515	1							
5.	0.712384	0.737492	0.565085	0.507539	1						
6.	0.993307	0.973855	0.60443	0.815673	0.737826	1					
7.	0.791582	0.726703	0.269158	0.91066	0.456736	0.810029	1				
8.	0.911033	0.952691	0.566726	0.577503	0.627597	0.868936	0.571081	1			
9.	0.799779	0.845179	0.72227	0.578188	0.946754	0.800069	0.465604	0.795193	1		
10.	0.950635	0.968269	0.561644	0.708525	0.847577	0.94449	0.719372	0.916651	0.911012	1	
11.	0.794224	0.782858	0.794955	0.878736	0.771125	0.806373	0.711961	0.621311	0.820234	0.7863	

Source: Calculated by the researchers based on Table 3.12.

Variables indicated from Row 1 to Row 11 are as follows.

Row 1= Crop Loans, Row 2= Agricultural Term Loans, Row 3= Allied Agricultural Terms Loan, Row 4 = Self-Help Groups, Row 5= Retail Trade/Small Business, Row 6= Transport Operators, Row 7= Small Scale Industries, Row 8= Housing, Row 9= Education Loan, Row 10= Others, Row 11= Total Credit

5.11 Growth Performance of MRB: A Comparison with RRBs

The comparative performance of MRB as well as RRBs as a whole has been summarized on the basis of parameters as presented in Table 3.14 during 2000-2011.

Table 3.14: Comparative Performance of MRB vis-à-vis RRBs

Sl. No	*Performance Indicators*	*MRB*			*RRB*		
		2000-01	*2005-06*	*2010-11*	*2000-01*	*2005-06*	*2010-11*
1	Number of RRBs	1	1	1	196	94	82
2	Branch Expansion of banks (number)	51	51	58	14,301	14,494	15,658
3	Population served per office ('000)	58,118	58,118	51,104	84,623	83,496	77,289
4	No of employee per branch	3.6	3.5	4.4	4.90	4.73	4.14
5	Total Deposits (₹ In crores)	122.63	250.41	677.42	37,027	71,329	16,3928
6	Deposit per branch (₹ In crores)	2.40	4.91	11.68	2.59	4.92	10.47
7	Per Capita deposit (₹ In thousand)	0.41	0.85	2.87	0.31	0.59	1.35
8	Total loans & advances (₹ In crores)	30.34	66.67	216.25	15,794	38,520	98.244
9	Loans & Advances per branch (₹ In crores)	0.59	1.31	3.73	1.10	2.66	6.27
10	Per capita loans & advances (₹ In thousand)	0.10	0.23	0.73	0.13	0.32	0.81
11	Credit-Deposit ratio (%)	30.0	26.63	31.91	41.0	55.6	59.6
12	Priority sector advances per branch (₹ In crores)	0.12*	0.24@	0.93#	0.50*	1.80@	4.40#
13	Share of priority sector advances (%)	61.97*	48.29@	58.79#	67.6*	79.3@	83.1#

*figures for March 2000, @ figures for March 2005, # figures for March 2010

Source: Calculated and computed from:

(i) Basic Statistical Returns, Reserve Bank of India, Various Issues

(ii) Trend and Progress of Banking in India, RBI, Various Issues.

(iii) Annual Report of Meghalaya Rural Bank, Various Issues.

It has been observed that during 2000-01, population served per MRB branch was 58,118 which declined to 51,104 in 2010-11. The same has declined to 77,289 in 2010-11 from 84,623 in 2000-01 for RRB as a whole. The growth of deposit per branch in MRB as well as RRBs is more or less same. During the period, the advances per branch in MRB have remained lower than that of the RRBs at national level. The net result of discrepancies reflected in the C/D ratio. It slightly rose to 31.9 per cent in 2010-11, from 30.0 per cent in 2000-01 in the context of the national average of RRBs which increased from 41.0 per cent in 2000-01 to 59.6 per cent in 2010-11. The percentage share of priority sector lending in RRBs of the country is better than the MRB. The priority sector lending by MRB was 58.79 per cent as compared to 83.1 per cent for RRBs as on March 2010.

The above comparison indicates that the existing branches of MRB are inadequate to serve the population in the area under study. Therefore, major areas are still remaining not served by the RRBs and the rural masses are yet to access the banking services. It is further confirmed by the analysis relating to the population per branch.

Hypothetically, the low credit deposit ratio is detrimental since it will adversely affect the profitability performance of the banks. Thus, it is high time to revamp the working and performance of MRB in the area. In order to reduce the transaction cost and increase the bank's productivity, the process of computerization and IT methods in the branches need to be accelerated. This would lead to nourishment of a new entrepreneurial culture in the area with positive strokes from the banks and thereby it will help for socio economic and rural development of the region.

Notes

1. RBI (2007); Task Force on Empowering RRB Boards for Operational Efficiency, (31st January, 2007).
2. The names of RRBs in NER are (1) Assam Gramin Vikas Bank (2) Langpi Dehangi Rural Bank (3) Arunachal Pradesh Rural Bank (4) Manipur Rural Bank (5) Meghalaya Rural Bank (6) Mizoram Rural Bank (7) Nagaland Rural Bank (8) Tripura Grameen Bank.
3. RBI (2010); *Basic Statistical Return of SCBs in India*, Vol. 39, p. 30 (Table 2.2).
4. Report of the committee on Man Power Norms in RRBs (Agarwal Committee, 2000).

4

Profitability Analysis of Meghalaya Rural Bank

The preceding chapter has devoted to assess the operational activities of Meghalaya Rural Bank (MRB) in terms of branch expansion, deposit mobilization, channelization of advances, credit deposit ratio, priority sector lending etc in the context of performance of RRB as a whole. It has been observed that banks are facing a severe competition in deposit mobilization in the personal sector with opening up the floodgate to its competitors. There is an apprehension among the bankers that the profitability of banks, an essential requirement for the healthy operation and survival, has adversely affected due to mounting over dues, poor recovery of advances and asset quality. This has further been fuelled by continuous reduction in their margins. However, MRB should not give up developmental role. The present chapter has therefore, discussed developments of the MRB in detail in a comparative standpoint to bring out the financial performance and profitability based on data of 58 branches of MRB during 2000-01 to 2010-11.

1. Introduction

Profitability is the basic objective of every business as well as motivating force behind the running of a firm. Opinions differ sharply with regard to the definition of profit. But in general, it is the difference between total revenue and total cost over a period of time (Gupta, 1977)[1]. There is mostly universal agreement with the definition that profit is primarily a residue or surplus of prices over expenses of production or leaving above costs (Hasan, 1975)[2]. Profits may be accounting profit, economic profit and social profit. Accounting profit[3] is calculated by taking explicit costs while economic profit[4] is derived at after taking both explicit and implicit costs into consideration (Angadi, 1987)[5]. Social profit is the difference between social benefit and social cost. It is yet difficult to find out social profit due to absence of an accurate measuring concept. Profitability is the ability of a given investment to earn return from its use. It is otherwise known as earning power of concern investments; it is only through profitability that the performance and efficiency of a firm or industry is judged. The higher degree of profit earning capacity will entail prosperity of the concern. The profitability is the relative term and its measurement can only be achieved by profit. On the other-hand, its relation with other subjects is compared by profit too. Like profit, there are accounting profitability and value added profitability.

In accounting profitability[6] relative change is measured by measuring the output as proportion of the input and comparing with the result of the similar firm while value added profitability is measured by the excess of turnover plus income from services over the cost of bought in-goods or services (Gupta, 1989)[7].

The profitability is a significant index of operational efficiency of banks. The higher degree of profit earning capacity will entail prosperity of the organization. The banks are highly responsive organization open to public security and must continuously ensure their profitability, which is essential for their growth and viability as also for infusing public confident (Uppal, 2011)[8]. The profitability is the most important indicator of financial performance. The level of efficiency, productivity, and cost effectiveness is reflected through the bank's profit which can be considered as a composite index of the bank's performance in its various areas of operation (Angadi and Devraj, 1983)[9]. Therefore, banks particularly RRBs at the present juncture have to ensure equilibrium between community banking and profitability and earned reasonable return to defend their survival. Hence, a detailed analysis of profitability is required to have an understanding of the present trend.

Although the banking sector works for the socio-economic development of an economy, it is also a commercial institution which mobilizes deposit and gives loans out of its collection and thereby tries to earn profit for its smooth functioning. At the same time, being a financial institution and in order to sprint the business for long term sustainability and to pay the price of the capital to the share holders, certain amount of profits the bank always needs to be targeted.

The RRBs though operate with a rural focus are primarily scheduled commercial banks with a commercial orientation. The literature provides mixed evidence on the impact of liquidity on profitability. Beginning with the seminal contribution of Haslem (1968)[10], the literature probing into factors influencing performance of banks recognizes two broad sets of factors, i.e., internal factors and factors external to the bank. The internal determinants originate from the balance sheets and/or profit and loss accounts of the bank concern and are often termed as micro or bank-specific determinants of profitability. The external determinants are systematic forces that reflect the economic performance of RRBs. Banking Enquiry Commission (1972)[11] on the analysis of cost structure and profitability observed that the present method of working out of branch profitability are not appropriate and suggested the use of certain ratios for the measure of operational efficiency. Shah (1979)[12] opined that mere increasing the margin between lending and borrowing will not improve the profitability. Any increase in income will be observed by latest efficiencies in cost structure. In the same line, The 9th Economist meets (1986)[13] at New Delhi pointed out the issue related to profitability and profit planning in banks. It recommended the professionalization of credit management, diversification of business, computerization and better cost management, etc. introducing the relationship between bank profitability and inflation. Revell (1979)[14] noted that the effect of inflation on bank profitability depends on whether banks' wages and other operating expenses increase at a faster pace than inflation. Perry (1992)[15] and Chopra (1987)[16] in similar vein contend that the extent to which inflation affects bank profitability depends on whether inflation expectations are fully anticipated. Since nationalization, banks acted over enthusiastically in observing norms much to the margin of their profits and profitability (Verma, 2002)[17]. But it was realized that adequate profits were an essential requirement of survival and healthy operation of the banking system. It is, in this context, PEP Committee (1977)[18] observed that the profitability of the banking system had come under severe pressure due to increased costs and comparatively low earnings. In the context of low earning capacity of RRBs, Narasimham Committee (1991)[19] observed that RRBs have not been able to earn much profit in view of their policy of restricting their operations to target groups. The recovery position of RRBs is not satisfactory. There are a large number of defaulters. Their cost of operation has been high on account of the increase in the salary scales of the employees in line with the salary structure of the employees of commercial banks. In most cases, these banks followed the same methods of operation and procedures as followed by commercial banks. Therefore, these procedures have not found favour with the rural masses. In many cases, banks have not been located at the right place. Rangarajan (1996)[20] suggested that banks have to cut costs, improve productivity and ensure better recovery of loans. He pointed out that NPA as the major blockade on the profitability of banks. Criticizing the banking sector reform, Joshi (1999)[21] viewed that banking sector reforms has been over emphasized on profits neglecting distributive role of banks and is contradicting the objectives of bank nationalization to spread the banking system in the nook and corners of the country.

In the era of financial sector reforms of 1991-92 the commercial viability of the RRBs in the country was in a serious strain. The RRBs have limited business flexibility and rare scope of diversification and expansion. Simultaneously, the lack of manpower expertise-ness for utilizing the fund in an efficient manner always posed a question of earning profitability and sustainability of the RRBs in the country. In order to strengthen the performance of the RRBs in the country the Government along with the RBI had undertaken the restructuring strategies. As a part of the restructuring programmes, recapitalization of the RRBs was taken up in the year 1994-95 and it continued till 1999-2000 and in the process around 187 RRBs were given the financial support to the aggregate amount of ₹ 2,188.44 crore. In order to enhance the performance of the RRBs other than recapitalization several steps like liberalization of branch licensing policy, opening of extension counters at the premises of the institution, installation of ATM branches, etc. were made liberal by the Government At the same time, RRBs were given permission of merging or close down of unviable business offices in the country. Similarly, it has been emphasized that the sponsor banks could be responsible for the performance of RRBs and would provide support in the matters of efficient management, training of staff, computerization and networking of RRBs in the country.

In the above light, Das and Ghosh (2004-05)[22] found that commercial banks are likely to have greater flexibility to rationalize their operations and diversify their activities than RRBs with limited option to rationalize branches. The study developed indicators of potential excess capacity in the RRB segment and illustrates its application to individual banking firms. Bose (2005)[23] concluded that the inception and expansion phase (1976-1990) shows rapid growth of the RRBs activities; the reform phase (1991-2002/3) raised the profitability of these banks at the cost of massive rural disintermediation, particularly of the targeted borrower categories; and the most recent phase of stock taking and perhaps some repositioning to strike a balance in the conundrum of `viability versus outreach'. Batra and Dangwal (2005)[24] observed a better performance of RRBs after the introduction of prudential norms in 1996-97 and recommended for further improving the efficiency in the present competitive era.

The Committee on Financial Sector Assessment was constituted by the Government of India (2006)[25] under the Chairmanship of Dr. Rakesh Mohan to identify appropriate ideas, methodologies for financial sector assessment. In order to review the efficacy of existing framework of money lending a technical group, was constituted under the Chairmanship of S.C. Gupta, submitted its report on July 2007 and recommended measures pertaining to the institutional reform, alternative avenues of credit dispensation such as micro finance institutions (RBI, 2007)[26].

Profitability has become the parameter that gives a competitive edge to banks. In this context, Rajkumar (2007)[27] analyses the earning performance of 28 private banks using the parameters like income, expenditure and profits. He identified some of the banks as best performer than the others. Rao (2007)[28] examined the performance of commercial banks with some established parameters like, Business per branch, operating profit per branch, return on assets, return on equity, credit deposit ratio, etc. The study suggested some measures to improve the operational and financial performance to face the challenges in transition. In the background of high level of international commitment, Pati and Shome (2007)[29] suggested to ensure a strong regulatory and supervisory mechanism for banking sector to assemble a flexible financial system. Khankhoje and Sathye (2008)[30] considering the variables i.e., interest income and non-interest income as outputs and interest expenses and non-interest expenses as inputs found that efficiency of rural banks has significantly improved after amalgamation and restructuring strategies. This finding was endorsed by Ibrahim (2010)[31] that the performance of RRBs has significantly been improved after amalgamation process which was initiated by GoI on the basis of various committees' recommendations. On the other side, the changing landscape of banking in the era of deregulation, globalization and technological advancement necessitated adequate operational risk management framework by the bank (Sinha, 2008)[32]. Under this situation particularly where the RRBs are struggling hard for achieving higher degree of performance, it is imperative to analyze the profitability performance of the rural banks in backward regions of the country in the context of national scenario of RRBs.

2. Objectives of the Chapter

The main objective of this chapter is to examine the profitability performance of MRB operating in Meghalaya. The chapter, however, proceeded with the following objectives:

- To study the growth of profits of MRB in the context of RRBs as a whole.
- To establish the relationship between volume of business and profitability of MRB.
- To assess the impact of total earnings on the profitability of MRB.
- To compare the profitability performance of banks with financial ratios in the context of RRBs as a whole.
- To identify the determinants of profitability of MRB.

3. Profitability of Regional Rural Banks in India

The profitability is a significant index of operational efficiency of banks. The higher degree of profit earning capacity will entail prosperity of the organization. The total profit is derived by subtracting total expenditure from its total income. In order to analyze profitability of RRBs at all India level, data relating to total income and total expenditure as well as figures of profit making and loss making RRBs in the national level has been considered. The position of income, expenditure and profits of the RRBs as a whole is shown in Table 4.1.

Table 4.1 showed that during the period 2000-2011, the income of the RRBs have increased on a continuous basis. The total income of the RRBs in the year 2000-01 was ₹ 4,756.31 crore and it reached to the level of ₹ 16,220.0 crore in 2010-11 recording a 3.41 fold increase. Similarly, the expenditure has also increased from ₹ 4,167.21 crore in 2000-01 to ₹ 14,232 crore in 2010-11. During the period, the increase in the expenditure of RRBs has gone up by 3.42 times which is almost equal to the increase in income level. As a result, the net profit of the RRBs was standing a meagre amount of ₹ 589.04 crore in 2000-01 which has increased to ₹ 1,988 crore in 2010-11. The net profit however, recorded a moderate growth of 3.37 times. The aggregate amount of operating profit[33] of the RRBs was ₹ 715.43 crores in 2000-2001 which has increased to ₹ 2,703 crore in 2010-11. The total assets of the RRBs as a whole increased to ₹ 2,15,359 crore from ₹ 48,569.41 crore during the period under consideration.

Table 4.1: Growth of Income, Expenditure and Profits of RRBs

(Amount ₹ in Crore)

Year	Total Income	Total Expenditure	Net Profit/ Loss	Operating Profit	Total Assets	Nos. of Loss making RRBs	Nos. of profit making RRBs	Total nos. of RRBs
2000-01	4,756.31	4,167.21	589.10	715.43	48,569.41	25	167	192
2001-02	5,564.19	4,956.31	607.88	774.08	56,803.84	29	167	196
2002-03	5,931	5,407	524	714	63,614	40	156	196
2003-04	6,244	5,475	769	1,055	70,278	33	163	196
2004-05	6,137	5,387	750	1,009	77,866	29	167	196
2005-06	6,546	5,929	617	928	89,645	22	111	133
2006-07	7,663	7,038	625	1,242	1,05,768	15	81	96
2007-08	9,406	8,379	1,027	1,859	1,25,194	8	82	90
2008-09	11,388	10,053	1,335	2,123	1,50,654	—	—	86
2009-10	13,835	11,951	1,884	2,913	1,84,093	—	—	82
2010-11	16,220	14,232	1,988	2,703	2,15,359	—	—	82

Source: 1. Basic Statistical Return of Scheduled Commercial Banks, Various Issues.
2. Report on Trend and Progress of Banking in India, Various issues.

During 2000-01, out of 196 RRBs in all India level, 167 were making profit and rest 25 numbers were loss making. The situation, however improved in 2007-08. The number of profit making RRBs appeared to 82 out of total 90. It is also found that during the period under study, the number of loss making RRBs has declined. The profit making RRBs has also declined from 167 in 2000-01 to 82 numbers in 2007-08.

4. Profitability of Regional Rural Banks: Component-wise Analysis

The component-wise growth of income, expenditure and profits of RRBs is presented in Table 4.2. The total income of the banking institution can be classified into interest income and income earned from other sources. The RRB has no exception to this. The overall income of the RRBs is classified into interest income and other income. During the year 2000-01, the interest income of the RRBs was ₹ 4,528.07 crore (i.e., 95.20% of total income). In 2010-11, the aggregate amount of interest income of the RRBs has increased to ₹ 15,225 crore (i.e., 93.87% of total income). Although, there has been quantum increase in interest income, the percentage share has declined. In case of other income, the figure was ₹ 228.24 crore in 2000-01 which increased to ₹ 995.0 crore in 2010-11. But during the years, there has been increase in the other income of the RRBs from 4.8 per cent of total income to 6.13 per cent. The total income (is the sum of interest income and other income) of the RRBs was ₹ 4,756.31 crore in 2000-01 which has increased to ₹ 16,220 crore in 2010-11.

The total expenditure of RRBs is sub-divided into interest expenditure, provisions and contingencies and operating expenditure of the banks. In 2000-01, the total amount of interest expenditure was ₹ 2,901.74 crore which was 69.63 per cent of total expenditure. This has increased to ₹ 8,612 crore in 2010-11 (i.e., 60.51% of total expenditure). The provisions and contingencies was ₹ 126.39 crore in 2000-01 (3.03% of total expenditure) has increased to a sum of ₹ 715 crore (5.02%) in 2010-11. Similarly, the operating expenditure has increased from ₹ 1139.14 crore to ₹ 4,905 crore during the period under consideration. The total expenditure of the RRBs was ₹ 4,167.27 crore in 2000-01 and its quantum increased to ₹ 14,232 crore in 2010-11. As a result, the total profits of RRB as a whole appeared as ₹ 589.10 crore in 2000-01 which has increased to ₹ 1,988 crore in 2010-11 recording a 3.38 fold increase during 11 years under consideration.

Table 4.2: Component-wise profitability of RRBs in the National Scenario

(Amount ₹ in Crore)

Year	Income			Expenditure				Profits (3-7)
	Interest Income	Other Income	Total (1+2)	Interest Expended	Provisions and Conti-ngencies	Operating Expenses	Total (4+5+6)	
	1	2	3	4	5	6	7	8
2000-2001	4,528.07 (95.20)	228.24 (4.80)	4,756.31 (100)	2,901.74 (69.63)	126.39 (3.03)	1,139.14 (27.34)	4,167.27 (100)	589.10
2001-2002	5,191 (93.30)	373 (6.70)	5,564 (100)	3,329 (67.17)	166 (3.35)	1,461 (29.48)	4,956 (100)	608.00
2002-2003	5,501 (92.75)	430 (7.25)	5,931 (100)	3,513 (64.98)	190 (3.51)	1,703 (31.50)	5,406 (100)	525
2003-2004	5,538 (88.69)	706 (11.31)	6,244 (100)	3,360 (61.37)	286 (5.22)	1,829 (33.41)	5,475 (100)	769
2004-2005	5,676 (92.49)	461 (7.51)	6,137 (100)	3,161 (58.68)	259 (4.81)	1,967 (36.51)	5,387 (100)	750
2005-2006	5,222 (93.27)	377 (6.73)	6,546 (100)	2,784 (54.71)	278 (5.46)	2,028 (39.85)	5,929 (100)	617
2006-2007	7,123 (92.95)	540 (7.05)	7,663 (100)	3,716 (52.80)	617 (8.77)	2,705 (38.43)	7,038 (100)	625
2007-2008	8,739 (92.91)	667 (7.09)	9,406 (100)	4,757 (56.77)	832 (9.93)	2,790 (33.30)	8,379 (100)	1,027
2008-2009	10,579 (92.90)	810 (7.11)	11,388 (100)	6,100 (60.68)	788 (7.83)	3,165 (31.48)	10,053 (100)	1,335
2009-2010	12,945 (93.57)	890 (6.43)	13,835 (100)	7,375 (61.71)	1020 (8.53)	3,547 (29.68)	11,951 (100)	1,884
2010-2011	15,225 (93.87)	995 (6.13)	16,220 (100)	8,612 (60.51)	715 (5.02)	4,905 (34.46)	14,232 (100)	1,988

Note: Figures in the brackets indicate percentage to total.
Source: Statements of Financial Performance of RRBs, various issues of Report on Trend and Progress of Banking in India.

In order to assess the inter-relationship between growths of interest income (X^1), other income (X^2) and total income (X^3), the correlation matrix analysis have been employed. The results are presented in Table 4.3.

Table 4.3: Correlation Matrix Analysis of the Components of Income

Variables	X^1	X^2	X^3
X^1	1		
X^2	0.91* (6.66)	1	
X^3	0.99* (21.06)	0.91* (6.66)	1

$t_{0.05}$ *(9 d f) = 1.833,* $t_{0.01}$ *(9 d f) = 2.821*

*significant at both 5 per cent and 1 per cent level
Source: Self-calculated by the researchers.

The above econometric analysis manifests that positive correlation coefficient (*r*) values are statistically significant at 5 per cent and 1 per cent level of significance in their respective degree of freedom. This indicates that with the expansion of total income, both interest income and non-interest income have increased in the same proportion. This however, signifies a positive growth trend of income of RRBs in India.

In the same line, an attempt has been made in the following paragraph to assess the inter-relationship among the component of total expenditure with the help of correlation matrix analysis. The results obtained are presented in Table 4.4. The analysis reveals that the positive correlation values are statistically significant at 1 per cent and 5 per cent level of significance at their respective degree of

Table 4.4: Correlation Matrix Analysis of the Components of Total Expenditure

Variables	*Interest expended*	*Provisions and contingencies*	*Operating expenses*	*Total expenditure*
Interest expended	1			
Provisions and contingencies	0.80* (3.99)	1		
Operating Expenses	0.94* (8.06)	0.82* (4.32)	1	
Total Expenditure	0.98* (14.7)	0.85* (4.81)	0.98* (14.7)	1

$t_{0.05}$ *(9 df.) =1.833,* $t_{0.01}$ *(9 df.) =2.821*

*significant at both 5 per cent and 1 per cent level.
Source: Self-calculated by the researchers.

freedom for each of the components of expenditures. Since calculated values of '*t*' are greater than the critical value, the relationship between total expenditure and its individual components is due to change. Hence, there is a positive relationship exists among the variables. This implies that with the increase in total expenditures, there has been corresponding increase in their components. Thus a matching growth trend in expenditure of RRB is observed.

Further, in order to measure the impact of income and expenditure on profitability of RRBs, we have calculated correlation between—(a) incremental income with incremental profit, and (b) incremental expenditure with incremental profit during 2000-01 to 2010-11. The results obtained as under:

Incremental Correlations

Variable	*Correlation (r)*	*'t' value (cal.)*
r_a	0.70*	2.78
r_b	0.53**	1.76

$t_{0.05}$ *(8 df.) = 1.860 (tab),* $t_{0.01}$ *(8 df.) = 2.896 (tab)*

* significant at both 5 per cent but not at 1 per cent level

** Insignificant

Source: Calculated by the researchers.

It is observed that there is positive correlation (*r*) between incremental income and incremental profit is significant at 5 per cent level not at 1 per cent level of significance at 8 df. Thus, it implies that with the increase of total income, there has been increase in the profits of the RRBs at the national level but rate of increase may not be proportionate. The insignificant coefficient of correlation between incremental expenditure and incremental profit (i.e. $r_b = 0.53$) at 8 df indicating that the total expenditure of RRBs has a direct bearing in the decrease of profit of the RRBs at the national level.

5. Profitability Performance of RRBs: The Ratio Analysis

The ratio analysis has been employed to examine the profitability of RRBs. The commonly used ratios are selected for measuring the profitability performance of RRBs in India. The profitability ratios are calculated by relating to various components of income, expenditure and operating and manpower expenses to a common denominator i.e., volume of business for the period 2000-01 to 2010-11. The following commonly used ratios are used for measuring the profitability performance of RRBs.

(I) Interest earned ratio (e) $= \dfrac{\text{Total Interest earned}}{\text{Volume of business}} \times 100$

(II) Interest paid ratio (p) $= \dfrac{\text{Total Interest paid}}{\text{Volume of business}} \times 100$

(III) Manpower expenses ratio (m) $= \dfrac{\text{Manpower expenses}}{\text{Volume of business}} \times 100$

(IV) Other establishment expenses ratio (o)

$$= \frac{\text{Other establishment expenses}}{\text{Volume of business}} \times 100$$

(V) Non-Interest income ratio (n) $= \dfrac{\text{Non-interest income}}{\text{Volume of business}} \times 100$

(VI) Spread ratio (s) = Interest earned ratio – interest paid ratio $(e-p)$

(VII) Burden ratio (b) = Manpower expenses ratio + other establishment expenses ratio – non-interest income ratio $(m+o-n)$ and

(VIII) Profitability ratio (p) = Spread ratio – burden ratio $(s-b)$

The commonly used ratios have been calculated and presented in Table 4.5. It is revealed from Table 4.5 that the interest earned ratio of the RRBs was 8.57 per cent in 2000-01, which declined to 5.83 per cent in 2010-11. In the same manner the interest paid ratio of the RRBs has declined from 5.49 to 3.30 per cent during the period. As a result, spread ratio (interest earned ratio – interest paid ratio) has declined from 3.08 to 2.53 per cent. The variations in interest earned and interest paid ratio resulted a decline in spread ratio of RRBs. Similarly, the establishment and manpower ratio found to be 2.16 per cent in 2000-01 which subsequently declined to 1.88 per cent in 2010-11. The non-interest income ratio of RRBs was 0.43 per cent in the year 2000-01 which has went down to 0.38 per cent in 2010-11. The burden (manpower and establishment expenses minus non-interest income) ratio of RRBs decreased to 1.50 per cent in 2010-11 from 1.73 per cent in 2000-01. As a result, the profitability ratio (spread ratio minus burden ratio) of the RRBs has remained as low during the period. The ratio was 1.35 per cent in 2000-01 declined to 1.03 per cent in 2010-11.

Table 4.5: Profitability Ratios of Regional Rural Banks in India

(Ratios in percentage)

Year	*Interest Earned Ratio (a)*	*Interest paid Ratio (b)*	*Spread Ratio (c)*	*Establishment and Manpower Ratio (d)*	*Non-Interest Income Ratio (e)*	*Burden Ratio (f = d–e)*	*Profitability Ratio (p = c–f)*
2000-01	8.57	5.49	3.08	2.16	0.43	1.73	1.35
2001-02	8.39	5.38	3.01	2.36	0.60	1.76	1.25
2002-03	7.80	4.98	2.82	2.42	0.61	1.81	1.01
2003-04	6.67	4.04	2.63	2.20	0.85	1.35	1.28
2004-05	5.97	3.33	2.64	2.07	0.49	1.58	1.06
2005-06	4.75	2.53	2.22	1.85	0.34	1.51	0.71
2006-07	5.46	2.85	2.61	2.07	0.41	1.66	0.95
2007-08	5.58	3.04	2.54	1.78	0.43	1.35	1.19
2008-09	5.69	3.28	2.41	1.70	0.44	1.26	1.15
2009-10	5.77	3.29	2.28	1.58	0.40	1.18	1.10
2010-11	5.83	3.30	2.53	1.88	0.38	1.50	1.03
Grand Mean	**6.41**	**3.77**	**2.62**	**2.01**	**0.49**	**1.52**	**1.10**
Variance	**1.64**	**1.09**	**0.07**	**0.07**	**0.02**	**0.05**	**0.03**

Source: Calculated by the researchers based on earlier tables of RRBs.

It is also observed that the average profitability ratio of the RRBs during the study period in the national level is around 1.10 per cent. This indicates that RRBs recorded on an average yearly profit of ₹ 1.10 per hundred rupee volume of business. This may be due to higher burden ratio and lower spread ratio of RRBs as a whole. The RRBs are earning a minimum level of profits while compared with the earning of public sector commercial banks in India. During 2008-09, the commercial banks in India have earned a profit of ₹ 1.50 in per hundred rupee volume of business (RBI, 2008-09)[34].

6. Profitability of Meghalaya Rural Bank: The Empirical Analysis

The foregoing analysis regarding profitability of RRBs revealed that RRBs were remained profitable on the basis of the parameters, i.e., average annual profit per hundred rupee volume of business. The gravity of the situation will be clear from the fact that net profit as per cent total asset, most telling measure of profitability performance, was 0.82 in 2000-01 augmented to 1.08 in 2010-11[35]. However, the number of profit making RRBs declined during the period under study. This apart, RRBs are earning a low level of profits while compared with the earning of public sector commercial banks in India. It is also observed that total expenditure of RRBs has a direct bearing on the decrease of profitability of the RRBs as a whole. With this backdrop, an attempt has been made hereunder to analyze the profitability of 58 number of branches of MRB operating in Meghalaya particularly to test whether the banks are achieving their desired profitability performance in the present day competition.

6.1 The Growth of Profitability of MRB

The profit is the chief barometer of efficiency and productivity of banks. It is the major objective of survival and growth of an enterprise. The excess of income over expenditure form the profit. In this context, Ganesh (1979)[36] pointed out that the effectiveness of monitoring system would depend upon profit plan, identification of profit centres and a proper Management Information System (MIS). Therefore, banks at the present juncture have to ensure equilibrium between social banking and profitability, and earned reasonable return to defend their survival. Hence, a detailed analysis of profitability of MRB is required to have an in-depth scrutiny of the burning problem. The growth of profitability of MRB is presented in Table 4.6.

It is observed from Table 4.6 that income of the MRB in the year 2000-01 was ₹ 1,40,126 thousand, which increased to ₹ 5,72,436 thousand in 2010-11 recording 4.08 times increase during 11 years. Similarly, the expenditure of the MRB was ₹ 1,13,865 thousand in 2000-01 and this has gone up to ₹ 4,52,519 thousand in 2010-11 recording a 3.97 fold increase over the years. It is found that over the years, increase in income is higher than the increase in expenditure.

Table 4.6: Growth of Income, Expenditure and Profits of Meghalaya Rural Bank

(Amount ₹ in thousand)

Year	Total Income	Total Expenditure	Net Profit	Operating Profit	Total Assets
2000-01	1,40,126	1,13,865	26,261	34,440	3,03,392
2001-02	1,71,133	1,32,406	38,727	52,891	3,52,205
2002-03	1,71,017	1,40,008	31,009	35,759	4,06,167
2003-04	1,68,975	1,46,843	22,132	30,864	4,62,521
2004-05	1,78,539	1,63,597	14,942	20,138	5,42,439
2005-06	1,69,725	1,50,402	19,323	26,534	6,66,700
2006-07	2,08,555	1,73,656	34,899	43,162	8,25,357
2007-08	2,69,043	2,09,826	59,217	73,420	9,73,316
2008-09	3,91,945	2,76,427	1,15,518	1,23,732	11,86,677
2009-10	4,22,974	3,06,612	1,16,362	1,26,767	16,04,869
2010-11	5,72,436	4,52,519	1,19,917	1,50,815	21,61,545
No of times increase	**4.08**	**3.91**	**4.56**	**4.37**	**7.12**

Source: Annual Reports of Meghalaya Rural Bank, Various Issues.

As a result, the profit of the bank which was ₹ 26,261 thousand in 2000-01, increased to ₹1,19,917 thousand in 2010-11. The profit of MRB recorded an increase of 4.57 times during the period. The scenario of growth of profits of MRB (4.57 times) is better than the RRBs (3.37 times) as a whole. The amount of operating profit was ₹ 34,440 thousand in the year 2000-01 and its aggregate amount has increased to ₹ 1,50,815 thousand in 2010-11. The total assets of the MRB were ₹ 3,03,392 thousand in 2000-01, this figure has increased to the aggregate amount of ₹ 21,61,545 thousand indicating a higher increase of 7.12 times over the years.

In order to examine the relationship between the volume of business (deposit + advances) and profitability growth of Meghalaya Rural Bank, we have calculated incremental volume of business and incremental profits during the period 2000-01 to 2010-11. In this respect, we have framed the hypothesis "Incremental volume of business has a direct and positive bearing on the profitability of MRBs". The hypothesis is tested by the correlation coefficient (r) analysis. The result is found as under.

$$r = 0.156$$
$$t = 0.447 \text{ (cal.)}$$
$$t_{0.05} \text{ (8 df.)} = 1.860 \text{ (tab)}$$
$$t_{0.01} \text{ (8 df.)} = 2.896 \text{ (tab)}$$

The '*r*' value between incremental volume of business and incremental profits is 0.156. This association indicates low relationship between the variables and statistically not significant both at 5 per cent and 1per cent level of significance at 8 degree of freedom[37]. It indicates that the volume of business does not have direct bearing on the volume of profits of MRB. Thus the hypothesis is found to be incorrect. It may be inferred that with the increase in volume of business (deposits + advances), the quantum of profits are not increasing at the same pace. This necessitates a further enquiry of component wise analysis of profitability of MRB.

6.2 Profitability of MRB: Component-wise Analysis

The income of MRB normally divided into interest income and other income. Likewise, the total expenditure is sub-divided into interest paid, provisions and contingencies and operating expenses.The component-wise profitability of the MRB may be had from Table 4.7. The table exhibits that interest income of the MRB in quantitative term increased from ₹ 1,39,082 thousand in 2000-01 to ₹ 5,52,534 thousand in 2010-11, but the percentage share of its total income dwindled from 99.25 to 96.52 per cent during the span. However, the share of miscellaneous income/other income of the MRB increased from 0.75 to 3.48 per cent. In the expenditure side, although there is a quantum increase of the interest expended its percentage share to total expenditure declined from 66.25to 58.94 per cent. In 2000-01, provisions and contingencies of the MRB was ₹ 8,179 thousand, increased to ₹ 30,898 thousand in 2010-11.

The operating expenses to total expenditure swelling from 26.56 to 34.23 per cent during the period covered. Table exhibits that over the years there has been 5.12 times increase in the operating expenditure of the MRB in comparison with 3.91 times in total expenditures. The higher rate of increase in operating expenditure of MRB may be due to infrastructural bottleneck and weak e-communication network of the area in which MRB is operating its business. Hence, an urgent step is required in this respect to control the unnecessary operating expenditure of banks.

Table 4.7: Component-wise profitability of Meghalaya Rural Bank

(Amount ₹ in thousand)

Year	Income			Expenditure				Profits (3-7)
	Interest Income	Other Miscell-aneous Income	Total (1+2)	Interest Expended/ paid	Provisions & Contingencies	Operating Expenses	Total (4+5+6)	
	1	2	3	4	5	6	7	8
2000-01	1,39,082	1,044	1,40,126	75,438	8,179	30,248	1,13,865	26,261
	(99.25)	(0.75)	(100)	(66.25)	(7.18)	(26.56)	(100)	
2001-02	1,63,150	7,983	1,71,133	84,444	14,164	33,798	1,32,406	38,727
	(95.34)	(4.66)	(100)	(63.78)	(10.70)	(25.53)	(100)	
2002-03	1,67,629	3,388	1,71,017	94,369	4750	40,889	1,40,008	31,009
	(98.02)	(1.98)	(100)	(67.40)	(3.39)	(29.21)	(100)	
2003-04	1,66,784	2,191	1,68,975	81,755	8,732	56,356	1,46,843	22,132
	(98.70)	(1.30)	(100)	(55.68)	(5.95)	(38.38)	(100)	
2004-05	1,75,315	3,224	1,78,539	86,843	5,196	71,558	1,63,597	14,942
	(98.19)	(1.81)	(100)	(53.08)	(3.18)	(43.74)	(100)	
2005-06	1,64,684	5,041	1,69,725	90,151	7,211	53,040	1,50,402	19,323
	(97.03)	(2.97)	(100)	(59.94)	(4.79)	(35.27)	(100)	
2006-07	2,02,956	5,599	2,08,555	99,481	8,263	65,912	1,73,656	34,899
	(97.32)	(2.68)	(100)	(57.29)	(12.54)	(37.96)	(100)	
2007-08	2,62,430	6,613	2,69,043	1,30,824	14,293	64,709	2,09,826	59,217
	(97.54)	(2.46)	(100)	(62.35)	(6.81)	(30.84)	(100)	
2008-09	3,61,774	30,171	3,91,945	1,92,367	8,214	75,846	2,76,427	1,15,518
	(92.30)	(7.70)	(100)	(69.59)	(2.97)	(27.44)	(100)	
2009-10	4,12,042	10,932	4,22,974	2,08,507	10,405	87,700	3,06,612	1,16,362
	(97.42)	(2.58)	(100)	(68.00)	(8.94)	(75.37)	(100)	
2010-11	5,52,534	19,902	5,72,436	2,66,730	30,898	1,54,891	4,52,519	1,19,917
	(96.52)	(3.48)	(100)	(58.94)	(6.83)	(34.23)	(100)	
CAGR	13.36	30.73	13.65	12.17	12.84	16.01	13.36	14.81

Source: Annual Report of Meghalaya Rural Bank, Various Issues

In order to assess the relationship among the components of income of MRB, the correlation matrix analysis is employed between growth of interest income (X^1), other income (X^2) and total income (X^3) during 11 years from 2000-01 to 2010-11. The results are presented in Table 4.8.

Table 4.8: Correlation Matrix Analysis of the Components of Income

Variables	X^1	X^2	X^3
X^1	1		
X^2	0.75* (3.41)	1	
X^3	0.99* (21.06)	0.78* (4.76)	1

$t_{0.05}(9\ df) = 1.833,\ t_{0.01}(9\ df) = 2.821$

*significant at both 5 per cent and 1 per cent level

Source: Self-calculated by the researchers.

The above econometric analysis shows that positive correlation coefficient (*r*) values are statistically significant at 5 per cent and 1 per cent level of significance at their respective degree of freedom and thereby, indicates that with the growth of total income, both interest income and non-interest income have increased in the same proportion. But the comparatively higher correlation (0.99) between total income and interest income indicates that the growth of interest income is exactly proportional to total income. This signifies a positive growth trend of income of the MRB. It may be inferred that MRB are performing as good as RRBs of the country.

Having analyzed the relationship of components of income, here an attempt has been made to assess the inter-relationship among the component of total expenditure viz, interest expended, provisions and contingencies, and operating expenses during period under consideration. The results obtained are shown in Table 4.9.

Table 4.9: Correlation Matrix Analysis of the Components of Expenditure

Variables	*Interest expended*	*Provisions and contingencies*	*Operating expenses*	*Total expenditure*
Interest expended	1			
Provisions & contingencies	0.71* (4.23)	1		
Operating Expenses	0.88* (6.25)	0.77* (4.69)	1	
Total Expenditure	0.98* (14.7)	0.78* (4.76)	0.95* (9.68)	1

$t_{0.05}$ *(9 df.) = 1.833,* $t_{0.01}$ *(9 df.) = 2.821*

*significant at both 5 per cent and 1 per cent level.
Source: Self-calculated by the researchers.

It is observed that all the correlation values are significant at 5 per cent and 1 per cent level of significance at their respective degree of freedom. This implies that with the increase of total expenditures, there has been corresponding increase in the individual components of total expenditure which reveals a matching growth trend. In other words, MRB is expensing the required amount in each expenditure head like RRBs of the country. However, a diagnosis in respect of influence of expenditure on profitability of MRB will be effective at this juncture to undertake strategies for future operation of the bank.

Hence, in order to assess the relationship between the growth of expenditure and the volume of profits of MRB, the analysis of correlation coefficient '*r*' between incremental amount of expenditure and incremental amount of profits are made. In this respect, our hypothesis is "Incremental expenditure has a negative impact on the profitability of MRB". The result obtained is as under:

$$r = 0.29$$
$$t = 0.858 \text{ (cal.)}$$
$$t_{0.05} \text{ (8 df.)} = 1.860 \text{ (tab)}$$
$$t_{0.01} \text{ (8 df.)} = 2.896 \text{ (tab)}$$

The analysis shows that there exist a low positive correlation ($r = 0.29$) between incremental expenditure and the incremental profitability of MRB. To test the significance level, 't' value has been calculated and found that the correlation is neither significant at 5 per cent level of significance nor at 1 per cent level of significance. It indicates that the MRB has not yielded higher profit due to an increase in expenditure over the years. Thus hypothesis is found to be true indicating thereby that incremental expenses have mounted over the years and not resulted in increasing profits. The reason may be attributed to involvement of excess staff in the branches and the volume of business has not increased over the years.

Similarly, an attempt has been made here under to identify the impact of total earnings on the profitability of MRB. For this purpose, the incremental growth of total income and incremental growth of profits has been calculated for the period 2000-01 to 2010-11. In this context our hypothesis is that "incremental flow of total income has a direct and positive bearing on the profitability of MRB". The hypothesis is tested with the help of correlation coefficient (r) between incremental income and incremental profits of MRB for the aforesaid period. The result obtained is as under:

$$r = 0.61$$
$$t = 2.179 \text{ (cal.)}$$
$$t_{0.05} \text{ (8 df.)} = 1.860 \text{ (tab)}$$
$$t_{0.01} \text{ (8 df.)} = 2.896 \text{ (tab)}$$

The correlation coefficient is found to be 0.61. It indicates a positive relationship between incremental income and incremental profits. The 'r' value is significant at 5 per cent level but not at 1 per cent level of significance. Hence, the hypothesis is partially true. It indicates that total earning might have a bearing on profitability but does not have a direct impact on the profitability of MRB. It means that the increase in total income does not result in the rise of profits.

6.3 Profitability Performance of MRB: The Ratio Analysis

The foregoing analysis relating to profitability of MRB leads us to scan further. Hence, the profitability ratios of the MRB have been calculated by using the common formulas, as used in ratio analysis of RRBs as a whole. The calculated ratios are shown in Table 4.10.

Table 4.10: Profitability Ratios of Meghalaya Rural Bank

(Ratios in percentage)

Year	Interest Earned Ratio (a)	Interest paid Ratio (b)	Spread Ratio (c)	Establishment and Manpower Ratio (d)	Non-Interest Income Ratio (e)	Burden Ratio (f = d-e)	Profitability Ratio (p = c-f)
2000-01	9.09	4.93	4.16	1.98	0.07	1.91	2.25
2001-02	9.14	4.73	4.41	1.89	0.45	1.44	2.97
2002-03	8.55	4.81	3.74	2.09	0.17	1.92	1.82
2003-04	7.51	3.68	3.83	2.54	0.10	2.44	1.39
2004-05	6.39	3.17	3.22	2.61	0.12	2.49	0.73
2005-06	5.19	2.84	2.35	1.67	0.16	1.51	0.84
2006-07	5.60	2.74	2.86	1.82	0.15	1.67	1.19
2007-08	6.35	3.17	3.18	1.57	0.16	1.41	1.77
2008-09	6.92	3.68	3.24	1.45	0.58	0.87	2.37
2009-10	5.95	3.01	2.94	1.27	0.16	1.11	1.83
2010-11	6.18	2.98	3.20	1.73	0.22	1.51	1.69
Grand Mean	**6.99**	**3.61**	**3.38**	**1.87**	**0.21**	**1.66**	**1.71**
Variance	**1.94**	**0.69**	**0.36**	**0.17**	**0.02**	**0.25**	**0.44**

Source: Calculated by the researchers based on earlier Tables of MRB.

During 2000-01, the interest earned ratio of the MRB was 9.09 per cent. This however, declined to 6.18 per cent in 2010-11. The position of interest earned ratio of MRB is better than the ratio of RRBs as a whole (5.83%) during 2010-11. The interest paid ratio was 4.93 per cent which has gone down to 2.98 per cent in 2010-11. The lower interest paid ratio of MRB (2.98%) than the RRB as a whole (3.30%) indicates better position of MRB in Meghalaya. As a result, the spread ratio was 4.16 per cent in 2000-01, has reduced to

3.20 per cent in 2010-11. The establishment and manpower ratio was 1.98 per cent in 2000-01, which decreased to 1.73 per cent in 2010-11. The average fall in the establishment and manpower ratio over the years is 1.87 per cent. The non-interest income ratio of MRB was 0.07 per cent in 2000-01 which increased to 0.22 per cent in 2010-11. The average non-interest earned ratio over the years is 0.21 per cent. The burden ratio of MRB also declined during the period. The profitability ratio of MRB was 2.25 per cent in 2000-01 which declined to 1.69 per cent in 2010-11. The average profitability ratio during the study period stand at 1.71 per cent is far better than the RRBs as whole i.e., 1.10 per cent. This indicates MRB are performing well as it recorded on an average yearly profit of ₹ 1.71 per hundred rupee volume of business where as RRBs recorded ₹ 1.10.

However, a further enquiry on identification of factors influencing profitability of MRB will definitely lead the bank in a better platform.

6.4 Determinants of Profitability of Meghalaya Rural Banks

In order to assess the factors affecting the profitability of MRB, regression analysis has been employed. For this purpose, various factors like priority sector lending, C/D ratio, operating expenses, spread, total deposits and NPA are considered as independent variables and profit earned as dependent variables in the regression model. The regression equation has been fitted over the data pertaining to the period of 11 years, 2000-01 to 2010-11 exhibited in Table 4.11. To assess the interdependency among the factors, we have used the following regression model.

$$\pi = b_o + b_1\,(\mathrm{PSL})_t + b_2\,(\mathrm{C/D})_t + b_3\,(\mathrm{OT})_t + b_4\,(\mathrm{S})_t + b_5\,(\mathrm{TD})_t + b_6\,(\mathrm{NPA})_t + U_t$$

where,

p = Profit
PSL = Priority Sector Lending
C/D = Credit/Deposit Ratio
OT = Operating Expenses
S = Spread
TD = Total Deposits
NPA = Non-Performing Assets
U_t = Error Term
b_o = Intercept

and b_1 = $(i = 1,2,3,\ldots 6)$ = Co-efficient of regression parameters

Table 4.11: Data Relating to the Determinants of Profitability of MRB

Year	Profit (π) (thousand)	Priority Sector Advances (PSL) (In thousand)	C/D Ratio (percent) (C/D)	Operating Exp (OT) (in thousands)	Spread (S) (In thousand)	Total Deposit (TD) (in thousand)	NPA (in Thousand)
2000-01	26,261	37,311	30.00	30,248	63,644	12,26,293	1,17,651
2001-02	38,727	71,450	25.00	33,798	78,706	14,32,184	1,24,995
2002-03	31,009	78,646	26.00	40,889	73,260	15,53,924	1,36,316
2003-04	22,132	77,281	26.31	56,356	85,029	17,58,127	1,36,280
2004-05	14,942	97,531	24.67	71,558	88,472	21,99,196	1,49,062
2005-06	19,323	1,20,051	26.63	53,040	74,533	25,04,085	1,50,264
2006-07	34,899	2,01,848	29.36	65,912	1,03,475	28,01,385	1,70,463
2007-08	59,217	2,58,688	30.80	64,709	1,31,606	31,59,848	1,53,258
2008-09	1,15,518	2,73,253	29.37	75,846	1,69,407	40,39,445	93,112
2009-10	1,16,362	3,92,945	30.15	87,700	2,03,535	53,23,070	1,05,318
2010-11	1,19,917	5,39,552	31.91	1,54,891	2,85,804	67,74,188	1,33,660

The ANOVA of dependent variable shows that F ratio (80.439) is found to be statistically significant at 5 per cent level indicating that the independent variables considered may be the perfect determinants the profitability of MRB.

ANOVA of Dependent Variables

Model	*SS*	*df*	*MS*	*F*	*Sig.*
Regression	17538452676	6	2923075446	80.439	0.0004009
Residual	14535433.1	4	36338583.28		
Total	1017683807009	10			

The other results found are presented as under:

Regression Co-efficient

Variables	β *coefficients*	*'t' value*	*Sig.*	R^2	*Adjusted* R^2	*SE.*
β_o (Constant)	—	2.925	0.043	0.991	0.979	6028.15
Priority Sector Lending (PSL)	1.5116	2.681	0.055			
Credit Deposit ratio (C/D)	–2645.04	–1.743	0.156			
Operating Expenses (OT)	1.911	1.742	0.156			
Spread (S)	–2.201	–1.990	0.117			
Total Deposit (TD)	–0.0673	–2.284	0.084			
Non-Performing Assets (NPA)	–2.362	–3.020	0.039			

It is revealed from the regression analysis that variation in the dependent variable viz. profitability of MRB is explained about 99 per cent by independent variables ($R^2 = 0.991$). This implies that independent variables viz. priority sector lending, credit deposit ratio, operating expenses, spread, deposits and NPA are to be considered as perfect determinants of dependent variable i.e., profitability of MRB. In order to assess the influence of individual factors on profits, we have calculated '*t*' value on individual regression coefficients. The priority sector lending and operating expenses have turned to be statistically significant which indicates that profitability of MRB have been mounted due to bank exposure to priority sector lending and more operating expenditure incurred by banks. This has confirmed the fact that MRB has deployed more amount of loans to the priority sector and spend a huge of money for its recovery which leads to increase the operating expenditure of banks. However, the negative regression coefficients of CD ratio (-2645.03), deposits (-0.067) and NPA (-2.361) implies that more exposure of banks towards lending activities, higher amount of mobilization of deposits and the level of NPAs are the determinants of profitability. Thus an urgent step is warranted to arrest the uncontrolled expenditure in comparison with volume of business made by MRB over the period under consideration.

Notes

1. Gupta, L.N. (1977); *Profitability and Public Sector*, Oxford and IBH Publishing Company, New Delhi, p. 23.
2. Hasan, Z. (1975); "*Theory of Profit*", Vikash Publishing House Pvt. Ltd., New Delhi, p. 9.
3. Accounting Profit $= (E_A + E_s) - (I_c + O_c)$
   where, E_A = Earning from assets,
   E_s = Earning from other services.
   I_c = Interest cost,
   O_c = Operating cost.
4. Economic Profit $= (E_A + E_s) - (I_c + O_c) + S_c + K_c)$
   where, S_c = Solvency cost
   K_c = Opportunity cost of capital and reserve.
5. Angadi, V.B. (1987); "Integrated Approach to Study of Banks Profitability", *Prajyan,* (October-December) XVI (4) 524.
6. Accounting Profitability $= \frac{\text{Operating profit}}{\text{Capital employed}} \times 100$
7. Gupta, M. C. (1989); *Profitability Analysis; An Empirical Approach*, Pointer Publisher, Jaipur, p. 7-9.
8. Uppal, R.K. (2011); *Profitability and Productivity Analysis of Various Bank Groups in Liberalization Era: Emerging Issues*, APJRBM, Sri Krishna International Research and Educational Consortium, 2(2): (February) http://www.skirec.com (Date of visit: 16/04/11).

9. Angadi, V.B. and Devraj, V.J., (1983); "Productivity and Profitability of Banks in India", *Economic and Political Weekly,* (Nov. 26), 18 (48).
10. Haslem, John (1968); "A Statistical Analysis of the Relative Profitability of Commercial Banks", *Journal of Finance,* Vol. 23, pp. 167-176.
11. Report of the Banking Enquiry Commission, 1972, New Delhi.
12. Shah, S.G. (1979); "Bank Profitability: The Real Issues", *The Journal of the Indian Institute of Business,* July-Sep. (59)3, 1998.
13. PNB (1986); *Profitability and Profit Planning in Banks,* Bank Economists Meet, (Collection of Papers), New Delhi, 1986.
14. Revell, J. (1979); "Inflation and Financial Institutions", *Financial Times,* London.
15. Perry, P. (1992); "Do Banks Gain or Lose from Inflation", *Journal of Retail Banking,* 14(2), pp. 25-30.
16. Chopra, K. (1987); *Managing Profits, Profitability and Productivity in Public Sector Banking*, ABS Publication, Jalandhar, 1987.
17. Verma, S. and Verma, S. (2002); *Determinants of Profitability of SBI Groups, Other Nationalized Banks and Foreign Banks*, Banking and Financial Sector Reforms in India, Deep and Deep Publications, p. 321.
18. PEP Committee popularly known as Productivity, Efficiency and Profitability Committee appointed by RBI under the Chairmanship of J.C. Lathur, submitted its Report on 1977.
19. Government of India (1991); Report of the Committee on Financial System 1991 (Narasimham Committee), Ministry of Finance, p. 54.
20. Rangarajan, C (1996), "The Role of Rural Credit", *RBI Bulletin*, Vol. 1, No. 5, May, 1996.
21. Joshi, P.N. (1999), "Banking Sector Reforms: The Other Side of Coin". *Economic and Political Weekly,*: XXXIV (14); 797-798.
22. Das, A. and Ghosh, S. (2004-05): Examining Excess Capacity in Regional Rural Banks: Some Empirical Insights for India, *Prajnan,* Vol. XXXIII, No. 4, 2004-05, NIBM, Pune.
23. Bose, Sukanya (2005): "Regional Rural Banks: The Past and the Present Debate", Macro Scan, *URL: http://www. macroscan. Com/ fet/jul05/fet200705RRB_Debate.htm.*(visited on 4-5-10).
24. Batra, G.S. and Dangwal, R.C. (2005); "Management of Non-Performing Assets in RRBs" in Jain, S.C. (eds) *Management of Non-Performing Assets in Banks*, RBSA Publishers, Jaipur, pp. 1-19.
25. Government of India (2006); Committee on Financial Sector Assessment (CFSA), September 2006.
26. RBI (2007); Report of the Technical Group to Review Efficacy of Existing Legislative Framework Governing Money Lending and its Enforcement Machinery.

27. Rajkumar, K.P., (2007); "The Earning Performance of Private Sector Banks During 2005-06", *The Journal of Accounting and Finance*, 21(2): 66-77.
28. Rao, D.S. (2007); "Reforms in Indian Banking Sector: Evaluation Study on the Performance of Commercial Banks", *Finance India*, XXI(2): 591-597, (June).
29. Pati, A.P. and Shome, D. (2007); "International Commitment and Transformation in Indian Banking", *Business Vision*, Serial Publication, New Delhi, 3(1): 45-61.
30. Khankhoje, D. and Sathye, M. (2008) "Efficiency of Rural Banks: The Case of India" *International Business Research*, l(2): 140-149, April.
31. Ibrahim, M.S. (2010): "Performance Evaluation of Regional Rural Banks in India", *International Business Research*, 3(4) (November).
32. Sinha, T. (2008); "Operational Risk Management: A Paramount Importance for Banks", *The Management Accountant*, (January).
33. In operating profit, the aggregate amount of provisions and contingencies is not subtracted from the total income of the bank which is usually done in case of net profit. This is why the operating profit is always higher than the net profit.
34. Calculated from the figures available in Reserve Bank of India, Report on Trend and Progress of Banking in India, 2008-09 considering deposit plus loans and advances as volume of business.
35. Calculated on the basis of the data provided in RBI Trend and Progress of Banking in India.
36. Ganesh, K. (1979); "Monitoring Profitability in Banks", *The Commerce*, July 1979.
37. Since we have considered incremental figures, the eleven number of observations is deduced to ten and hence, the degree of freedom ($n-2$) is eight.

5

Productivity of Meghalaya Rural Bank

An Analysis

The previous episode recognized that the profitability performance of MRB in the context of RRBs performance has been improved over the years. It has identified some of the factors that influence the profitability of MRB. In order to survive in the present competitive environment, the banks should be strengthened adequately and would attain competitiveness through the use of its existing resources and managing business in effective manner. Therefore, it is imperative to assess the productivity performance of MRB. In this chapter, an attempt has been made to study the effectiveness of MRB in the productivity performance keeping in view the trends of rural banks in the national context. The productivity measured in terms of labour, branch, ROI, ROA, profit on business volume etc have been calculated to examine the innovativeness of MRB.

1. Introduction

In economics, productivity is the ratio of output produced by per unit of input (Ahuja, 2006)[1] . It may also refer to the technical efficiency of production relative to the allocation of resources of enterprises. If the goal is to increase productivity, enterprises must produce more with the same level of input. The goal can also be achieved by maintaining the same level of output using fewer inputs. The drive to increase productivity can be caused by various factors, but perhaps the most apparent is the aspiration of an enterprise to increase profitability. There are certain factors affecting the productivity of entities. General categories of the factors concerning productivity include the labour force, product, quality, process, capacity, and external influences. The resources are also important to consider in assessment of productivity of an entity.

The increased productivity will directly result in improved profitability for the company that achieves it, but the relationship between productivity and profit is more complicated over the long term. The relationship between productivity and profitability can best be explained with a hypothetical example. Assume a situation where two companies compete in the same regional market with access to the same input factors. Both have similar levels of productivity and profitability. If one company manages to increase its productivity, it will by definition be able to produce the same quantity of goods and services at the same quality level with less input, thereby enjoying a cost advantage. The company then can use the resulting profit for new investments, or it can distribute profit to shareholders as dividends. The company may also choose to offer lower prices in order to gain market share or pay higher wages in order to attract higher skilled labour. A one time increase in productivity, however, will usually not lead to a sustainable profitability advantage. In order to stay in business, the other company will have to follow suit and improve its productivity. Once the two competitors reach the same productivity levels, they will start to compete on price until the original profitability advantage has disappeared.

In the present competitive environment, the most sustainable source of profitability is constant productivity improvement. In other words, profitability is the fleeting reward of productivity improvement. This dynamic also holds true in more complex market situations. Two companies that are located in different regional environment, but which compete directly in a global market may face different input factor costs (i.e., higher wages or cost of capital). In a state of equilibrium, the company that faces higher input factor costs will be able to compensate for this disadvantage through higher productivity. Higher wages, for example, reflect the greater productivity of the labour force in that region. In a competitive environment, where there is a level playing field, an increase in productivity by one company will start the same process as described above, where the company's competitor is forced to make productivity improvements. In fact, this process may eventually lead to a convergence in input factor costs between the two countries (Leade, 2009)[2]. The pressure for ever-increasing profits is intense and unrelenting today and accommodating Wall Street, coping with local competitors and thriving in the global economy make bottom-line efficiency an absolute day-to-day business essential (Frei and Mader, 2008)[3].

The productivity analysis may be said as an evaluative activity of the performance of an entity. The purpose of it being employed is to provide the appropriate solution to a problem that hinders the attainment of production goals in the present and future of the company. The findings from productivity analysis being undertaken are indeed of great help in providing an entity the necessary changes to be implemented for the realization of its production goals (Miller, 2010)[4]. Profitability analysis is the assessment of the impact of various marketing strategies on the profit contribution that can be expected from a product or product line whereas productivity analyses is the assessment of the sales or market share consequences of a marketing strategy. The following paragraphs are highlighted the conceptual outline and measuring techniques of productivity of banks.

2. Productivity Analysis: The Conceptual Framework

In the present changing economic scenario, the importance of productivity has assumed a crucial significance for the viability of banks. Productivity is one of the factors affecting the profitability among others like expansion of bank's operations in areas where the avenues for profitable deployment of funds are less, increased overdraft, higher overhead expenses, increase in sickness in industrial units faced by the banks, NPAs, etc. Higher the productivity, proportionately lower will be the establishment cost. It also indicates the kind of business a particular bank may be doing. A high productivity indicates that, along smaller transactions, a bank does high volume of transactions too. A lower productivity increases relative operational cost and often becomes the cause of losses as intermediary returns are directly related to the quantum of productivity. Bank, as a business concern, can not overlook the profitability aspects since profit signifies efficiency. For the long term survival and growth of banks, profit is imperative. The banks have, of late, demonstrated a remarkable ability to adjust to the new operating environment and acquired a high level of business strength.

3. Definition and Meaning of Productivity

Productivity is a universal concept refers to an organization's effectiveness in using all its resources viz., labour, financial resources, fixed assets and premises. It indicates the relationship between output and input expended in any work situation (Monga, 1992)[5]. In this respect, Peter Drucker (1980)[6] articulated "without productivity objectives, a business does not have direction. Without productivity measurement, it does not have control." Productivity is an efficiency index that measures the rate of output per unit of input like man, material, machine, money and space. It explains the efficiency in the use of factors of production employed by an organization.

Productivity is the corner stone of banking growth and economic development. In simple sense, it means efficiency and effectiveness of services. In fact, productivity is an essential part of our urge for self-improvement and achievement of excellence that is a part of our dynamic society. Optimum productivity is reached when there is a balance between all factors of production that yield maximum output for least effort (Choudhary, 1998)[7]. The productivity measures the extent to which the actual input consumption exceeds the minimum input necessary to produce the actual output level (Ahmed, 2003)[8]. The minimum input consumption is determined in a manner consistent with other current knowledge of the available production technology (Diwan, 1997)[9] but there are difficulties in measuring productivity in service industries where quality of services assumes greater importance.

A bank is described as a financial institution generating a stream of financial services in order to sustain a stock of assets and liabilities. The financial services are produced delivered and consume instantaneously. In the process, the consumer is exposed to an experiential quality that is part of the service. In case of banks, the distinction between input and output is not clear (Athma and Srinivas, 1997)[10]. One aspect of productivity is the measurement of business (deposit + advances) per branch and per employee and the other aspect is cost responsiveness and return on working fund (Angadi, 1984)[11].

The RRBs were established to mobilize rural savings and its use especially for the development of the village economy of the nation through agriculture, small industry, etc. and in the process of utilization of village potential resources. Therefore, it is an urge to understand whether the resources accumulated by the RRBs are utilized effectively for achieving overall productivity. With the initiation of financial sector reforms there have been several changes in the working of RRBs because various measures have been undertaken by the government to improve the commercial viability of the RRBs and their level of productivity. The various committees also apprehended that RRBs have always important for changing the ground reality of village economy but necessary is to improve the operational viability of the institution and thereby to bring higher productivity and profitability.

4. Previous Studies

In the context of institutional dimension, Nitin and Thorat (2004)[12] observed that efforts taken during the reform era have limited impact because the reform process change in institutional dimension has not been given adequate importance. Few efforts were made to redesign the perverse institutional arrangements that gave rise to incompatible incentive structures for key stakeholders, such as political leaders, policy-makers, stockholders, bank staff, and clients and suggested to bring change further to increase productivity of the bank. Hosmani (2002)[13] studied on performance of RRBs related to Malaprabha Grameen Bank observed that the managerial efforts in terms of imparting recent banking know-how, knowledge and skills helped to improve the business performance of the bank by way of increased deposits, advances, business, recovery and profitability. Joshua and Nahm (2006)[14] studied on cost and profit efficiency for Australian banks between 1995 and 2002 by using Data Envelopment Analysis (DEA) to construct an efficient frontier for ten banks listed on the Australian Stock Exchange. Empirical results indicate the major banks have improved their cost and profit efficiency, while the regional banks have experienced little change in cost efficiency, and a decline in profit efficiency.

Banking sector efficiency is considered as a pre-condition for macro-economic stability, monetary policy execution, and economic growth. In this respect, Qayyum and Khan (2006)[15] investigated empirically the efficiency, scale economies, and technological progress of commercial banks operating in Pakistan. They observed that the domestic banks operating in Pakistan are relatively less efficient than their foreign counterparts. Sathye (2003)[16] measured the productive efficiency of banks in India. He found that the mean efficiency score of Indian banks compares well with the world mean efficiency score and the efficiency of private sector commercial banks as a group is, paradoxically lower than that of public sector banks and foreign banks in India. The study recommended that the existing policy of reducing non-performing assets and rationalization of staff and branches may be continued to obtain efficiency gains and make the Indian banks internationally competitive. Das (2002)[17] analyzed the level of risk and productivity of public sector banks and observed interrelationship of the fact that the productivity, capital base and risk taking tend to be jointly determined and reinforced. Cheema and Agarwal (2002)[18] observed the productivity is a measure for efficient resource use and showed that commercial banks operating in India are below the average level of efficiency. Ahmed (2003)[19] analyzed empirically the bank's productivity performance and inferred that wicked nature of clientele resulted in lower productivity of banks. The factors like lower contribution to priority sector lending, lesser involvement in private sector lending and profitable activities are mainly responsible for this state of affairs. In the liberalized environment, Pati (2005)[20] has referred financial parameters in almost all the states of NER are far below the national level. He observed that many RRBs in this region are on the verge of financial collapse due to the level of business volume. Reddy (2006)[21] examined total factor productivity technical and scale efficiency changes in regional rural banks by using data from 192 banks for the period 1996 to 2002. It observed that total factor productivity growth of rural banks was higher than the service provision during liberalization. Banks located in economically developed as well as low banking density regions exhibited significantly higher productivity growth. It also observed that parent PSBs have no influence on the efficiency and productivity growth of rural banks.

Khanokoje and Sathye (2008)[22] measured the efficiency of rural banks with the help of non-parametric technique of Data Envelopment Analysis (DEA). Efficiency scores were calculated for the years 1990 to 2002; thereafter, these scores were compared for before and after the restructuring year (1993-94). The study found that productive efficiency of RRBs has increased. Ibrahim (2010)[23] observed that performance of rural banks have significantly improved after amalgamation process which has been initiated by the Government of India. Credit-deposit ratio has increased over the years showing a remarkable deployment of credit by these banks in rural areas. It also observed that during the post merger period although the number of RRBs have decreased but the number of branches and districts covered by the RRBs in the country have increased.

Reddy and Prasad (2011)[24] observed that the banks have penetrated into every corner of the country and have been extending helping hand in the growth of the economy. Despite the RRBs journeyed over three decades, they have achieved performance to the expected level turning towards sound financial management and productivity. Moreover, the achieved performance is not uniform though they are working under the approach of same management. Bhaskar (2011)[25] observed that RRBs have to be repositioned and carry out their entrusted responsibility of meeting the credit requirement in rural sector, their various constraining factor such as low credit off take, small ticket business, low recovery rate and high employee cost. In order to reposition RRBs, loss making RRBs should take step for enhancing productivity by improving the skill and performance of their employees by better and specialized training in the areas of banking and finance, IT, management, etc.

5. Productivity of RRBs: The Measuring Techniques

The productivity ratios of banks are worked out by relating the total deposits, total advances and the total business (deposit plus advances) of the banks to the total number of branches and also total number of employees. The following are the commonly used ratios measuring productivity of the banks.

A. Labour Productivity

1. Deposit per employee = $\frac{\text{Total Deposits}}{\text{No. of employees}}$

2. Advance per employee = $\frac{\text{Total Deposits}}{\text{No. of employees}}$

3. Business per employee = $\frac{\text{Deposits + Advances}}{\text{No. of employees}}$

B. Branch Productivity

1. Deposit per branch = $\frac{\text{Total Deposits}}{\text{No. of branches}}$

2. Advances per branch = $\frac{\text{Total Advancecs}}{\text{No. of branches}}$

3. Business per branch = $\frac{\text{Deposits + Advances}}{\text{No. of branches}}$

C. Return on Investment, Return on Assets and Profit as Percentage of Volume of Business

The productivity of banks can also be measured with Return On Investment (ROI) and profit as percentage of volume of business. The return on investment enables us to know profitability of the funds used for investment. It shows the productivity of capital employed. Higher the profits as a percentage of volume of business, the better will be the productivity performance of a bank. The Return On Investment (ROI), profit as per cent of assets (ROA) and profit as percentage of volume of business can be calculated with the help of following formulas.

1. Return on investment (ROI) = $\frac{\text{Net Profits}}{\text{Investment}} \times 100$

2. Profit as per cent of assets (ROA) = $\frac{\text{Net Profits}}{\text{Total assets}} \times 100$

3. Profit as per cent of volume of business

$$= \frac{\text{Net Profits}}{\text{Volume of Business}} \times 100$$

6. Productivity of Regional Rural Banks

The consequence of productivity analysis has assumed a crucial implication for the viability of banks. The high productivity indicates that a bank does high volume of transactions. A lower productivity increases relative operational cost and often becomes the cause of losses as intermediary returns are directly related to the quantum of productivity. The RRBs can not overlook the profitability aspects since profit signifies efficiency. The increase in productivity decreases the costs per unit produced and leads to better profitability. Productivity improvement is one means among others for increasing the profitability of actions. Therefore, it is imperative to assess the productivity performance of RRBs. An attempt has been made in the following paragraphs to study the effectiveness of RRBs in their productivity performance. The productivity measured in terms of labour productivity, branch productivity, return on assets and profit as per cent of volume of business etc have been calculated to examine the footing of rural banks for the period 2000-01 to 2010-11.

6.1. Labour Productivity of RRBs

The widely used parameters like deposit per employee, advance per employee and business per employee have been used to measure the labour productivity in RRBs as a whole. The accompanying Table 5.1 exhibits labour productivity and branch productivity of RRBs.

The deposit per employee in 2000-01 was ₹ 0.53 crore which increased to ₹ 2.53 crore in 2010-11. In case of advance per employee of the RRBs, it was ₹ 0.23 crore in 2000-01, has increased to ₹ 1.52 crore in 2010-11. Although there has been continuous increase in the level of advance per employee, the average deposit per employee is higher than the average advances per employee throughout the

Table 5.1: Productivity Ratios of Regional Rural Banks

(Amount ₹ in Crore)

Year	Labour Productivity			Branch Productivity		
	Deposit per employee	Advance per employee	Business per employee	Deposit per branch	Advances per branch	Business per branch
2000-01	0.53	0.23	0.75	2.59	1.10	3.69
2001-02	0.62	0.27	0.89	3.00	1.29	4.30
2002-03	0.70	0.32	1.01	3.35	1.54	4.88
2003-04	0.82	0.38	1.20	3.94	1.81	5.75
2004-05	0.90	0.48	1.38	4.29	2.27	6.56
2005-06	1.04	0.56	1.60	4.92	2.66	7.58
2006-07	1.22	0.69	1.91	5.73	3.26	8.99
2007-08	1.46	0.85	2.30	6.71	3.90	10.61
2008-09	1.75	0.96	2.71	7.92	4.32	12.24
2009-10	2.22	1.21	3.43	9.37	5.12	14.49
2010-11	2.53	1.52	4.04	10.47	6.27	16.74
Grand Mean	1.25	0.68	1.93	5.66	3.05	8.71

Source: Self-calculated by the researchers.

period. Similarly, the business (deposit plus advances) per employee was ₹ 0.75 crore in 2000-01 which increased to 4.04 crore in 2010-11 recording 5.39 fold increases.

6.2. Branch Productivity of RRBs

The parameters like deposit per branch, advances per branch and business per branch are used to measures the branch productivity. It is observed from the table that the average productivity per branch in terms of deposits, advances and total business has increased considerably. The deposit per branch in 2000-01 was ₹ 2.59 crore which has increased to ₹ 10.47 crore in 2010-11. Over the years there is 4.04 times increase in the deposit per branch of RRBs. In case of advances per branch, it increased from ₹ 1.10 crore to ₹ 6.27 crore recording 5.70 times increase. As a result, the business per branch increased from ₹ 3.69 core to 16.74 crore between the periods 2000-01 to 2010-11 recording 4.54 times increase over the years. It is evident from the table that there has been continuous growth of deposit per branch, advances per branch and the business per branch. The growth of deposits per branch is higher than growth of advances per branch throughout the period under consideration. This is a positive sign for productivity performance of RRBs. However, the RRBs performance in business volume per branch while compared with Scheduled Commercial Banks (SCBs) of the country is not up to the mark. The figure for business per branch for SCBs at the national level was ₹ 88.15 crore in 2009-10 (RBI, 2010-11)[26].

6.3. Relationship between Per Employee Income, Expenditure and Productivity

To attain higher productivity by the banking institution it needs to be highly competitive in the present market environment. After the reform in 1991, the nature of competition and the mode of operation of the rural banks have changed. The strategy of enhancing volume of business per branch and as well as reducing per employee expenditure of the bank became the need of the hour. In case of RRBs for attaining higher productivity and its healthy growth in the backward economy of the country, it required to have own strategy for their survival.

Therefore, an attempt has been made to examine the relationship between income, expenditure and productivity. For this purpose, per capita employee income, per capita employee expenditure, per employee profits and per branch income, expenditure and profits, etc. are calculated and presented in Table 5.2. It is revealed from Table 5.2 that the per capita employee income of the RRBs as a whole was ₹ 0.07 crore in 2000-01 which increased to ₹ 0.25 crore in 2010-11. Similarly, the income per bank branch was ₹ 0.33 crore in 2000-01 and it improved to ₹ 1.04 crore in 2010-11. In the same way, the per capita employee expenditure increased from ₹ 0.06 crore to ₹ 0.21 crore during the years of study. The expenditure per bank branch increased from ₹ 0.29 crore to ₹ 0.91 crore. In 2000-01, the profit per employee was ₹ 0.008 crore which increased to ₹ 0.031 crore in 2010-11. The increase in profit per employee is 3.88 times over the years. Lastly, the increase in profit per bank branch is swelled to ₹ 0.13 crore from ₹ 0.04 crore during the period 2000-01 to 2010-11.

The correlation matrix analysis has been employed to examine the nature of relationship among the aforesaid variables viz, per capita

Table 5.2: Per Capita and Per Employee Income, Expenditure and Profits of RRBs

(Amount ₹ in Crore)

Year	Per capita employee income	Income per bank branch	Per capita employee expenditure	Expenditure per bank branch	Profit per employee	Profit per bank branch
2000-01	0.07	0.33	0.06	0.29	0.008	0.04
2001-02	0.08	0.39	0.07	0.34	0.009	0.04
2002-03	0.09	0.41	0.08	0.37	0.008	0.04
2003-04	0.09	0.43	0.08	0.38	0.011	0.05
2004-05	0.09	0.42	0.08	0.37	0.011	0.05
2005-06	0.10	0.45	0.09	0.41	0.009	0.04
2006-07	0.11	0.53	0.10	0.48	0.009	0.04
2007-08	0.14	0.64	0.12	0.57	0.015	0.07
2008-09	0.17	0.75	0.15	0.66	0.019	0.09
2009-10	0.21	0.89	0.18	0.77	0.029	0.12
2010-11	0.25	1.04	0.21	0.91	0.031	0.13

Source: Self-calculated by the researchers.

employee income, per capita employee expenditure, per employee profits, per branch income, per branch expenditure and per branch profits. The results obtained are displayed in Table 5.3

Table 5.3: Correlation Matrix of the Variables

Variables	PEI	IPB	PEE	EPB	PPE	PPB
PEI	1					
IPB	0.99	1				
PEE	0.99	0.99	1			
EPB	0.99	0.99	0.99	1		
PEB	0.97	0.97	0.97	0.96	1	
BPB	0.98	0.97	0.97	0.96	0.99	1

where,

PEI = Per Capita Employee Income
IPB = Income per Bank Branch
PEE= Per Capita Employee Expenditure
EPB= Expenditure per Bank Branch
PPE= Profit per Employee
PPB= Profit per Bank Branch

The correlation matrix discerned that the '*r*' values between the variables are highly positive indicating a high degree of relationship exists among the variables. The level of per employee income is associated with the level of per employee business. With the increasing volume of expenditure there will be corresponding increasing increase in volume of business. Thus incentives to employees, automation of branches, facilities to the customers are the pre requisites for the growth of productivity of the employees and the branches of RRBs.

6.4 Return on Assets, Investment and Volume of Business

The productivity of RRBs may further be examined on the basis of the parameters viz, profit as per cent of investment, profit as per cent of total assets and profit as percentage of volume of business. The Table 5.4 depicts the aforesaid productivity ratios.

Table 5.4: Return on Investment (RoI), Profit as per cent of Assets (RoA) and Profit as percentage of Volume of Business

Year	*Profit as % of volume of business*	*Profit as % of Investment*	*Profit as % of total Assets*
2000-01	1.12	7.81	1.21
2001-02	0.98	8.98	1.07
2002-03	0.74	4.19	0.83
2003-04	0.93	4.41	1.09
2004-05	0.79	3.23	0.96
2005-06	0.56	2.48	0.69
2006-07	0.48	2.37	0.59
2007-08	0.66	3.40	0.82
2008-09	0.72	3.51	0.89
2009-10	0.84	3.98	1.02
2010-11	0.76	3.60	0.92
Grand Mean	**0.78**	**4.36**	**0.91**

Source: Self-calculated by the researchers.

Table 5.4 reveals that during the year 2000-01 the profit as per cent of investment was 7.81 per cent which declined to 3.60 per cent in 2010-11. Similarly, the profit as per cent of volume of business was 1.12 per cent in the year 2000-01. In 2010-11 this has decreased to 0.76 per cent. The lowest percentage was in the year 2006-07 i.e., 0.48 per cent. The average of profit as percentage of volume of business of RRBs is 0.78 per cent. The profit as per cent of total assets has declined with extreme fluctuation, throughout the period. The above ratio indicates that the RRBs productivity performance has been declined leading to an adverse effect on profitability of banks. This may be due to repositioning strategies of RRBs at national level in one hand, and also due to character of rural clients for non repayment of loans and advances they gain, on the other.

7. Productivity Performance of RRBs in North East

Table 5.5 presents the position of branch and labour productivity of all the RRBs in NER. It is observed that branch productivity (volume of business per branch) of Tripura Gramin Bank (₹ 2567.42 lakh) is highest in north east which is followed by Assam Gramin Vikas Bank (₹ 1427.13 lakh), Meghalaya Rural Bank (₹ 1259.63 lakh), Mizoram Rural Bank (₹ 1166.05 lakh), Arunachal Pradesh Rural Bank (₹ 963.53 Lakh), Langpi Dehangi Rural Bank (₹ 864.90 lakh), Manipur Rural Bank (₹ 438.33 lakh) and Nagaland Rural Bank (₹ 418.86 lakh).

Table 5.5: Productivity of RRBs of NER as on March, 2010

(Amount ₹ in Lakh)

Name of RRBs	*Branch Productivity (Business per branch)*	*Staff Productivity (Business per employee)*
1. Arunachal Pradesh Rural Bank	963.53	298.56
2. Assam Gramin Vikas Bank	1427.13	298.68
3. Langpi Dehangi Rural Bank	864.90	205.23
4. Manipur Rural Bank	438.33	140.89
5. Meghalaya Rural Bank	1259.63	317.80
6. Mizoram Rural Bank	1166.05	333.94
7. Nagaland Rural Bank	418.86	113.20
8. Tripura Gramin Bank	2567.42	437.76
RRBs at NER	1138.23	268.26
RRBs as a Whole	1471.93	330.02

Source: RRB Monitoring, Key Performance Indicators of RRB, Key Statistics 2009-10.

In case of labour productivity (business per employee), Tripura Gramin Bank (₹ 437.76 lakh) is highest in the north east region which is followed by Mizoram Rural Bank (₹ 333.94 lakh), Meghalaya Rural Bank (₹ 317.80 lakh), Assam Gramin Vikas Bank (₹ 298.68 lakh), Arunachal Pradesh Rural Bank (₹ 298.56 lakh), Langpi Dehangi Rural

Bank (₹ 205.23 lakh), Manipur Rural Bank (₹ 140.89 lakh) and Nagaland Rural Bank (₹ 113.20 lakh).

It is clear from the regional level analysis of productivity of RRBs that MRB placed in 3rd rank among the RRBs in NER in terms of both labour and branch productivity. However, average productivity of MRB is higher than the productivity of RRBs in NER as on March 2010. With this backdrop, a further analysis on productivity performance of MRB is undertaken on the basis the similar parameters to have in depth study of the problem.

8. Productivity of Meghalaya Rural Bank: The Empirical Analysis

The foregoing analyses clearly reveal that efforts are being made to improve the productivity of RRBs in India during the period under consideration as reflected from branch and labour productivity parameters. In the following paragraph, an attempt has been made to analyze the productivity performance of MRB. For this purpose, we have considered all the branches of MRB operating in Meghalaya. To analyze the productivity of bank branches under consideration we have considered labour productivity, branch productivity, return on assets and profit as per cent of volume of business. The data have been collected from the various issues of annual reports of MRB during the period 2000-01 to 2010-11.

8.1 Labour Productivity of MRB

We have used deposit per employee, advance per employee and business per employee, widely used parameter to measure the labour productivity. The accompanying Table 5.6 exhibited the productivity ratio of MRB.

It reveals that deposit per employee in 2000-01was ₹ 6,701.05 thousand and it increased to ₹ 26,461.67 thousand in 2010-11. Over the years, the increase in deposit is ₹ 3.95 thousand per employee. Similarly, in case of advance per employee it was ₹ 1,657.88 thousand in 2000-01 and increased to ₹ 8443.54 thousand in 2010-11. Over the years it increased by 5.09 times. In the same manner, the business per employee was ₹ 8, 358.93 thousand in 2000-01 which increased to ₹ 34,905.21 thousand in 2010-11 recording 4.18 times lift up. The

Table 5.6: Productivity Ratios of Meghalaya Rural Bank

(Amount ₹ in thousand)

Year	Labour Productivity			Branch Productivity		
	Deposit per employee	Advance per employee	Business per employee	Deposit per branch	Advances per branch	Business per branch
2000-01	6,701.05	1,657.88	8,358.93	24,044.91	5,948.86	29,993.82
2001-02	7,912.62	1,945.88	9,858.50	28,082.02	6,905.98	34,988.02
2002-03	8,445.24	2,207.43	10,652.67	30,470.00	7,964.06	38,433.16
2003-04	9,555.04	2,513.71	12,068.74	34,473.08	9,069.06	43,542.14
2004-05	12,017.46	2,964.14	14,981.61	43,121.49	10,636.04	53,757.53
2005-06	14,067.89	3,745.51	17,813.40	49,099.71	13,072.55	62,172.25
2006-07	15,916.96	4,689.53	20,606.49	54,929.12	16,183.47	71,112.59
2007-08	14,904.94	4,591.11	19,496.06	61,957.80	19,084.63	79,483.92
2008-09	19,608.96	5,759.60	25,368.55	74,804.54	23,264.26	96,776.33
2009-10	24,417.75	7,361.78	31,779.54	96,783.09	29,179.44	1,25,962.52
2010-11	26,461.67	8,443.54	34,905.21	1,16,796.34	37,268.02	1,54,064.36
Grand Mean	14,546.33	4,170.92	18,717.25	55,869.28	16,234.22	71,844.02

Source: Self-calculated by the researchers.

MRB maintained the similar trend of business growth of per employee with the per employee business growth of RRBs. During 2000-01, the business per employee of RRB was ₹ 7,500 thousand which swelled to ₹ 40,400 thousand in 2010-11.

8.2 Branch Productivity of MRB

The branch productivity of the MRB reveals that the deposit per branch in 2000-01 was ₹ 24,044.91 thousand which increased to ₹ 1,16,796.34 thousand in 2010-11. Over the years, the increase is 4.88 times per branch. The advance per branch in 2000-01 was ₹ 5,948.86 thousand and it has increased to ₹ 37,268.02 thousand in 2010-11. During the period, there has been 6.24 times increase in advance per branch. Lastly, the business per branch was ₹ 29,993.82 thousand in 2000-01 which increased to ₹ 1,54,064.36 thousand in 2010-11 recording 5.14 times increase. The MRB is doing better in terms of volume of business per branch while compared with RRBs a whole. The business per branch of RRB was ₹ 36,900 thousand in 2000-01, swelled to ₹ 1,67,400 thousand in 2010-11. The better productivity performance of MRB is due to the fact that they are able to mobilize more deposit from the area (as discussed in the appropriate chapter). This indicates that the MRB is utilizing efficiently the resources that they mobilized.

Further, we have considered correlation analysis for labour and branch productivity between MRB as well as RRB in order to examine the extent of productivity of MRB. The result found is as under:

Correlations between MRB and RRB

Labour productivity	*Branch Productivity*
0.989	0.991

The high positive '*r*' values for both the parameters indicate a close relationship between MRB and RRBs in respect of their productivity performance. It is observed that MRB is performing as good as RRBs as a whole particularly for acquiring business per bank branch and business per employee during 2000-01 to 2010-11. It means that the MRB in the state of Meghalaya is performing its volume of business at par with RRB of the country.

8.3 Per Employee and Per Branch Income, Expenditure and Productivity of MRB

The data relating to per employee income, expenditure, profits and per branch income, expenditure, profits of MRB have been collected from the annual reports of Meghalaya Rural Bank for the period of 2000-01 to 2010-11. On the basis of collected data, employee income, expenditure and branch productivity ratios are calculated which is shown in Table 5.7.

The per capita employee income of MRB was ₹ 765.72 thousand in 2000-01 which increased to ₹ 2,236.08 thousand in 2010-11 recording 2.92 times increase. Similarly income per branch was ₹ 2,747.57 thousand in 2000-01 which increased to ₹ 9,869.59 thousand in 2010-11 recording 3.59 times raise. In the expenditure side, the per capita employee expenditure in 2000-01 was ₹ 622.21 thousand and it increased to ₹ 1,767.65 thousand in 2010-11. During period under consideration, per capita employee expenditure of the MRB has increased roughly 2.84 times. The expenditure per branch was ₹ 2,232.65 thousand in 2000-01, has increased to ₹ 7,802.05 thousand in 2010-11. Similarly, the profit per employee in the MRB in 2000-01 was ₹ 143.50 thousand which increased to ₹ 468.43 thousand in 2010-11. Over the period, profit per employee has increased by 3.26 times. Lastly, the profit per branch was ₹ 514.92 thousand in 2000-01 and it has increased to ₹ 2067.53 thousand in 2010-11.

Table 5.7: Per Capita and Per Employee Income, Expenditure and Volume of Business of MRB

(Amount ₹ in thousand)

Year	Per capita employee income	Income per bank branch	Per capita employee expenditure	Expenditure per bank branch	Profit per employee	Profit per branch
2000-01	765.72	2,747.57	622.21	2,232.65	143.50	514.92
2001-02	945.49	3,355.55	731.52	2,596.20	213.96	759.35
2002-03	929.44	3,353.27	760.91	2,745.25	168.53	608.02
2003-04	918.34	3,313.23	798.06	2,879.27	120.28	433.96
2004-05	975.62	3,500.76	893.97	3,207.78	81.65	292.98
2005-06	953.51	3,327.94	844.96	2,949.06	108.56	378.88
2006-07	1,184.97	4,089.31	986.68	3,405.02	198.29	684.29
2007-08	1,269.07	5,173.90	989.75	4,035.12	279.33	1,138.79
2008-09	1,902.65	7,258.24	1,341.88	5,119.02	560.77	2,139.22
2009-10	1,940.25	7,690.44	1,406.48	5,574.76	533.77	2,115.67
2010-11	2,236.08	9,869.59	1,767.65	7,802.05	468.43	2,067.53

Source: Self-calculated by the researchers.

8.4 Relationship Among Income, Expenditure and Profits of MRB

The above table of the MRB showed that income and expenditure for both per employee and per branch have increased over the years. However, to assess the interrelationship between the variables, correlation has been calculated considering a period of 11 years from 2000-01 to 2010-11. The results obtained are presented in Table 5.8.

The correlation matrix discerned that the '*r*' values between the variables are highly positive and statistically significant. Thus, it can be argued that –

- A high positive association between per capita employee income and per branch income indicates that MRB is doing a tremendous job of increasing their productivity.

- Low level of expenditure per branch is associated with the low level profit per branch. With the increase in volume of expenditure, there will be corresponding increase in profitability.
- Low level of correlation exists between per capita employee expenditure and profit per employee. This indicates that employee productivity of MRB can increase only by controlling the unnecessary expenditure.

Table 5.8: Correlation Analysis of the Variables

Variables	*PEI*	*IPB*	*PEE*	*EPB*	*PPE*	*PPB*
PEI	1					
IPB	0.99	1				
PEE	0.98	0.99	1			
EPB	0.97	0.99	0.99	1		
PPE	0.93	0.90	0.85	0.83	1	
PPB	0.96	0.94	0.89	0.88	0.99	1

Source: Calculated by the researchers.
where,
PEI = Per Capita Employee Income
IPB = Income per Bank Branch
PEE = Per Capita Employee Expenditure
EPB = Expenditure per Bank Branch
PPE = Profit per Employee
PPB = Profit per Bank Branch

8.5 Return On Investment and Profit as Percentage of Volume of Business of MRB

The productivity of MRB has also been assessed with the Return On Investment (ROI) and profit as percentage of volume of business and the calculated figures are presented in Table 5.9.

Table reveals that during the year 2000-01 the return on investment was 2.48 per cent which increased to 4.11 per cent in 2010-11. The return on investment in 2002-03 was only 0.22 per cent indicated a wide variation in MRBs productivity. The average return on investment is 2.20 per cent throughout the period. Similarly, the profit as per cent of volume of business in 2000-01 was 1.72 per cent. In 2010-11, this has decreased to 1.34 per cent. The highest percentage was in the year 2008-09 which is 2.21 per cent. The lowest

Table 5.9: ROI and Profit as Per Cent of Volume of Business of MRB

Year	*Return on Investment*	*Profit as % of Volume of Business*
2000-01	2.48	1.72
2001-02	3.07	2.17
2002-03	0.22	1.58
2003-04	1.56	0.99
2004-05	0.91	0.55
2005-06	1.09	0.61
2006-07	1.68	0.96
2007-08	2.53	1.43
2008-09	3.01	2.21
2009-10	3.58	1.68
2010-11	4.11	1.34
Average	**2.20**	**1.39**

Source: Calculated by the researchers.

was in the year 2004-05 which is 0.55 per cent. The average profit as percentage of business volume of MRB (1.39%) is better than the RRBs as a whole (i.e., 0.78%). This is a positive sign for the MRB operating in rural Meghalaya.

The above analysis indicates that although MRB has been doing relatively better than that of the RRBs, there has been a wide variations in the productivity, as per the indicators identified, which might have adverse effect on profitability of the said bank. This variation may be due to lesser involvement of banks in profitable activities, wicked nature of rural clients for non repayment of loans and advances they obtain.

Notes

1. Ahuja, H.L. (2006) *Advanced Economic Theory: Microeconomic Analysis*, S. Chand & Co Ltd, New Delhi, India; (14th Edn.).
2. Leade, R., (2009), *Productivity and Competitiveness* Retrieved from http://www.mckinsey com/mgi/ publications/europe/profitability.asp (Date of visit, 12/04/11)
3. Frei, B. and Mader, M., (2008), *The Power of Done,* Retrieved from

http://www.smartsheet. com/ productivity/chapter9 (date of visit: 10/7/10).

4. Miller, S. (2010), *Profitability and Productivity Analysis*, Retrieved from http://ezinearticles.com/? Productivity-and-Productivity-Analysis&id=1033522 (Date of visit: 10.12.10).
5. Monga, R.C. (1992), "Dynamics of Productivity Management", *Productivity*, 33 (1), National Productivity Council, New Delhi.
6. Drucker, P.F. (1980), *Managing in Turbulent Times*, New York, Harper – Row.
7. Choudhary, A.K. (1998); *Bank Management*, Rajat Publication, New Delhi, pp, 172,173.
8. Ahmed, J.U. (2003); "The Productivity of Public Sector Banks", *Productivity,* National Productivity Council, New Delhi.
9. Diwan, P. (1997); *Productivity and Technology Management*, A Pentagon Press Publication, Hari Nagar, New Delhi, pp. 34 -39.
10. Athma, P. and Srinivas P. (1997); "Productivity in Commercial Banks", *Productivity,* (October-November), 38 (3): 441.
11. Angadi, V.B. (1984); "Some Issues Relating to Productivity of Indian Scheduled Commercials Banks", *The Journal of the Indian Institute of Bankers*, 58 (4): 184.
12. Nitin Bhatt. and Thorat Y.S.P. (2004); "India's Regional Rural Banks: The Institutional Dimension of Reforms", *National Bank News Review*, NABARD, April-September, 2004.
13. Hosmani, S.B. (2002); *Performance of Regional Rural Banks*, Anmol Publications Pvt. Ltd., New Delhi.
14. Joshua K. and Nahm, D., (2006); *Australian Banking Efficiency and Its Relation to Stock Returns*, The Economic Record, The Economic Society of Australia, 82(258), p. 253-267.
15. Qayyum, A. and Khan, S. (2006); *X-efficiency, Scale Economies, Technological Progress and Competition of Pakistani's Banks*, MPRA Paper 2654, University Library of Munich, Germany.
16. Sathye, M. (2003); "Efficiency of Banks in a Developing Economy: The Case of India", *European Journal of Operational Research,* 148(3): 662-67.
17. Das, A. (2002); "Risk and Productivity Change of Public Sector Bank", *Economic and Political Weekly*, (February 2). pp. 437- 447.
18. Cheema, C.S. and Agarwal, M. (2002); "Productivity in Commercial Banks: A DEA Approach", *The Business Review*, 8(1-2): 15-17.
19. Ahmed, J.U., (2003), "Productivity of Public Sector Banks", *Productivity, National Productivity Council,* CBS Publishers and Distributors, New Delhi.

20. Pati, A.P. (2005), *Regional Rural Banks in Liberalized Environment*, Mittal Publications, New Delhi.
21. Reddy, A.A: (2006), "Productivity Growth in Regional Rural Banks", *Economic and Political Weekly*, (March 18, 2006).
22. Khankhoje, D. and Sathye, M. (2008), "Efficiency of Rural Banks: The Case of India", *International Business Research,* l(2):140-149, (April).
23. Ibrahim, M.S. (2010), "Performance Evaluation of Regional Rural Banks in India", *International Business Research*, 3 (4) (Nov).
24. Reddy, D.M and Prasad, K.V.N (2011), "Evaluating Performance of Regional Rural Banks: An Application of Camel Model", Research World, *Journal of Arts, Science and Commerce*, II (4) (Oct. 2011).
25. Bhaskar, C.S. (2011), "Problems and Prospects of Regional Rural Banks in India", *Indian Streams Research Journal,* 1 (X), pp. 1-4, (November, 2011).
26. RBI (2010-11); Trend and Progress of Banking in India.

6

Loan Recovery and Asset Quality of Meghalaya Rural Bank

An Analytical Study

The analyses relating to productivity of MRB on the basis of the parameters viz, labour productivity, branch productivity, return on assets and profit as per cent of volume of business, etc., has identified the reasons for the variations in productivity is the lesser involvement of banks in commercial activities and wicked nature of rural clients for non-repayment of advances as presented in earlier Chapter 5. In this sequence, the present chapter has diagnosed the recovery performance and asset quality of MRB in the context of performance of rural banks at the national level. This has also covered the impact of NPA on profitability and productivity of MRB.

1. Introduction

The loan recovery of banks is the essential criteria for the liquidity of funds. The recovery performance of RRBs is more crucial for deploying more advances to the rural people for their economic upliftment. Loan recovery is the main factor which determines the quality of loan assets of banks. The lower recovery indicates erosion of banks profitability and blocking up bank credit meant from developmental project of the area. The mounting overdues lead to high level of Non-Performing Assets (NPA) and thereby deteriorate the asset quality. It consequently restricts the bank's lending capacity and stands in the way of dilution of funds to developmental activities and hence the socio economic development of the area. Thus,

improving the quality of loan assets is the true test of improved efficiency of banking system (Trivedi, 2012).[1]

The Non-Performing Assets (NPA) of banks is an important criterion to assess the financial health of banking sector. It reflects the asset quality, credit risk and efficiency in the allocation of resources to productive sectors. Since the reform regime, there have been various initiatives to contain growth of NPAs of banks to improve the asset quality of banking sector. Commercial banks have envisaged the greatest renovation in their operation with the introduction of new concepts like income recognition, prudential accounting norms and capital adequacy ratio, etc. which placed them in a new platform. The growing competition from internal and external constituents and sluggish growth in economy coupled with poor credit deposit ratio, the large volume of NPAs in the balance sheet and lack of automation and professionalization in operation have been flaring up the banking situation in the country.

High level of NPAs in banks and financial institutions are a cause of worry to the public as bank credit is the catalyst to the economic growth and any bottleneck in the smooth flow of credit is bound to create adverse effect on economic development due to mounting NPAs (Sinha, 2006)[2]. The management is seriously concerned about the growing NPA menace, which is taking its toll on efficiency and profitability. NPAs are serious strain on the profitability because the banks can not book income on such accounts. Further, they are required to charge the funding cost and provision requirement to their profits. High level of NPAs adversely affects the financial strength of banks and enforces the government to recapitalize the weak banks from time to time. On the other hand, the banks have failed to conform to stringent international standard.

The Narasimham Committee has expressed concern over the erosion in the quality of assets of which non-performing advances constitutes the bulk. The fund lock up in the NPAs is not available for productive use. When banks write them off, it becomes a charge on their profits. In order to write off NPAs, banks are compelled to charge higher rate of interest on productive loans. In the present scenario, NPAs have been the most vexing problem faced by public sector banks (Reddy *et al.*, 2006)[3]. The Government of India and Reserve Bank of India have initiated various measures to control NPAs

in the post reform years. But the banks are still unable to solve the dilemma. This needs to be remedied. With this backdrop, an attempt has been made to study the loan recovery and treatment of NPA of MRB in the context of the performance of RRBs.

2. Definition of Non-Performing Assets (NPA)

After introduction of Narasimham Committee recommendations all advances and loans are classified into two categories i.e., performing assets and non-performing assets (NPA). Generally an asset became NPA when it ceases to generate income for the bank. When a borrower fails to repay the instalment of principal and interest within the first quarter, it becomes non-performing in the next quarter (GoI, 1991)[4]. If the past due amount of advance remains outstanding for the second quarter, it becomes non-performing in the third quarter and the past due amount remaining un-recovered for the last quarter the amount would be classified as NPA for the whole year. However, it may so happen that a past due amount remaining non-performing in first quarter or second quarter may become performing in the next quarter. It is thus required to compute and report the segregated amount of NPA for each quarter and then assign specified percentage for provisioning in accounts (Sikidar,1997)[5].

The Narasimham Committee in this respect recommended uniform accounting practices for banks particularly in respect of income recognition, classification of assets and provisioning of bad-debt. The Committee holds that a proper system of income recognition and provisioning is fundamental to the preservation of strength and stability of banking system. In this context, it recommended international practice of recognizing an asset as 'non-performing' as 'when interest was overdue for at least two quarters and where interest was not recognized on accrual basis but was booked as income only when actually received'. An NPA would thus be considered as an advance where as on the balance sheet date:

(i) In respect of term loans, interest remains past due when it remains outstanding 30 days beyond the due date for a period of more than 180 days;

(ii) In respect of overdraft and cash credits, accounts remain out of order for a period of more than 180 days;
(iii) In respect of bills purchased and discounted, the bill remains overdue and unpaid for a period of more than 180 days; and
(iv) In respect of other accounts, any amount to be received remains past due when it remains outstanding 30 days beyond the due date for a period of more than 180 days.

The Committee recommended a transition period of three years, commencing from the year 1991-92, to be given to the banks and financial institutions to harmonize their accounting practices with the new norms. The banks and financial institutions were advised to classify their assets into four categories, namely standard assets, substandard assets, doubtful assets and loss assets for the purpose of provisioning (Shajahan, 1998).[6] The broad categories were defined as follows:

1. Sub-standard assets are those assets that exhibit problems and would include assets classified as non-performing for a period not exceeding two years.
2. Doubtful assets are those NPAs which remain as such for a period exceeding two years and would also include loans in respect of which installments are overdue for a period exceeding two years.
3. Loss assets are accounts where loss has been identified but the amounts have not been written off.

An asset is considered to have gone bad when the borrower has defaulted on principal and interest repayments for more than two quarters or 180 days. Globally this cut off has been set at 90 days and RBI is trying to implement the same (RBI, 2001)[7]. With effect from April 2004, an asset will become NPA if a borrower fails to pay interest for 90 days. With effect from March 31, 2005 banks will have to classify assets as 'doubtful', if they remained under the sub-standard category for 12 months (currently at 18 months).

3. Prudential Norms for RRBs

The introduction of prudential norms has been a turning point in the reform process of the Indian Banking Industry. The income recognition and asset classification norms were introduced in 1992-93 to commercial banks were also applicable with exception of provisioning to RRBs from 1995-96 in a phased manner with the provisioning norms from 1996-97. NPAs are those loans given by a bank or financial institution where the borrower defaults or delays interest and principal payments. According to RBI guidelines, any loan repayment that is delayed beyond 180 days has been identified as an NPA.

The RBI has advised to the regional rural banks to make a general provision at a minimum rate of 0.25 per cent on standard assets from the year ending March 31, 2000. However, RRBs should classify an asset as doubtful if it has remained in the sub-standard category for 18 months instead of 24 months as at present by March 31, 2001. In case of accounts with potential threat of recovery on account of erosion in the value of security, etc, such assets straightway classified as doubtful or loss assets, irrespective of the period of its non-recovery.

4. Calculation of NPAs

According to RBI directives, banks are required to maintain two sets of NPAs figure in the annual account from 1995-96. They are also required to calculate two categories of figures on gross and net basis for easy reference by the RBI. While gross NPA will be of NPAs both on the gross and net basis as a percentage of bad-loans to the total advances. On the other hand, net NPA would be arrived at after deducting provisions and claims received from the Deposit Insurance and Credit Guarantee Corporation (DICGC) from the gross NPA figure. It can be calculated as under:

$$\text{Non-Performing Assets} = \frac{\text{Gross/Net NPA}}{\text{Total advances}} \times 100$$

$$\text{Net NPA} = \text{Gross NPA} - \text{Provision for NPAs}$$

Total advances = Total advances are taken as per the amount shown in the assets side of the balance sheet.

5. Capital Adequacy Ratio (CAR)

The CAR is the parameter to reflect the financial soundness of banks. Banks maintain capital to cushion the risk of loss in value of exposure, businesses, etc. so as to protect the depositors and general creditors against losses. Bank has a well defined Internal Capital Adequacy Assessment Policy (ICAAP) to comprehensively evaluate and document all risks and substantiate appropriate capital allocation so as to evolve a fully integrated risk/capital model for both regulatory and economic capital. In line with the guidelines of the Reserve Bank of India, the bank has adopted Standardised Approach for Credit Risk, Basic Indicator Approach for Operational Risk and Standardized Duration Approach for Market Risk for computing CRAR.

Capital Adequacy Ratio (CAR) or Capital to Risk Weighted Asset Ratio (CRAR) is the ratio of capital fund to risk weighted assets. Capital reserves and tier II bonds are components of capitals fund. On the other hand risk weighted assets include fund based loans and non fund based credit exposure of the banks. Higher NPAs require higher provisions to be made out of profits, resulting in lower reserves, leading to lower CRAR, keeping other things to be same. The CAR was introduced from 1992 after acceptance of Narasimham Committee Report, which recommended observance of prudential norms by commercial banks and financial institutions, in respect of income recognition, assets classification, prescribed by Bank of International Settlement (BIS). The motive behind was that the banks should attain its competitiveness as well as remain sound in their operation. They have to maintain minimum capital funds against their risk-weighted assets and other exposure on an ongoing basis. The Basle Committee prescribed minimum 8 per cent capital adequacy standard with a view to regulate banking operation on a global basis in 1987. However, it was open to national authorities to adopt more stringent requirements. Banks in India were required to attain this ratio on an incremental basis in phased manner 9 per cent with effect from 31st March, 2000 to 10 per cent from March 2001. The CAR is derived as under:

$$CAR = \frac{\text{Capital fund of the bank}}{\text{Risk Weighted Assets (RWA)}} \times 100$$

However, the proposed accord, Basel-II, revised in January, 2000 has added operational risk in the RWA. It is defined as the risk of direct or indirect loss resulting from inadequate or failed internal processes, people and systems or from external events. However, it was observed that operational risk would constitute approximately 20 per cent of overall capital requirement. Thus under the new method, RWA constitutes credit risk along with market risk and operational risk.

$$\text{CAR} = \frac{\text{Tier-I} + \text{Tier-II} + \text{Tier-III}}{\text{Credit risk} + \text{market risk} + \text{operational risk}}$$

Risk Weighted Assets and other exposures may be calculated as–

(Assets * Risk weight) + (Off balance sheet items i.e., contingent credit exposure * conversion factors)

The minimum capital maintained by banks on implementation of Basel-II norms is subject to a prudential floor computed with reference to the requirement as per Basel-I framework for credit and market risks. The floor has been fixed at 100 per cent, 90 per cent and 80 per cent for the position as at end-March for the first three years of implementation of the revised framework. Hence, in the context of the robust capital adequacy of Indian banks, there were some emerging concerns with regard to NPAs which need to be remedied. The 2007-09 financial crisis which began in the United States and spread to other developed countries exposed substantial weakness in the Basel-II rules for regulating commercial banks. In particular, large bank holding companies suffered large declines in their return on equity from losses on off-balance sheet activities despite maintaining the capital ratios required under Basel-II. As a result, the BIS (2010a)[8] developed a new set of regulations, Basel-III, designed to alleviate the shortcomings of the previous regulations. There has been much speculation concerning the increase in the cost to banks and borrowers due to these more stringent regulations. Banks' responses will vary considerably from one advanced economy to other reflecting cross-country variations in the tightness of capital constraints, banks' net cost of raising equity, and elasticity of loan demand with respect to changes in loan rates (Cosimano and Hakura 2011)[9]. An additional feature of Basel-III is a counter-cyclical capital requirement which can lead to an additional 2.5 per cent increase in the capital ratios under a declaration of 'excessive credit growth'.

The GoI had constituted a Committee in September 2009, under the Chairmanship of Dr. K.C. Chakrabarty, Deputy Governor, Reserve Bank of India, to examine the financials of RRBs with capital to Risk-Weighted Assets Ratio (CRAR) of less than 7 per cent and suggest measures to bring it to at least 9 per cent in a phased manner. The committee had constituted a sub-committee to analyse the financials of RRBs in detail for assessing capital required to attain 7 per cent CRAR by March 2011 and 9 per cent by March 2012.

6. Studies on Non-Performing Assets of Banks

Various studies have been conducted on the loan recovery and NPA management of banks in Indian context. Some of which deserve a mention to pinpoint the significance of this chapter.

In view of the increasing overdues and willful defaulting, Hosmani (2002)[10] observed that the insurance coverage should be encouraged and effectively implemented in place of loan waiver during aberrant weather conditions. Adopting appropriate insurance schemes and linking with marketing should evolve fool proof system for recovery of loans. The incentives may be provided to encourage prompt repayment of loans. Raul (2004)[11] suggested that an appropriate set of substantial financial sector regulation clarity including changes in tax laws is imperative for the banking system to get rid of NPAs to look forward to the investment opportunity. Pati (2005)[12] in his study of Subansiri Gaonlia Bank in the Lakhimpur district of Assam suggested that credit appraisal should be properly taken care of to avoid incidence of NPA. In each branch at least one trained staff should be recruited. In this regard, the branches should go for rating the borrowers on a scientific basis rather than sanctioning loan on the need basis of the borrower. Further, he suggested the bank can go for securitization of its loan assets and can transfer some of its bad loans to the Asset Reconstruction Company (ARC). Singh and Singh (2009)[13] in their paper examined the recovery performance of Manipur Rural Bank. The study observed that the repayment of loans mainly depends on proper utilization of the loan amount, supply of quality assets, generation of sufficient income from schemes, availability of infrastructural and marketing facilities, willingness to repay, continuous supervision and follow-up visits etc. Akhan (2009)[14] attempted to study the NPA Management of NBFC in India during 2002-2007 and suggested that pre-sanctioned scrutiny and post sanctioned supervision, effective recovery steps and fully compliance with the prudential norms of RBI help to control NPA.

Ghosh and Ghosh (2011)[15] established that NPA is an important parameter in the analysis of financial performance of a bank as it results in decreasing margin and higher provisioning requirements for doubtful debts. Various banks from different categories together provide advances to different sectors like agriculture, SSI, priority sector, public sector and others. These advances require pre-sanctioning appraisal and post-disbursement control to contain increasing NPAs in the Indian banking sector. The reduction of NPA is necessary to improve profitability of banks and comply with the capital adequacy norms as per the Basel Accord. Unny (2011)[16] considered about effectiveness of remedies available for banks in a Debt Recovery Tribunal, and originate that, banking in India faces the difficulty of mounting NPA, which is unfavourable for the bank's financial health. Banks have had to wait for very long time in Civil Courts to get cases concerning debt-recovery disposed and recovered. This led to the trapping of crores of rupees in litigation proceedings, which the bank could not re-advance, forcing the Government to establish a Debt Recovery Tribunal (DRT) to assure expeditious recovery proceedings and speedy adjudication of matters concerning debt recovery of banks. Yadab (2011)[17] studied about Impact of NPAs on profitability and productivity of PSBs and opined that an adverse impact on profitability of banks at aggregate or sectoral level indicating high degree of riskiness in credit portfolio and raising question mark on the credit appraisal.

Poongavanam (2011)[18] opined that the banking industry has undergone a sea change after the first phase of economic liberalization in 1991 and hence credit management. In recent times, the banks have become very cautious in extending loans, this is due to mounting NPAs. Therefore, an NPA account not only reduces profitability of banks by provisioning in the profit and loss account, but their carrying cost is also increased which results in excess and avoidable management attention. Apart from this, a high level of NPA also puts strain on a bank's net worth. Considering all the above facts banking industry has to give more importance to NPA and to structure proper remedial solutions. Kumar and Sharma (2011)[19] on the comparative study of Himachal Gramin Bank and Parvatiya Gramin Bank found that the Parvatiya Gramin Bank is more conservative as compared to the Himachal Gramin Bank with regard to NPAs' management. It is because of the fact that NPAs to total assets ratio for the Parvatiya Gramin Bank has decreased.

From the review of earlier studies, it is revealed that not many studies based exclusively on the loan recovery and management of NPAs of RRBs. Most of the studies relate to the quality of bank assets and loan portfolio.

7. Recovery Performance of RRBs

The recovery performance of RRB was estimated at 80.03 per cent, as on 30 June 2010, as compared to 77.85 per cent as on 30 June 2008. The NER has remained lower in terms of recovery percentage throughout the period under consideration. The RRBs have emerged as a strong intermediary for financial inclusion in rural areas by opening a large number of "No Frills" accounts and financing under General Credit Cards (GCC). RRB as a group in the northern and southern region registered a recovery performance above the national average throughout the entire period. Table 6.1 presents the region-wise recovery position of RRBs in India.

Table 6.1: Recovery Positions of RRBs As on March

(Percentage)

Region	2004	2005	2008	2009	2010
1. North-Eastern	59.2	65.8	65.51	72.47	74.82
2. Eastern	68.8	71.5	68.10	74.58	73.10
3. Northern	85.9	88.3	85.01	85.69	88.70
4. Central	77.4	78.1	76.24	75.45	75.01
5. Western	74.9	75.5	77.85	76.64	77.36
6. Southern	80.0	82.8	81.51	82.83	81.40
All India	**77.7**	**79.8**	**77.85**	**80.09**	**80.03**

Source: NABARD Annual Report, Various Issues.

Table 6.2 shows frequency distribution of states according to the levels of recovery of RRBs. A recovery of above 80 per cent was achieved by 39 RRBs in the country, while 37 RRB had recovery levels ranging above 60 per cent but less than 80 per cent. Six RRB had recovery more than 40 per cent but below 60 per cent. None of the RRBs is having recovery of less than 40 per cent.

Table 6.2: Frequency Distribution of States according to Levels of Recovery of RRBs (As on 30 June, 2010)

Recovery percentage	*Number of RRBs*	*States*
Less than 40	0	Nil
Between 40 and 60	6	Bihar (1), Madhya Pradesh (1), Manipur (1), Odisha (1), Jharkhand (1), Karnataka (1)
Between 60 and 80	37	Andhra Pradesh (3), Arunachal Pradesh (1), Assam (1), Bihar (2), Chhattisgarh (2), Gujarat (1), Jammu & Kashmir (1), Jharkhand (1), Karnataka (2), Madhya Pradesh (5), Maharashtra (2), Meghalaya (1), Nagaland (1), Orissa (3), Tripura (1), Uttar Pradesh (7), West Bengal (3)
More than 80	39	Andhra Pradesh (2), Assam (1), Bihar (1), Chhattisgarh (1), Gujarat (2), Haryana (2), Himachal Pradesh (2), Jammu & Kashmir (1), Karnataka (3), Kerala (2), Madhya Pradesh (2), Maharashtra (1), Mizoram (1), Orissa (1), Pondicherry (1), Punjab (3), Rajasthan (6), Tamil Nadu (2), Uttar Pradesh (3), Uttarakhand (2)

Note: Figures in parentheses against each state indicate number of RRBs.
Source: NABARD Annual Report, 2010-11.

7.1 Magnitude of NPAs in RRBs

The Indian banking system had acquired a large quantum of NPAs, which can be termed as legacy NPAs. The high level of NPA of the Indian financial sector reflects country's poor bankruptcy laws. The gross NPAs of scheduled commercial banks in absolute term reduced from ₹ 60,841 crore in March 2000 to ₹ 50,486 crore in March 2007 and thereafter started to increase and reached to 89,017 crore in March 2011 (RBI, 2010-11)[20]. This has been largely possible because of the huge provisioning that most of these banks could make as a result of growth in treasury income and, therefore profits.

The gross NPAs of RRBs in absolute term reduced from ₹ 3067 crore in 2001-02 to ₹ 3084 crores in 2009-2010. It has been observed that the percentage of net NPAs to total advances of RRBs declined from 11.13 per cent in March 2001-02 to 3.19 per cent in 2007-08 and further to 1.80 per cent in 2009-10 (NABARD)[21]. The gross NPAs as per cent of total advances also declined to 3.72 per cent from 16.46 per cent during the same period. This significant reduction of NPAs may be due to the definitional changes of NPAs and appropriate strategy for controlling the fresh accretion of NPAs. Table 6.3 presents the gross and net NPAs of RRBs and PSBs in India.

Table 6.3: Gross and Net NPA of RRBs vs PSBs

(Percentage)

Year	*Regional Rural Bank*		*Public Sector Banks*	
	Gross NPA to advances	*Net NPA to advances*	*Gross NPA to advances*	*Net NPA to advances*
2001-02	16.46	11.13	11.1	5.8
2002-03	14.44	9.51	9.4	4.5
2003-04	12.63	8.51	7.8	3.0
2004-05	8.53	4.84	5.4	2.1
2005-06	7.28	3.92	3.7	1.3
2006-07	6.55	3.46	2.7	1.1
2007-08	6.04	3.19	2.8	0.8
2008-09	4.13	1.98	3.1	0.7
2009-10	3.72	1.80	2.19	1.09

Source: 1. RRB Monitoring, Key Statistics of RRBs 2009-10 and Annual Report of NABARD, Various Issues.
2. Trend and progress of Banking in India, Various Issues.

It is revealed that though NPAs maintaining a declining trend across all segments of banking sector, RRBs position are inferior as compared to PSBs. The reasons of decline of NPAs to total advances may be attributed to change in the composition of assets in favour of investment in government and other approved securities and the banks unwillingness or inability to assume higher exposure to small and medium enterprises and farm sector.

7.2 Asset Classification of RRBs

Table 6.4 exhibits that the total amount of loan outstanding of the RRBs in all India level was ₹ 82,81,910. 28 lakh in March 2010 whereas the total amount of loan outstanding of MRB in 2010 was ₹ 16,048.69 lakh.

Table 6.4: Asset Classification of RRBs in North-East and All India, March 2010

(Amount ₹ in Lakh)

Banks	Total Loan	Standard Asset	Non-Performing Assets (NPA)				Total Assets
			Sub-standard Asset	Doubtful Asset	Loss Assets	Total NPA	
Arunachal Pradesh Rural Bank	4211.85	3492.41 (82.92)	328.27 (7.79)	243.31 (5.78)	147.86 (3.51)	719.44 (17.08)	4211.85
Assam Gramin Vikas Bank	161823.28	150740.24 (93.15)	3013.10 (1.86)	8069.94 (4.99)	0.00 (–)	11083.04 (6.85)	161823.28
Langpi Dehangi Rural Bank	13422.04	12812.11 (95.46)	348.54 (2.60)	258.59 (1.93)	2.80 (0.02)	609.93 (4.54)	13422.04
Manipur Rural Bank	3080.76	1562.77 (50.73)	359.60 (11.67)	1156.51 (37.54)	1.88 (0.06)	1517.99 (49.27)	3080.76
Meghalaya Rural Bank	16048.69	14995.51 (93.44)	295.03 (1.84)	607.32 (3.78)	150.83 (0.94)	1053.18 (6.56)	16048.69
Mizoram Rural Bank	23452.67	21783.07 (92.88)	1208.93 (5.15)	415.17 (1.77)	45.50 (0.19)	1669.6 (7.12)	23452.67
Nagaland Rural Bank	871.62	729.39 (83.68)	69.85 (8.01)	72.38 (8.30)	0.00 (–)	142.23 (16.32)	871.62
Tripura Rural Bank	79964.76	77083.43 (96.40)	443.53 (0.55)	2400.80 (3.0)	37.0 (0.05)	2881.33 (3.60)	79964.76
All India RRBs	8281910.28	7973428.85 (96.28)	118175.44 (1.43)	171322.48 (2.07)	18983.51 (0.23)	308481.43 (3.72)	8281910.28
All RRBs in NE Region	302875.67	283198.93 (93.50)	6066.85 (2.0)	13224.02 (4.37)	385.87 (0.13)	19676.74 (6.50)	302875.67

Note: Figures in brackets indicate percentage to total loans and advances.
Source: RRB Monitoring, Key Statistics of RRBs 2009-10 and Annual Report of NABARD, Various Issues.

It is observed that the NPA as per cent of advances of RRBs in NER was 6.50 per cent in March 2010 while the corresponding figure for RRBs of the country as a whole was 3.72 per cent. The NPA as per cent of advances of MRB is however, higher than the RRBs of NER and RRBs as a whole. The NPA was 6.65 per cent of total advances of MRB during March 2010.

The foregoing analysis aptly demonstrates that the malady of high level of NPAs eroding the profitability of banks is not confined to RRBs alone, but it is severely present in the RRBs of NER also. The RBI in this respect proposed Prompt Corrective Action (PCA) mechanism for arresting the menace of NPAs. On the other hand, RBI has introduced various measures like credit risk management models, Compromise Settlement methods, effective use of Debt Recovery Tribunals (DRT's), Asset Reconstruction Companies (ARC) and Recovery of Debts[22], Securitization and Reconstruction of Financial Assets and Enforcement of Security Interest (SRFAESI) Act-2002[23], Circulation of information on defaulters, Corporate Debt Restructuring (CDR), Lok Adalats and so on.

With a view to provide an additional option and developing a healthy secondary market for NPAs, the guideline relating to sale/purchase of NPAs were issued in July 2005 covering the procedure for purchase/sale of NPAs by banks valuation aspects, prudential norms. The guideline were partly modified in May 2007 whereby it was stipulated that atleast 10 per cent of the estimated cash flows should be realized in the first year and atleast 5 per cent in each half year thereafter subject to full recovery within three years.

8. Loan Recovery and Asset Quality of MRB: The Analysis of Data

It has been observed from the foregoing discussion that there are a number of factors causing NPAs which became great concern of the planners in the context of the country as a whole. However, during reform era there has been a declining proportion of NPAs in the asset portfolio of RRBs in India. Now the reason for NPAs may be studied in MRB particularly to find out the growth trend of NPAs and to identify whether similar factors are amounting to NPAs. In this respect, we have conducted an empirical study over the branches of MRB in Meghalaya. The major objectives are:

- To study the recovery performance of MRB over the years.
- To study the nature and growth of NPAs of MRBs.
- To study the impact of NPAs on profitability and productivity.

For this purpose, 58 branches of MRB operating in Meghalaya have been considered. An attempt has also been made to cross section analysis of NPAs of bank branches pertaining to 11 years i.e., from 2000-01 to 2010-11. The statistical techniques have been used to analyze the data relating to and associated with NPAs.

8.1 Demand and Recovery Performance of Credit in Meghalaya Rural Bank

The loan recovery[24] performance of banks is the *sin qua non* for their liquidity of funds. The lower recovery indicates erosion of bank's profitability and blocking up of bank credit meant for developmental projects of the area. It consequently restricts the bank's lending capacity and stands in the way of dilution of funds to developmental activities and hence, the socio-economic and rural development of the area. The demand, recovery and overdue position of MRB during the study period from 2000-01 to 2010-11 is presented in Table 6.5. From Table 6.5, it is observed that the recovery amount of credit in the year 2000-01 was ₹ 92,096 thousand which increased to ₹ 6,84,187 thousand in 2010-11. The recovery position evidenced 7.43 times increase over the years. At the same time, the total credit overdue was ₹ 1,21,165 thousand in 2000-01, increased to ₹ 1,84,111 thousand in 2010-11 recording 1.51 fold increase. Thus, it indicates that the increase in recovery performance of the bank during the period is better than the proportionate increase in the overdues amount of the bank.

The percentage share of loan recovery to total demand has been increased during the period; the figure was 43.18 per cent in 2000-01 which increased to 78.8 per cent in 2010-11. Again in case of overdues, the percentage share has declined from 56.82 per cent in 2000-01 to 21.20 per cent in 2010-11. Hence, it confirms the fact that the MRB is doing a reasonably better management of its recovery of loans.

However, MRB is lagging behind in its recovery position while compared with the RRBs of the country as a whole. As on March 2010, average recovery of RRB was 80.03 per cent while the same for MRB was 78.22 per cent. Hence, a further examination of sector-wise recovery position of MRB has been done in the following paragraphs.

Table 6.5: Demand and Recovery Performance of Credit of the MRB

(Amount Rupees in Thousand)

Year	Total Recovery	Total Overdues	Total Demand	Recovery Percentage	Percentage of Overdues
2000-01	92,096	1,21,165	2,13,261	43.18	56.82
2001-02	1,07,392	1,17,498	2,24,890	47.75	52.25
2002-03	1,29,560	1,23,688	2,53,248	51.16	48.84
2003-04	1,59,351	1,34,977	2,94,328	54.14	45.86
2004-05	2,14,023	1,43,514	3,57,537	59.86	40.14
2005-06	2,30,660	1,47,829	3,78,489	60.94	39.06
2006-07	2,55,650	1,62,799	4,18,449	61.09	38.90
2007-08	2,94,750	1,79,325	4,74,075	62.17	37.83
2008-09	5,48,805	1,53,939	7,02,744	78.09	21.91
2009-10	5,18,628	1,44,379	6,63,007	78.22	21.76
2010-11	6,84,187	1,84,111	8,68,298	78.80	21.20

Source: Annual Report of Meghalaya Rural Bank and Calculated by the researchers.

8.2 Recovery Performance of Farm and Non-Farm Sector Advances of MRB

The recovery performance of farm and non-farm sector of MRB can be well grasped from the Table 6.6. It has been observed that the recovery position was poor in farm sector than the non-farm sector. In 2000-01, it was 17.61 per cent for farm sector and 63.47 per cent for non-farm sector.

The lower recovery indicates erosion of banks profitability and blocking up bank credit from developmental projects of the area. The gravity of the situation will be cleared when we found ₹ 1,57,594 thousand (64.37%) was realized against the total outstanding dues of ₹ 2,44,835 thousand under farm sector and ₹ 5,26,593 thousand (84.46%) against the total outstanding dues of ₹ 6,23,463 thousand under non-farm sector during 2010-11. However, in percentage term, the recovery position of MRB has improved steadily in both the sectors during 2010-11.

The recovery position in farm sector is relatively discouraging. The noteworthy facet of banks lending is that, despite mounting overdues in each year, the farm sector e.g., agriculture and allied activities, enjoyed a notable quantum of bank credit. The agriculturists and poor people of the area could not repay the loans because they

Table 6.6: Farm and Non-Farm Sector Performance of Meghalaya Rural Bank

(Amount ₹ In thousand)

Year	Farm Sector					Non-Farm Sector				
	Demand	Recovery		Overdues		Demand	Recovery		Overdues	
		Amount	Per cent	Amount	Per cent		Amount	Per cent	Amount	Per cent
2000-01	94,322	16,608	17.61	77,714	82.39	1,18,939	75,488	63.47	43,451	36.53
2001-02	92,160	17,941	19.47	74,219	80.53	1,32,730	89,451	67.39	43,279	32.61
2002-03	97,581	20,030	20.53	77,551	79.47	1,55,667	1,09,530	70.36	46,137	29.64
2003-04	1,04,356	20,970	20.09	83,386	79.91	1,89,972	1,38,381	72.84	51,591	27.16
2004-05	1,18,158	27,304	23.11	90,854	76.89	2,39,379	1,86,719	78.00	52,660	21.99
2005-06	1,21,602	29,915	24.60	91,687	75.40	2,56,887	2,00,745	78.15	56,142	21.85
2006-07	1,43,933	43,965	30.55	99,968	69.45	2,74,516	2,11,685	77.11	62,831	22.89
2007-08	1,68,888	62,790	37.18	1,06,098	62.82	3,05,178	2,31,960	76.00	73,227	23.99
2008-09	2,06,706	1,54,785	74.88	51,921	25.12	4,96,038	3,94,020	79.43	1,02,018	20.57
2009-10	1,95,018	1,46,274	75.00	48,744	24.99	4,67,989	3,72,354	79.56	95,635	20.44

Source: Annual Report of Meghalaya Rural Bank.

spend their loan on consumption purposes rather than productive purposes without bothering the liability of making repayment because of illiteracy. Further, there have been numerous disparities in the region for distribution of resources. Hence, the flow of institutional loans has particularly benefited the richer section of the society. In that context, the priority sector lending provides privileges to the poor people in order to lift their economic structure and condition. Indeed, they get subsidy by government on this loan. But they do not use the loan in the proper way for productive use. So, the loanee cannot return loan. The constant failure of monsoon, natural calamities as famine, drought, willful default, etc. is the chief reasons for non-recovery of loans. The reasons for poor recovery may also be attributed to various other factors such as lack of supervision of end use of fund, defective processing of loan applications, communication gap between banker and customer, etc. In the absence of any suitable step for recovery from the loans sanctioning authority, the loan is never recovered and it becomes difficult to pay back by the borrowers due to heavy amount. As a result, the mounting overdues restricted the bank's lending capacity. Therefore, an immediate action from appropriate authority to accelerate the recovery position in all sectors is necessary.

8.3 Asset Classification of Meghalaya Rural Bank

Table 6.7 demonstrated the position of NPAs of MRB during 2000-2011. Table 6.7 unfolds that the proportion of total NPAs to total advances declined to 6.18 per cent in 2010-11 from 38.78 per cent in 2000-01. The MRB is not in a position reduce its NPAs as like as RRBs as a whole. As on March 2010, the NPA as per cent to advances of RRBs was 3.72 per cent as compared to 6.52 per cent for MRB. This may be due to inappropriate remedial measures and improper recovery mechanism undertaken by the MRB.

Table 6.7 exhibits that the quantum of standard asset of the MRB and the percentage share to total advances has been increased throughout the period. The amount of standard assets was ₹ 1,85,741 thousand in 2000-01 has increased to ₹ 20,27,885 thousand in 2010-11. This indicates that the performance of MRB in terms of enhancing standard asset has augmented by 10.92 fold. The total NPA

Table 6.7: Asset Classification of Meghalaya Rural Bank

(Amount Rupees in Thousand)

Year	Standard Asset	Non-Performing Assets				Total Loans and Advances Outstanding
		Sub-Standard Asset	Doubtful Asset	Loss Assets	Total NPA	
2000-01	1,85,741 (61.22)	31,328 (10.33)	62,416 (20.57)	23,907 (7.88)	1,17,651 (38.78)	3,03,392 (100)
2001-02	2,27,210 (64.51)	24,985 (7.09)	76,098 (21.61)	23,912 (6.79)	1,24,995 (35.49)	3,52,205 (100)
2002-03	2,69,851 (66.44)	31,857 (7.84)	77,314 (19.04)	27,145 (6.68)	1,36,316 (33.56)	4,06,167 (100)
2003-04	3,26,242 (70.54)	24,226 (5.24)	79,375 (17.16)	32,678 (7.07)	1,36,279 (29.46)	4,62,521 (100)
2004-05	3,93,377 (72.52)	29,608 (5.46)	81,980 (15.11)	37,474 (6.90)	1,49,062 (27.48)	5,42,439 (100)
2005-06	5,16,436 (77.46)	24,326 (3.65)	77,497 (11.62)	48,441 (7.27)	1,50,264 (22.54)	6,66,700 (100)
2006-07	6,54,894 (79.35)	41,673 (5.05)	88,022 (10.66)	40,768 (4.94)	1,70,463 (20.65)	8,25,357 (100)
2007-08	8,20,058 (84.25)	29,108 (2.99)	89,797 (9.23)	34,353 (3.53)	1,53,258 (15.75)	9,73,316 (100)
2008-09	10,93,366 (92.14)	22,077 (1.86)	49,475 (4.17)	21,759 (1.83)	93,311 (7.86)	11,86,677 (100)
2009-10	14,99,551 (93.44)	29,503 (1.84)	60,733 (3.78)	15,082 (0.94)	1,05,318 (6.52)	16,04,869 (100)
2010-11	20,27,885 (93.82)	64,917 (3.00)	54,011 (2.50)	14,732 (0.68)	1,33,660 (6.18)	21,61,545 (100)

Source: Annual Reports of Meghalaya Rural Bank, Various Issues.

of the MRB are classified into sub-standard asset, doubtful asset and loss asset. It is observed that the aggregate amount of the sub-standard asset of the bank was ₹ 31,328 thousand in 2000-01 which increased to ₹ 64,917 thousand in 2010-11. Although, the aggregate amount has increased, the percentage share has decreased from 10.33 per cent in 2000-01 to 3.00 per cent in 2010-11 of total loans and advances outstanding. In the same manner, the doubtful asset of the MRB was ₹ 62,416 thousand in 2000-01 (which is 20.57 per cent of total loans and advances outstanding) and it decreased to ₹ 54, 011 thousand in 2010-11 (i.e., 2.50 per cent of total loans and advances outstanding). The loss asset of the MRB has declined both in quantum and percentage share. It was ₹ 23,907 thousand in 2000-01 which decreased to ₹ 14,732 thousand in 2010-11. Over the years, the percentage figure of loss asset decreased from 7.88 to 0.68 per cent of total loans and advances outstanding. There have been 1.14 fold increases of NPAs of MRB while loans and advances of MRB recorded 7.12 times increase during the period under consideration. Hence, it may be inferred that MRB is not in a position to manage and contain its NPAs as reflected from the NPAs as per cent to advances and comparative growth of NPA and advances. This necessitates a further investigation in the relationship between NPAs and advances.

In order to assess the interrelationship between the advances and NPAs along with its components, we have employed correlation matrix analysis. The following Table 6.8 exhibits the matrix of correlation co-efficient among the components of NPAs and advances.

Table 6.8: Correlation Matrix of Advances and NPA Components

Variables	*Sub-Standard*	*Doubtful*	*Loss*	*NPA*	*Loans and Advances*
Sub-Standard	1				
Doubtful	–0.23 (0.71)	1			
Loss	–0.33 (1.05)	0.76 (3.51)	1		
NPA	0.24 (0.74)	0.84 (4.67)	0.76 (3.51)	1	
Loans and Advances	0.65 (2.57)	–0.55 (1.96)	–0.52 (1.84)	–0.23 (0.71)	1

$t_{0.05}$ (9df.) = 1.833 & $t_{0.01}$ (9 df.) = 2.821

Source: Calculated by the researchers.

The negative correlation between advances and NPAs (–0.23) is statistically not significant at 5 per cent and 1 per cent level of significance. This indicates that there is lethargic relationship between the growth of advances and the growth of NPAs. The negative '*r*' values of advances with doubtful assets (-0.55) and loss assets (–0.52) is significant at 5 per cent level but not at 1 per cent while with sub-standard assets (0.65) is not statistically significant at 1 per cent level. This indicates that with the increase in NPAs, doubtful assets and sub-standard assets and loss assets increased but the increasing rates are not followed by the rate of increase of advances.

8.4. Interrelationship Between Growth of Advances and Growth of NPAs

A comparison of growth of standard assets, non-performing assets and advances per branch is presented in Table 6.9. For the purpose of comparison, the total advances, NPAs and standard assets per office and their standard deviation and skewness has been calculated. It is observed that positive skewness value of standard assets and advances indicates the more allocation of credit for the economic development. The negative skewness of NPA per branch gives the message for a reducing propensity of the level of NPAs in future years. The standard deviation analysis implies that the NPA per branch throughout the years associated with lower deviation than that of advances and standard assets. Hence, the MRB has committed towards reduction of the level of NPAs in the post merger period.

Table 6.9: Standard Asset and Non-Performance Asset of MRB

(Amount ₹ in thousand)

Year	Total Advances	Advances Per Branch	Standard Asset	Standard Asset Per Branch	Total NPA	NPA Per Branch
2000-01	3,03,392	5,948.86	1,85,741	3641.98	1,17,651	2306.88
2001-02	3,52,205	6,905.98	2,27,210	4455.10	1,24,995	2450.88
2002-03	4,06,167	7,964.06	2,69,851	5291.20	1,36,316	2672.86
2003-04	4,62,522	9,069.06	3,26,242	6396.90	1,36,280	2672.13
2004-05	5,42,438	10,636.04	3,93,377	7713.28	1,49,062	2922.78
2005-06	6,66,700	13,072.55	5,16,436	10126.20	1,50,264	2946.35
2006-07	8,25,357	16,183.47	6,54,894	12841.06	1,70,463	3342.41
2007-08	9,73,316	19,084.63	8,20,058	15770.35	1,53,258	2947.27
2008-09	11,86,477	23,264.26	10,93,366	20247.52	93,112	1727.98
2009-10	16,04,869	29,179.44	14,99,551	27264.56	1,05,318	1914.87
2010-11	21,61,545	37,268.02	20,27,885	34963.53	1,33,660	2304.48
Std Devi	**559159.5**	**9636.2**	**564493.1**	**9737.2**	**21414.0**	**459.0**
Skewness	**1.291**	**1.042**	**1.298**	**1.137**	**-0.309**	**–0.289**

Source: Calculated by the researchers on the basis of the Annual Reports of MRB.

An attempt has been made to determine whether growth of advances per branch is associated with growth of NPAs per branch of MRBs. In this connection, we have used coefficient of correlation (*r*) between advances per branch and NPAs per branch during 2000-01 to 2010-11. The '*r*' value is found as under:

$$r = -0.41$$
$$t = \text{(cal) } 1.35$$
$$t_{0.05}\text{ (9 df.)} = 1.833 \text{ (tab)}$$
$$t_{0.01}\text{ (9df.)} = 2.821 \text{ (tab)}$$

The analysis manifests that the correlation coefficient (–0.41) in respect to advances per office and NPA per office of MRB is negative. This implies that there is a discouraging relationship between advances per branch and NPAs per branch. In other words, it can be argued that high volume of advances does not lead to increase in the volume of NPAs.

8.5. Interrelationship between NPA and Priority Sector Advances

Due to non-availability of information relating to priority sector NPAs and non-priority sector NPAs in MRB, an attempt has been made hereunder to study the relationship, (a) between NPA and priority sector advances, and (b) NPA and non-priority sector advances to identify with contribution of the same to total NPA of MRB. Table 6.10 presents the position of the variables relating to non-performing assets and priority, non-priority sector advances per bank branch.

Table 6.10: Priority Sector, Non-Priority Sector Advances and NPA of MRB (As on March)

(Amount ₹ in Thousand)

Year	*NPA (₹)*	*Priority Sector Lending (₹)*	*Non-Priority Sector Lending (₹)*	*NPA Per Branch (₹)*	*Priority Sector Lending per Branch (₹)*	*Non-Priority Sector Lending per Branch (₹)*
2001	1,17,651	71,450	52,166	2,306.88	1,400.98	1,022.86
2002	1,24,995	78,646	73,515	2,450.88	1,542.08	1,441.47
2003	1,36,316	77,281	94,367	2,672.86	1,515.31	1,850.33
2004	1,36,280	97,531	92,580	2,672.16	1,912.37	1,815.29
2005	1,49,062	1,20,051	1,28,543	2,922.78	2,353.94	2,520.45
2006	1,50,264	2,01,848	1,34,775	2,946.35	3,957.80	2,642.65
2007	1,70,463	2,58,688	1,54,011	3,342.41	4,974.77	2,961.75
2008	1,53,258	2,73,253	1,94,927	2,947.27	5,060.24	3,609.76
2009	93,112	3,92,945	3,30,195	1,724.30	7,144.45	6,003.55
2010	1,05,318	5,39,552	3,78,190	1,914.87	9,302.62	6,520.52

Source: Annual Report of MRB, Various Issues.

For the purpose of the analysis, we have calculated '*r*' between (a) NPAs per branch and priority sector advances per branch (b) NPA per branch and non-priority sector advances per branch for the period 2000-01 to 2010-11. The results obtained are summarized as under –

Correlation Values

	Variables	*Correlation Value (r)*	*Calculated 't' Value*
1.	NPA per Branch and Priority Sector Lending per Branch	–0.41	1.28
2.	NPA per Branch and Non-Priority Sector Lending per Branch	–0.54	1.82

$t_{0.05}$ (8df.) = 1.860 & $t_{0.01}$ (8 df.) = 2.896

The analysis shows that the negative correlations –0.41 and –0.54 are statistically not significant at 1 per cent and 5 per cent level of significance for NPAs with priority sector advances and for NPAs with non-priority sector advances. This implies that with the increase of priority sector lending, there has not been corresponding increase in the volume of NPAs. However, it cannot be argued that priority sector lending is the sole factor in enhancing the volume of NPAs in the area under study. In other words, with the increase in priority sector lending per branch, the level of NPA per branch has declined. This has again confirmed by the fact that a significant reduction of NPAs to total advances of MRB to 6.18 per cent from 38.78 per cent during 2000-01 to 2010-11. Hence, the hypotheses "bank's exposure to priority sector advances lead to increase in NPA level of MRB" found to be incorrect.

8.6 NPA and Provisions Management in MRB

The provisioning of NPAs tends to follow a frequent pattern. Table 6.11 shows provisions maintained by the MRB against its non-performing assets. From Table 6.11, it may be observed that the aggregate amount of provision maintained by the bank against its NPA was ₹ 6,198 thousand in 2000-01 which increased to ₹ 29,025 thousand in 2010-11. Over the years, there has been 4.68 times increase in the provisions maintained by the MRB against its non-performing assets. In case of percentage of provisions against NPA, it was 5.27 per cent in 2000-01 which increased to 21.72 per cent in 2010-11. It indicates that over the years the percentage of provisions maintained by the MRB is striking. This again reveals the banks imitativeness and sensitiveness for management of NPA.

Table 6.11: NPA and Provisions in MRB

(Amount ₹ in Thousand)

Year	Provisions made against NPAs	% of provisions against NPA at the end of the year
2000-01	6,198	5.27
2001-02	10,594	8.48
2002-03	4,750	3.48
2003-04	8,732	6.41
2004-05	5,196	3.49
2005-06	6,780	4.51
2006-07	5,745	3.37
2007-08	8,328	5.43
2008-09	2,324	2.49
2009-10	8,243	7.83
2010-11	29,025	21.72

Source: Annual Reports of Meghalaya Rural Bank

8.7 Relationship of NPA, Profitability and Productivity of MRB

The NPA per branch of MRB was ₹ 2306.88 thousand in 2000-01 has increased till 2006-07 and reached to ₹ 3342.41 thousand and thereafter started to decline and reached to ₹ 2304.48 thousand in 2010-11. The MRB in the state mainly rely on loans and advances as source of income. As a result, the profitability of the bank has increased. The profit per branch and business per branch has increased but NPA per branch of MRB has roughly been identical amount throughout the period. This indicates that MRB is able to control the fresh accretion of the quantum of NPAs. Table 6.12 delineates the facts.

A further enquiry on impact of NPAs on profitability of bank has been undertaken particularly to verify whether NPAs has any influence for reducing the quantum of profits. In order to examine the impact of NPAs on profitability and productivity of MRB, the correlation analysis is employed between the– (a) profit per branch and NPA per

Table 6.12: NPA, Profits and Business of MRB

(Amount ₹ in Thousand)

Year	*NPA per branch*	*Profit per branch*	*Business per branch*
2000-01	2306.88	514.92	29993.82
2001-02	2450.88	759.35	34988.02
2002-03	2672.86	608.02	38433.16
2003-04	2672.13	433.96	43542.14
2004-05	2922.78	292.98	53757.53
2005-06	2946.35	378.88	62172.25
2006-07	3342.41	684.29	71112.59
2007-08	2947.27	1138.79	79483.92
2008-09	1727.98	2139.22	96776.33
2009-10	1914.87	2115.67	125962.52
2010-11	2304.48	2067.53	154064.36

Source: Calculated on the basis of Annual Report of MRB, Various Issues

branch, (b) business per branch and NPAs per branch for the period of 11 years i.e., from 2000-01 to 2010-11. The results of correlations are—

Correlation between NPA, Profitability and Productivity

Variables	*Correlation Value (r)*	*Calculated 't' Value*
(a) NPA per Branch and Profit per Branch	–0.73	3.17
(b) NPA per branch and Business per branch	–0.40	1.30
$t_{0.05}$ (9df.) = 1.833 and $t_{0.01}$ (9 df.) = 2.821		

Source: Calculated by the researchers.

The correlation coefficient between NPA per branch and profit per branch found to be –0.73, is highly negative and statistically significant at both 5 per cent and 1 per cent level of significance. It indicates that NPA has some negative impact on bank's profits. In fact, the level of NPA adversely affects the profitability of bank. In other words, per branch increase in NPAs resulted a decline in per branch profits. Hence, it may be inferred that the profitability of banks has been affected by the level of NPAs. The negative correlation coefficient value between NPA per branch and business per branch is statistically not significant at both 5 per cent and 1 per cent level of significance indicated that NPA has negative impact on bank's productivity. In other words, with per branch increase in NPAs the per branch productivity has declined. Hence, it may be inferred that the total business (deposit plus advances) has also been affected by the high level of NPAs of MRB.

Notes

1. Trivedi, J.H. (2012) "A Study of Business Operation of RRBs of Gujrat", *International Journal of Research in Computer Applications and Management*, 2(2): 85-86.
2. Sinha, R.P. (2006), "Asset Quality and Bank Efficiency: A Non-Parametric Approach", Kumar, C.V (Ed.) *Advances in Business and Finance Studies*, 2006, ICFAI University Press, III: 1-20.
3. Reddy, B.K, Babu, P.P., Mullikarjuna, V and Viswanathan, P. (2006), "Non-Performing Assets of Public Sector Banks: An Investigation", *ICFAI Journal of Financial Economics*, IV(1): 69-79.
4. Government of India (1991), Report of the Committee on Financial System 1991 (Narasimham Committee), Ministry of Finance, p. 54.
5. Sikidar, S. (1997), "Computation of NPA, Income Recognition and Impact on Reporting of Bank Account", *The Management Accountant*, (November), p. 811.
6. Shajahan, K.M. (1998); "Non-Performing Assets of Banks: Have They Really Declined? And on Whose Account", *Economic and Political Weekly*, (March 21), pp. 671.
7. RBI Tightens NPA Recognition Norm, *The Economic Times*, November 2001.
8. Bank of International Settlements, (2010a); "Basel-III: A Global Regulatory Framework for More Resilient Banks and Banking Systems." Available at http://www.bis.org/list/basel3/index.htm (Date of visit: 23/3/2011).
9. Cosimano, F.T. and Hakura, S. D. (2011); "Bank Behaviour in Response to Basel-III:A Cross Country Analysis" *International Monetary Fund Working Paper* WP/11/119, (May).
10. Hosmani, S.B. (2002); *Performance of Regional Rural Banks*, Anmol Publications Pvt. Ltd, New Delhi, pp. 182-83
11. Raul, R.K. (2004); "NPA Menace and ARCs: An Assessment in Indian Context", *The Management Accountant*, June, pp. 471-476.

12. Pati, A.P. (2005); *Regional Rural Banks in Liberalized Environment*, Mittal Publications, New Delhi, p. 121.
13. Singh, N.T. and Singh T.J. (2009); "Recovery Performance of RRBs: A Case Study of Manipur Rural Bank", *Journal of Accounting and Finance*, 23(1):66-74, October 08 – March 09.
14. Akhan, J.A. (2009); "Non-Performing Assets Management of Non-Banking Financial Companies: Introspection", *The Management Accountant*, (February).
15. Ghosh. D. and Ghosh, S. (2011); "Management of Non-Performing Assets in Public Sector Banks: Evidence From India", *International Conference on Management (ICM 2011)* (Proceeding).
16. Unny. P.M. (2011); *A Study on the Effectiveness of Remedies Available For Banks in a Debt Recovery Tribunal—A Case Study on Ernakulam DRT*, Centre for Public Policy Research Kochi, Kerala, 682 020 India.
17. Yadab, S.M. (2011); "Impact of Non-Performing Assets on Profitability and Productivity of Public Sector Banks In India" *Afbe Journal*, 4 (1) (June).
18. Poongavanam, S (2011); "Non-Performing Assets: Issues, Causes and Remedial Solution", *Asian Journal of Management Research*. Online Open Access Publishing Platform for Management Research, 2(1).
19. Kumar, R. and Manoj, S. (2011); "Rural banking in Himachal Pradesh: A Comparative Study of Himachal Gramin Bank and Parvatiya Gramin Bank", *Political Economy Journal of India*, (January-July, 2011).
20. RBI (2010-11); Trend and Progress of Banking in India, Mumbai.
21. NABARD, Annual Report, Various issues.
22. The committee on banking sector reforms (Narasimham Committee, 1998) suggested for constitutions of Asset Reconstruction Companies (ARC) for taking over the NPAs of banks which carry high NPA portfolio. The ARC is wrapped up in considerable ambiguity. It is to be noted that Indian banking system suffers from lack of inappropriate legal system for quick recovery of bank dues. The DRTs were set up to expedite disposal of high value claims of banks.
23. The problem of NPA is multidimensional and unless the same is checked and its level is brought down to international standard of 2-3 per cent of total loan assets the whole banking sector will definitely lose its grip in the competitive market. In this respect, the Securitization and Reconstruction of Financial Assets and Enforcement of Security Interest Act, 2002 is an important landmark in Indian banking scenario. With the passage of the Act, the banks and the Financial Institution (FIs) have been quick to initiate action against the defaulters on loans. The SRFAESI Act 2002, has given the much strong weapon to the

bankers, to fight the menace of NPAs and redress a historic imbalance between lenders and borrowers.

24. Loan recovery was calculated as the ratio of collection over demand. Since loan losses were seldom written off due to inappropriate asset classification and rescheduling policies, official estimates of may have overstated loan losses.

7

Findings and Suggestions

The foregoing discussions and analyses revealed various lacunas and rising issues relating to the performance of RRBs in general and MRB in particular covering almost all the important aspects of bank's performance. This final Chapter 7, brings the major findings pertaining to the performance of MRB in the context of ongoing RRB restructuring strategies. The chapter has been summarized into three parts viz, (a) the background, (b) major findings and hypotheses verifications, and (c) suggestions for future action.

1. Introduction

The genesis of the RRBs can be traced to the need for a stronger institutional arrangement for providing rural credit. The Narasimham Committee conceptualized the creation of RRBs in 1975 as a new set of regionally oriented rural banks, which would combine the local feel and familiarity of rural problems characteristic of cooperatives with the professionalism and large resource base of commercial banks. Subsequently, the RRBs were set up through the promulgation of RRB Act of 1976. RRBs were supposed to evolve as specialized rural financial institutions for developing the rural economy by providing credit to small and marginal farmers, agricultural labourers, artisans and small entrepreneurs. Over the years, the RRBs, which are often viewed as the small man's bank, have taken deep roots and have become a sort of inseparable part of the rural credit structure. They have played a key role in rural institutional financing in terms of geographical coverage, clientele outreach and business volume as also contribution to development of the rural economy. A remarkable feature of their performance over the past three decades has been the massive expansion of their retail network in rural areas. From a modest beginning of 6 RRBs with 17 branches covering 12 districts in December 1975, the numbers have grown into 196 RRBs with 14,446 branches working in 518 districts across the country in March 2004. Government of India initiated the process of structural consolidation of RRBs by amalgamating RRBs sponsored by the same bank within a State as per the recommendations of various committees. The amalgamated RRBs were expected to provide better customer service due to better infrastructure, computerization of branches, pooling of experienced work force, common publicity marketing efforts, etc. and also derive the benefits at large area of operation, enhanced credit exposure limits and more diverse banking activities.

As a result of the amalgamation, the number of RRBs was reduced from 196 to 133 as on March, 2006 and further to 82 RRBs with 15,658 branches operating in 621 districts as on March 2011. The population served per branch of RRBs is interestingly high i.e., roughly 84.6 thousand in 2000-01 which slightly improved and figured at 77.3 thousand populations served per branch in 2010-11. The scenario is extremely terrible while compared with the population per branch of commercial bank as a whole which covered 18 thousand populations by each branch during 2010-11. The average deposit per branch in 2000-01 was ₹ 2.59 crore which has gone up to ₹ 10.47 crore per office during the year 2010-11. The scenario of deposit per branch of Indian commercial banks is much higher than the RRB as a whole during the same span. The figure for commercial banks as a whole increased from ₹ 14.56 crore in 2000-01 to ₹ 44.65 crore in 2010-11. The per branch advances of RRBs was ₹ 1.10 crore in 2000-01 which has increased to ₹ 6.27 crore in 2010-11. The RRBs are not in a position deploy credit for socio-economic development alike commercial banks in India as the credit per office of RRBs is much lower while compared the figure for credit per commercial banks in India throughout the period. The credit per commercial bank branches increased to ₹ 41.55 crore in 2010-11 from ₹ 7.79 crore in 2000-01.

Thus, under the amalgamation process, a number of RRBs have been amalgamated but the branches have increased. The credit deposit ratio of RRBs has increased from 46.3 per cent in March 2004 to

59.6 per cent in March 2011. The RRBs have a large branch network in the rural area forming around 43 per cent of the total rural branches of commercial banks. The rural orientation of RRBs is formidable with rural and semi-urban branches constituting over 97 per cent of their branch network. The growth in the branch network has enabled the RRBs to expand banking activities in the un-banked areas and mobilize rural savings. The mandate of promoting bank with a rural focus, however, would be an enduring phenomenon only when the financial health of the RRBs is sound. With built in restrictions on their operations, it is common to expect that the financial health of the RRBs itself would be a matter of concern.

As regards to their financial status, during the year 2003-04, 163 RRBs earned profits amounting to ₹ 953 crore while 33 RRBs incurred losses to the tune of ₹ 184 crore. The aggregate income of RRBs during 2007-08 grew by 20 per cent on account of higher interest as well as non-interest income. The growth in expenditure during the year was relatively subdued. As a result, profitability of RRBs improved significantly. RRBs earned a net profit of ₹ 1,374 crore in March 2008 as compared to ₹ 625 crore in previous year. (Out of 90 RRBs, 82 RRBs earned a combined profit of ₹ 1,429 crore whereas 8 RRBs incurred a combined loss of ₹ 55 crore during 2007-08. The branch productivity (business per branch) of RRBs has increased from ₹ 4.48 crore in March 2003 to ₹ 16.74 crore in March 2011. Furthermore, non-performing assets of the RRBs in absolute terms stood at ₹ 3,299 crore as on March 2004. The percentage of net NPAs was 8.51 per cent during the year ending March 2004 reduced to 1.80 per cent in March 2010.

Given the multi-agency share holding and various restructuring strategies of RRBs introduced from time to time, the banks are under severe pressure to improve their foundation with a view to attain competitiveness. Given the attention at the policy level to restructure the RRBs, it is necessary that the functioning of RRBs be analyzed separately than the RRBs as a whole so that it helps in policy formulation. The present study is an attempt to enquire into such factors that influence the working of the RRBs in general and MRB in particular. This final chapter however, is an attempt to present the summery of the main findings, hypotheses verifications and suggestions. This chapter has been summarized into three parts viz.,

- Background,
- Major Findings and Hypotheses Verifications,
- Proposed suggestions.

2. Background

The foregoing observation clearly reveals that RRBs have moved away from the conditions and compulsions that were prevailing at the time of RRBs in 1975. Hence, the researchers are ventured with an investigation on the performance of RRBs in the present scenario. Having realised the need and significance of RRBs, the proposed study undertaken in MRB i.e., RRB of Meghalaya and sets forth the following specific objectives:

1. To study the growth performance of MRB in terms of branch expansion, deposit mobilization, credit channelization, C/D ratio in the context of RRB as a whole.
2. To examine the efficiency in respect of profitability and productivity of MRB on the basis of selected parameters.
3. To study the asset quality and the level of NPAs of MRB over the years.

The following hypotheses have been framed for the purpose of the study:

- MRB has made a special dent in the banking operation in Meghalaya over the years.
- Despite the onslaught of openness measures adopted in banking sector, MRB is performing efficiently.

However, suitable operational hypotheses have been framed in appropriate places to meet the objectives of the proposed study.

The research population comprised of the RRBs operating in the state of Meghalaya for the proposed study. As on March 2011 there is only one RRB i.e., Meghalaya Rural Bank with 58 number of branches operating in six districts of Meghalaya. The bank was established on 29th December 1981 under the RRBs Act 1976 as a joint undertaking of Government of India, the Government of

Meghalaya and the State Bank of India with the share capital at the ratio of 50: 15: 35. Prior to 1st May 2007, the name of this RRB was '*Ka Bank Nonkyndong Ri Khasi Jaintia*'. As per power conferred by sub-section (1) Section (3) of the RRB Act 1976 (21 of 1976) Department of Economic Affairs (Banking Division), Ministry of Finance, Government of India, in its notification dated 1st May 2007 substituted the name "*Ka Bank Nonkyndong Ri Khasi Jaintia*" as "Meghalaya Rural Bank". As on 2010-11, the East Khasi Hill constituted 25 number of branches, West Khasi Hills 14 branches, Jaintia Hills 13, Ri Bhoi district 4, West Garo Hill and East Garo Hill districts are having 1 branches in each district.

For the purpose of the proposed study, we have considered all the branches particularly for the analysis of working and efficiency of the bank. The sources of data collection are financial statements compiled by the head office of Meghalaya Rural Banks, RBI bulletin, RBI Annual Reports, RBI Trend and Progress of Banking in India, Annual Reports of Meghalaya Rural Bank, Annual Reports of NABARD, Directorate of Economics and Statistics, various reports, surveys, published and unpublished research papers and dissertations.

To assess the growth performance of the bank, we have taken the variables like total deposits, total advances, and credit deposit ratio. The variables like net profit, paid up capital plus retained earnings, advances outstanding, loan recovered etc have been considered for measuring the efficiency of bank. The variables includes interest earned, interest paid, manpower expenses, non-interest income, spread, burden, cost responsiveness, return on working fund, volume of business (deposit plus advances), labour productivity and branch productivity for assessing the profitability and productivity of banks. To assess the nature of unbridled virus of NPAs of bank, the variables considered are net and gross NPA, total standard asset, doubtful and loss asset. The variables for identifying the determinants of NPAs includes priority sector lending, capital adequacy ratio, net NPA to net advances, branch expansion and credit deposit ratio.

The financial ratios and statistical techniques have been used to test the proposed hypotheses of the study. The statistical techniques viz, correlation co-efficient, regression analysis, skewness, measure of central tendency and dispersion have been used. The parametric test i.e., '*t*' test, has been considered to test significance level in appropriate cases. The most popularly used financial ratios have been used which include return on assets, return on equity, net profit per employee, liquid asset ratio, advances to total assets, interest income, non-interest income, spread, burden, slippage ratio, NPA accretion ratio and so on.

The growth performance of banks has been tested with compound annual growth rate analysis. The correlation coefficient between incremental deposits and incremental advances has been used to find out the nature of growth of deposit as well as credit. Besides this, whether banks are deploying credit at the same rate what they have mobilized, researcher visited the branch managers of the bank for collecting necessary information and has discussed with them the present position, weaknesses, the problem being faced by them and future role of branch for the development of the operational area. The correlation matrix analysis has been employed to assess the relationship between advances and NPAs alongwith its components viz, sub-standard assets, doubtful assets and loss assets. The regression models have also been fitted in appropriate places.

3. Major Findings

On the basis of the analysis on the performance of MRB in the context of their feat of RRBs as whole, the important findings are summarised as under:

1. It is found that the branch expansion of MRB is not up to the mark as only 7 number of branches added during 11 years considered. There were 51 branches of MRB in 2000-01 functioning in the state whose number has increased to 58 in 2010-11. Although initiatives have taken in the area of renovation of branches with a view to improve the public image, the bank has not set up any satellite branch or extension counter. Roughly 50 per cent of the branches are computerised.
2. The study found that the existing branches of MRB are inadequate to serve the population in the area under study. Therefore, major areas are still remaining not served by the

MRB and the rural masses are yet to access the banking services. It is further confirmed by the analysis relating to the population per branch. The population served per branch of MRB is 58.1 thousand in 2000-01 which slightly improved and figured at 51.1 thousand population served per branch in 2010-11. The scenario is relatively better while compared with the population per branch of RRBs as a whole which covered 77.3 thousand populations by each branch during 2010-11.

3. The number of employee per branch found to be very low i.e., around 3 to 4 persons throughout the period due to the abolition of clerical cadre by converting the staff into multipurpose workers. The staff norms i.e., 4.2 number of staff per branch as recommended by Agarwal Committee (2000), has not been achieved by MRB till 2009-10. In 2000-01, the average number of employees per office was 3.6 which has risen to 3.9 in 2009-10 and a further increase of 4.4 during the year 2010-11.
4. The MRB have been doing at par with the RRBs in terms of mobilization of deposits. The amount of deposit per branch for MRB was ₹ 2.4 crore in 2000-2001 which has increased to ₹ 11.6 crore in 2010-11. The same for RRBs was ₹ 2.59 crore in 2000-01 which has gone up to ₹ 10.47 crore per office during the year 2010-11. However, scenario of per capita deposits indicates that MRB is performing better than the RRBs as a whole. The per capita deposit of MRB increased from ₹ 0.41 thousand in 2000-01 to ₹ 2.28 thousand in 2010-11; the corresponding figure for RRBs increased from ₹ 0.31 thousand to ₹ 1.35 thousand.
5. The analysis relating to loans and advances per branch indicate that MRB is lagging behind the RRB's loan performance. The loans and advances per branch of MRB was ₹ 0.59 crore in 2000-01 which increased to ₹ 3.72 crore in 2010-11; the corresponding figures for RRBs was ₹ 1.1 crore in 2000-01, increased to ₹ 6.27 crore in 2010-11. It is also observed that in terms of per capita loans and advances, the MRB has been maintaining the same rate at which RRBs of the country are deploying loans and advances.

6. The credit deposit ratio of the Meghalaya Rural Bank was 30 per cent in 2000-01 which increased to 31.91 per cent in 2010-11. The C/D ratio of MRB is significantly low while compared with RRB as a whole. The same for RRBs was 41.0 per cent in 2000-01, augmented to 59.6 per cent in 2010-11. The reason of significant low ratio of MRB may be attributed to non-recovery of loans, wilful non-payer, lack of supervision of end use of bank credit, lack of implementation of bankable schemes. This exhibited poor credit absorption capacity of the entire area alongwith lack of entrepreneurial zeal to undertake viable projects.
7. The type-wise deposit analysis found that the saving account has the highest rate of growth as it has Compound Annual Growth Rate (CAGR) i.e., 19.91 per cent which is followed by term deposit (16.71), current deposit (15.73), sundries (14.47), special term deposit (11.27) and recurring deposit (10.54). The result of growth rate analysis is contradicting with RRB as a whole where the growth rate in case of current deposit is higher than any other type of deposits. This may be due to the fact that the lower income group people inhabited in rural Meghalaya who are not having proper business opportunities.
8. The correlation analysis relating to the extent of credit deployment to various occupation groups like agriculture, trade, transport operator, personal loan etc found that '*r*' values are statistically significant at their respective degree of freedom indicating that there is close relationship between the variables considered. It can thus be inferred that all the sectors are getting proportionate amount of bank credit along with the rise of total credit of the MRB. Hence, the MRB has been performing a logical and genuine credit deployment practices in the present situation considering economic development of the area from where they mobilized the fund.
9. The study found that the coefficient of correlation between priority sector and non-priority sector advances ($r = 0.46$) is neither significant at 5 per cent level nor at 1 per cent level of significance. This indicates that the increase in non-priority sector lending is not followed the growth of priority sector

lending of MRB. In other words, there exist a difference in lending practices of MRB for priority and non-priority sector. The MRB shows a reverse trend in lending to priority and non-priority sector while compared with RRBs as a whole. In case of RRB, there is no difference in lending practices of priority and non-priority sector.

10. The analysis found that the coefficient of correlation between advances and priority sector lending ($r = 0.88$) is statistically significant. It indicates that along with the increase in advances, the priority sector lending is also increasing at the same pace. The coefficient of correlation between the advances and non-priority sector lending ($r = 0.61$) is statistically significant which suggests that along with the increase in advances of the MRB, the non-priority sector lending is also increasing but not in the proportionate rate. By and large, it inferred that the MRB is giving more weightage to the priority sector than the non-priority sector by providing proportionately more advances to fulfil the motto of rural economic development of the region.
11. The analysis relating to various sub sectors of priority sector found that the highest correlation is between total priority sector lending and self-help group loans ($r = 0.88$). It indicates that along with the increase in total credit, self-help group loan is also increasing highly in comparison to other sub-sectors. The '*r*' value between total priority sector lending and transport operators ($r = 0.81$) indicated a close nexus between priority sector lending and transport operators. The lowest correlation value observed with total lending is between priority sector lending and housing ($r = 0.62$). However, highly positive correlations among the variables signify that MRB has made a special dent in the banking operation in Meghalaya over the years.
12. It is found that increase in income is higher than the increase in expenditure. As a result, the profit of the bank increased from ₹ 26,261 thousand in 2000-01 to ₹ 1,19,917 thousand in 2010-11. The profit of MRB recorded an increase of 4.57 times during the period. The scenario of growth of profits of

MRB (4.57 times) is better than the RRBs (3.37 times) as a whole.

13. It is found that the operating expenses to total expenditure swelling over the years. There has been 5.12 times increase in the operating expenditure of the MRB in comparison with 3.91 times in total expenditures. The higher rate of increase in operating expenditure of MRB may be due to infrastructural bottleneck and weak e-communication network of the area in which MRB is operating its business. Hence, an urgent step is required in this respect to control the unnecessary operating expenditure of banks.
14. The econometric analysis relating to the components of income found that positive correlation coefficient (*r*) values are statistically significant at 5 per cent and 1 per cent level at their respective degree of freedom and thereby, indicates that with the growth of total income, both interest income and non-interest income have increased in the same proportion. But the comparatively higher correlation (0.99) between total income and interest income indicates that the growth of interest income is exactly proportional to total income. This signifies a positive growth trend of income of the MRB. It may be inferred that MRB is performing as good as RRBs of the country.
15. The ratio analysis found that the profitability ratio of MRB was 2.25 per cent in 2000-01 which declined to 1.69 per cent in 2010-11. The average profitability ratio stand at 1.71 per cent is far better than the RRBs as whole i.e., 1.10 per cent. This indicates MRB is performing well as it recorded on an average yearly profit of ₹ 1.71 per hundred rupee volume of business where as RRBs recorded ₹ 1.10.
16. The regression analysis has identified that the variables i.e., priority sector lending, credit deposit ratio, operating expenses, spread, deposits and NPA as perfect determinants of profitability of MRB ($R^2 = 0.991$). The influence of individual variables has been examined with '*t*' values on individual regression coefficients. The analysis established priority sector lending and operating expenses are the major deterrents. This has confirmed the fact that MRB has

deployed more amount of loans to the priority sector and spend a huge amount of money for its recovery which leads to increase the operating expenditure of banks. However, the negative regression coefficients of CD ratio (–2645.03), deposits (–0.067) and NPA (–2.361) implies that more exposure of banks towards lending activities, higher amount of mobilization of deposits and the level of NPAs are the determinants of profitability.

17. It is found that the MRB maintained the similar trend of business growth of per employee with business growth of RRBs per employee. The business per employee of MRB was ₹ 8,358.93 thousand in 2000-01 which increased to ₹ 34,905.21 thousand in 2010-11. The corresponding figures for RRB were ₹ 7,500 thousand which swelled to ₹ 40,400 thousand.
18. The MRB is also doing better in terms of volume of business per branch while compared with RRBs a whole. The business per branch of MRB was ₹ 29,993.82 thousand in 2000-01 which increased to ₹ 1,54,064.36 thousand in 2010-11. The figures for business per branch of RRB was ₹ 36,900 thousand in 2000-01, swelled to ₹ 1,67,400 thousand in 2010-11. The better productivity performance of MRB is due to the fact that they are able to mobilize more deposit from the area. This indicates that the MRB is utilizing efficiently the resources that they mobilized.
19. The high positive '*r*' values for both the parameters i.e., business per employee and business per branch indicate a close relationship between MRB and RRBs in respect of their productivity performance. It is observed that MRB is performing as good as RRBs as a whole particularly for acquiring business per bank branch and business per employee during 2000-01 to 2010-11. It means that the MRB in the state of Meghalaya is performing its volume of business at par with RRB of the country.
20. The productivity analysis relating to return on investment found that the average return on investment is 2.20 per cent throughout the period. The average profit as percentage of business volume of MRB (1.39%) is better than the RRBs

as a whole (i.e., 0.78%). This is a positive sign for the MRB operating in rural Meghalaya. The analysis also found that although MRB has been doing relatively better than that of the RRBs, there has been a wide variation in the productivity which might have adverse effect on profitability of the bank. This variation may be due to lesser involvement of banks in profitable activities, wicked nature of rural clients for non-repayment of loans and advances they obtain.

21. The loan recovery performance of MRB has improved. The figure was 43.18 per cent in 2000-01 which increased to 78.8 per cent in 2010-11. Hence, it confirms the fact that the MRB is doing a reasonably better management of its recovery of loans. However, MRB is lagging behind in its recovery position while compared with the RRBs of the country. As on March 2010, average recovery of RRB was 80.03 per cent while the same for MRB was 78.22 per cent.
22. It has been observed that the recovery position was poor in farm sector than that of the non-farm sector. In 2000-01, it was 17.61 per cent for farm sector and 63.47 per cent for non-farm sector. The lower recovery indicates erosion of banks profitability and blocking up bank credit from developmental projects of the area. The gravity of the situation is cleared when we find ₹ 1,57,594 thousand (64.37%) was realized against the total outstanding dues of ₹ 2,44,835 thousand under farm sector and ₹ 5,26,593 thousand (84.46%) against the total outstanding dues of ₹ 6,23,463 thousand under non-farm sector during 2010-11.
23. The reasons for poor recovery may also be attributed to various other factors such as lack of supervision of end use of fund, defective processing of loan applications, communication gap between banker and customer, etc. In the absence of any suitable step for recovery from the loans sanctioning authority, the loan is never recovered and it becomes difficult to pay back by the borrowers due to heavy amount. As a result, the mounting over-dues restricted the bank's lending capacity.
24. The matrix of correlation coefficient analysis found that the negative correlation between advances and NPAs (–0.23) is

statistically not significant at 5 per cent and 1 per cent level of significance. This indicates that there is lethargic relationship between the growth of advances and the growth of NPAs. The negative '*r*' values of advances with doubtful assets (–0.55) and loss assets (–0.52) is significant at 5 per cent level but not at 1 per cent while with sub-standard assets (0.65) is not statistically significant at 1 per cent level. This indicates that with the increase in NPAs, doubtful assets and sub-standard assets and loss assets have increased but the increasing rates are not followed by the rate of increase of advances.

25. The growth of advances and growth of NPA has been assessed with coefficient of correlation (*r*) between advances per branch and NPAs per branch during 2000-01 to 2010-11. The analysis found that the correlation coefficient (–0.41) in respect to advances per office and NPA per office of MRB is negative. This implies that there is a discouraging relationship between advances per branch and NPAs per branch. In other words, it can be argued that high volume of advances does not lead to increase in the volume of NPAs.
26. It is found that the profitability of MRB has been affected by the level of NPAs. The correlation coefficient between NPA per branch and profit per branch found to be –0.73, is highly negative and statistically significant at both 5 per cent and 1 per cent level of significance. It indicates that NPA has some negative impact on bank's profits. In fact, the level of NPA adversely affects the profitability of bank. In other words, per branch increase in NPAs resulted a decline in per branch profits.
27. The negative correlation coefficient value between NPA per branch and business per branch is statistically not significant indicates that NPA has negative impact on bank's productivity. In other words, with per branch increase in NPAs, the per branch productivity has declined. Hence, it may be inferred that the total business (deposit plus advances) has also been affected by the high level of NPAs of MRB.

4. Hypotheses Verifications

Further, major findings of the study related to the testing of following operational hypotheses are:

1. The hypothesis that "There is no difference in the growth of deposit as well as the growth of credit of MRB" is tested with correlation analysis and found as correct. The high correlation ($r = 0.997$) value between deposit per office and advances per office are statistically significant at 1 per cent and 5 per cent level of significance. This confirms that over the years deposit per office and advance per office of MRB has been increasing in the same proportion. The high correlation coefficient undoubtedly indicates more savings habit of the people as well as higher volume of credit deployment of MRB in the area.
2. The hypothesis that "The MRB is mobilizing the deposits at par with RRB over the years" found valid. The correlation analysis shows high correlation ($r = 0.83$) between the incremental deposit per office of RRBs and the incremental deposit per office of MRB is statistically significant. This indicates that the MRB is mobilizing the deposits at the same rate what the RRB at the national level does.
3. The hypothesis that, "There exists a close relationship between the extent of credit channelization of MRB as well as RRBs" found to be correct. The highly positive correlation ($r = 0.93$) between the incremental loans and advances per branch in the RRBs of India and the per branch loans and advances of MRB is significant both at 1 per cent and 5 per cent level of significance. It indicates that along with the increase in incremental credit in the national level RRBs, the incremental credit in the MRB is also increasing at the same pace. This implies that MRB has maintained the national tempo of credit channelization of rural banks. In other words, MRB is deploying credit for the economic growth of the area from which they have mobilized funds.
4. The hypothesis that "Incremental volume of business has a direct and positive bearing on the profitability of MRBs"

has examined the relationship between the volume of business and profitability growth of MRB and tested with correlation analysis between incremental volume of business and incremental profits during the period 2000-01 to 2010-11. The '*r*' value found to be 0.156 indicates low relationship between the variables and statistically not significant at 8 degree of freedom. It indicates that the volume of business does not have direct bearing on the volume of profits of MRB. Thus, the hypothesis is found to be incorrect. It may be inferred that with the increase in volume of business, the quantum of profits are not increasing at the same pace.

5. The hypothesis that, "Incremental expenditure has a negative impact on the profitability of MRB" has been tested with the analysis of correlation '*r*' between incremental amount of expenditure and incremental amount of profits during 2000-01 to 2010-11. The analysis found that there exist a low positive correlation ($r = 0.29$) between incremental expenditure and the incremental profits of MRB is not significant. It indicates that the MRB has not yielded higher profit due to an increase in expenditure over the years. Thus hypothesis is found to be true indicating thereby that incremental expenses have mounted over the years and not resulted in increasing volume of profits.
6. The hypothesis that "Incremental flow of total income has a direct and positive bearing on the profitability of MRB" found partially true. The hypothesis is tested with the help of correlation coefficient (*r*) between incremental growth of income and incremental growth profits of MRB for the period 2000-01 to 2010-11. The '*r*' value (0.61) found statistically significant at 5 per cent level but not at 1 per cent level indicates a positive relationship between incremental income and incremental profits. It indicates that total earning might have a bearing on profitability but does not have a direct impact on the profitability of MRB. It means that the increase in total income does not result in the rise of profits.
7. The hypothesis that "Bank's exposure to priority sector advances lead to increase in NPA level of MRB" found to be incorrect. The analysis established that the negative

correlations –0.41 and –0.54 are statistically not significant at 1 per cent and 5 per cent level of significance for NPAs with priority sector advances and for NPAs with non-priority sector advances respectively. This implies that with the increase of priority sector lending, there has not been corresponding increase in the volume of NPAs. However, it cannot be argued that priority sector lending is the sole factor in enhancing the volume of NPAs in the area under study. This has again confirmed by the fact that a significant reduction of NPAs to total advances of MRB to 6.18 per cent from 38.78 per cent during 2000-01 to 2010-11.

5. Suggestions for Future Action

Consequent upon the foregoing diagnosis and findings of the performance of MRB on the basis of selected parameters, the following suggestions may be offered for better performance of MRB.

1. There is also need to rationalize the branch network by consolidating the number of branches within a local area in to a single profit centre without affecting customer service to reduce the administrative expenditure. The introduction and operation of ATM facilities as per provision will boost the level of banking services in the state. Efforts may also be made for computerisation of cent per cent branches of MRB.
2. It is observed that due to limited number of employees, MRB is not in a position to compete with other commercial banks particularly for increasing its volume of business. Hence, the number of employees of MRB needs to be increased by recruiting qualified personnel for better banking services.
3. There is need of greater specialization by MRB in different niches of the market such as retail, agriculture, export and the small scale sector. Banks in the districts need a shift away from common banking to specialized banking and private banking. In order to reduce the transaction costs and increase the bank's productivity, the process of computerization and IT methods in the branches are to be accelerated.
4. The MRB in the districts under operation mainly rely on

loans and advances as source of income. It needs greater attention to the non-interest income particularly on the income from consultancy, etc. The cost consciousness among the branches needs to be developed in resource mobilization which should be guided by availability of opportunity for fund deployment in a profitable manner.

5. The MRB in consonance with and as per guidelines of RRBs should introduce new credit and deposit schemes which prove better than other banks. The service quality has to be improved so that the processing and transacting with the bank becomes faster and convenient compared to other banks.
6. The MRB should create awareness among the customers to avail different credit and deposit schemes. The proper advertisements should be given in television, newspapers, etc. so that people become aware of the products and facilities offered by the bank.
7. The MRB should insist in providing financial services such as portfolio management services under which the bank will provide suggestions and guidance to the customers regarding their investment. These will help the customers to choose the best alternative of investments where the return is maximum and the risk is minimum as compared to others.
8. For improving the profitability position, MRB should undertake an aggressive marketing of retail banking particularly consumer loan, car loans, housing loans, etc. It will ensure the return and prompt recovery of loans. The product range of banks has to be widened by introducing new loan-schemes to meet the changing needs of customers. MRB can market the products through e-commerce also.
9. The MRB is deploying more amount of loans to the priority sector and spend a huge of money for its recovery which leads to increase the operating expenditure of banks as confirmed by the regression analysis. Thus an urgent step is warranted to arrest the uncontrolled expenditure in comparison with volume of business made by MRB.
10. The interest expenses can be checked by improving the quality of deposit related services. It has been observed that customers do not mind to get a lower interest rate on deposit

if the overall quality of services and the attitude of the staffs are improved to their satisfaction. Further, there is much scope to convince the retail traders and other institutional customers to open their current account in the bank to avail of various services.

11. To solve the problem of mismatch of various components of expenditure, the disparity between manpower needed and manpower allocated should be corrected through reallocation. Since, it would not be possible to reduce various costs viz., man power and establishment cost through technological substitution, the attempt should be made on the optimum use of other type of inputs and reallocation of existing man power to increase overall effectiveness.
12. The effective steps need to be taken to increase the job satisfaction and morale of the employees. Efforts should be made to inculcate positive attitude and a feeling of conformity among them. The staff should also follow a humanistic approach to monitor, supervise and evaluate their work for enhancing productivity.
13. The analysis of various indicators of productivity reveals that there is wide disparity in profitability of MRB. The wicked nature of rural clientele in the districts resulted in lower productivity and profitability. In order to improve the performance of bank, it need to improve efficiency through introduction of electronic banking, consolidation and merger of branches; develop small and medium enterprises to catch better clientele in the area on which MRB is functioning.
14. The management must understand that to satisfy the customers, they first have to educate, train, motivate and satisfy their own staff because organizations can only meet its customer's expectations and needs only if the staffs are satisfied. Thus, MRB in this regard should inculcate proper marketing orientation in their work culture. There should be separate marketing cell which will specially deal with proper training and development of the bank staffs.
15. The mounting overdue thwarted the MRB's lending significantly in farm sector. Rare effort is made to improve the recovery performance. They are not encouraged to pay

the loan. Consequently, loan is not recovered in future; it becomes difficult to pay it back due to heavy amount. Therefore, an immediate action plan in the line of provisions made in various recovery channels is necessary to expedite the recovery position.

16. The timely edifice of loan portfolio is indispensable for effective management of NPAs of MRB. Keeping in view the present stipulation of sensitive sector where the instability is rising, the bank should diversify its services into consultancy, credit card, housing finance and insurance sector etc.
17. In the wake of expansion regime of credit although the asset quality of MRB has improved considerably, banks need to safeguard against any deterioration of credit quality. MRB need to have a comprehensive system in which the process of risk monitoring is combined with proper risk assessment.
18. The pre-arrangements must be made to contain the fresh accretion. The surest way of containing NPA is to prevent their occurrences. The tenet of this prevention policy lies on proper risk management system in bank, strong and effective credit monitoring, open and co-operative working relation between banks and borrowers.
19. The internal governing factors of banks are, possibly, responsible for current level of NPAs. The onus, therefore, rests with the bank itself. The organizational structuring, improvement in managerial efficiency, up-gradation of skilled for proper assessment of credit worthiness and a change in the bank's attitude towards legal action need to be called for.
20. The repayment ethics should be inculcated in the minds of the borrowers by optional utilization of various media i.e., television, video films, all India radio and press. The incentives could be offered to the regular payers by financing again or providing bonus or disincentives for the wilful defaulters in the form of public crime action or adverse publicity in the newspapers.

Bibliography

Books

Ahuja, H.L. (2006) *Advanced Economic Theory: Microeconomic Analysis*, Sultan Chand & Company Ltd, New Delhi, India; (14th Edition).

Batra, G.S. and Dangwal, R.C. (2005); "Management of Non-Performing Assets in RRBs" in Jain S.C. (Eds) *Management of Non-performing Assets in Banks*, RBSA Publishers, Jaipur.

Chopra, K. (1987); *Managing Profits, Profitability and Productivity in Public Sector Banking*, ABS Publication, Jalandhar.

Choudhary, A.K. (1998); *Bank Management*, Rajat Publication, New Delhi.

Desai, B.M. and N.V. Namboodiri (2001), *Organization and Management of Rural Financial Sector: Text, Cases and Exercises,* Oxford Publishing House, New Delhi.

Diwan, P. (1997); *Productivity and Technology Management*, A Pentagon Press Publication, Hari Nagar, New Delhi.

Drucker, P.F. (1980), *Managing in Turbulent Times*, New York, Harper- Row Education, New Delhi.

Green, Tull, Albaum, (1999); *Research for Marketing Decisions*, Prentice Hall Of India, New Delhi.

Gupta, L.N. (1977); *Profitability and Public Sector*, Oxford and IBH Publishing Company, New Delhi.

Gupta, M.C. (1989); *Profitability Analysis; An Empirical Approach*, Pointer Publisher, Jaipur.

Hadi, A. and Bagchi, K.K (2006); *Performance of Regional Rural Banks in West Bengal: An Evaluation*, Serial Publications, New Delhi.

Hartough, K.J. (1994); *Entrepreneurial Bankers; The Banker's Personal Action Plan for Building a Profitable Small Business Portfolio*, Probus Publishing, Chicago.

Hasan, Z. (1975); *Theory of Profit*, Vikash Publishing House Pvt. Ltd., New Delhi.

Hosmani, S.B. (2002); *Performance of Regional Rural Banks*, Anmol Publications Pvt. Ltd., New Delhi.

Indian Institute of Banking and Finance, *Risk Management,* Macmillan.

Kondle, Ramesh (1986), *Lead Bank Scheme in HP: Progress and Prospectives*, Ph.D Thesis, Himachal Pradesh University, Shimla.

Kothari, C.R., (2000), *Research Methodology*, Wishwa Prakashan, New Delhi.

Krishnaswamy, Sivakumar and Mathirajan, (2006), *Management Research Methodology: Integration of Principles, Methods and Techniques*, Pearson Education, New Delhi.

Maheshwari and Maheshwari, (2004), *Banking Law and Practice*, Kalyani Publishers, New Delhi.

Nandal, R.S. and Singh, A. (2002); *Banking Infrastructure in Haryana*, Banking and Financial Sector Reform in India, Deep and Deep Publication Pvt. Ltd.

Pandey, K.L., (1968); *Development of Banking in India Since 1949*, Calcutta Scientific Book Agency, Kolkata.

Pathak, Bharti, V., (2004); *Indian Financial System*, Pearson Education, New Delhi.

Pati, A.P. (2005); *Regional Rural Banks in Liberalized Environment*, A Mittal Publication, New Delhi.

Prasad, N. (1985); *The SBI and Rural Development*, Amar Prakasan, New Delhi.

Raul, R.K., (1997); *Industrial Finance in India*, Anmol Publications, New Delhi.

Sikidar, S. (1992); *Rural Banking: An Infrastructural Input for Hill Area Development*, Anmol Publication, New Delhi.

Sikidar, S. (1990); *Economic Development of Tribal India*, Ashish Publishing House, New Delhi.

Singh, S.P. and Singh, S., (1999); *Financial Analysis for Bank Lending in Liberalized Economy*, Himalya Publishing House, Mumbai.

Sinha, R.P. (2006); Asset Quality and Bank Efficiency: A Non-Parametric Approach, Kumar, C.V. (Edn) *Advances in Business and Finance Studies, 2006*, ICFAI University Press, Hyderabad.

Tasi, K. (2006); *Role of Regional Rural Banks in Economic Development*, Eastern Book Corporation, New Delhi.

Uddin, N. (2003); *Regional Rural Banks and Development*, Mittal Publications, New Delhi.

Vashisht, A.K., (1989) *Public Sector Banks in India*, H.K. Publishers, New Delhi.

Verma, S. and Verma, S. (2002); *Determinants of Profitability of SBI Groups, Other Nationalized Banks and Foreign Banks*, Banking and Financial Sector Reforms in India, Deep and Deep Publications, New Delhi.

Zikmund William G. (2003) *Business Research Methods*, Thomson Asia Pvt. Ltd., Singapore.

Research Papers and Articles

Ahmed, J.U. (2003); "The Productivity of Public Sector Banks", *Productivity,* National Productivity Council, New Delhi.

Akhan, J.A. (2009); "Non-Performing Assets Management of Non-Banking Financial Companies: Introspection", *The Management Accountant,* (February).

Angadi, V.B. and Devraj, V.J., (1983); "Productivity and Profitability of Banks in India", *Economic and Political Weekly,* (Nov. 26), 18 (48).

Angadi, V.B. (1984); "*Some* Issues Relating to Productivity of Indian Scheduled Commercials Banks", *The Journal of the Indian Institute of Bankers,* 58 (4): 184.

Angadi, V.B. (1987); "Integrated Approach to Study of Banks Profitability", *Prajyan,* (October-December), XVI (4), 524.

Athanasoglou, P.P., Brissimis, S.N. and Delis, M.D. (2005); "Bank-Specific, Industry- Specific and Macroeconomic Determinants of Bank Profitability", *Bank of Greece, Working Paper No. 25.*

Athma, P. and Srinivas, P. (1997); "Productivity in Commercial Banks", *Productivity,* (October- November), 38 (3): 441.

Banos, J.A.L. (2007); "Rural Banks, Resource Allocation Efficiency and Regional Economic Performance," *Philippine Management Review,* 14,115-126.

Barth, J.R., Caprio, G., Levine, R. (2004); "Bank Supervision and Regulation: What Works Best?" *Journal of Financial Intermediation,* 13 (2), 205-248.

Basu, S.K. (1991); "Credit Worthiness of Purpose: A Study on RRBs", *Kurukshetra* (May).

Bell, F.W. and Nell, Mushy (1969); "Impact of Market Structure on the Price of a Commercial Banking Service", *The Review of Economics and Statistics* (May).

Bhagawati, S.K. (1999); "Credit Deposit Ratio of Commercial Banks; A Case Study of North Eastern Region", *Journal of North Eastern Council,* (April, June) 19 (2): 14-19.

Bhaskar, C.S. (2011); "Problems and Prospects of Regional Rural Banks in India", *Indian Streams Research Journal,* 1(X), 1-4.

Bose, Sukanya (2005); "Regional Rural Banks: The Past and the Present Debate", Macro Scan, *URL: http://www. macroscan. Com/fet/jul05/ fet200705RRB_Debate.htm.*(visited on 4-5-10).

Bourke, P. (1989); "Concentration and other Determinants of Bank Profitability in Europe, North America and Australia", *Journal of Banking and Finance,* 13, 65-79.

Boyd, J.H. and M. Gertler (1994), "Are Banks Dead? Or Are Reports Greatly

Exaggerated?" Federal Reserve Bank of Chicago, *Conference on Bank Structure and Competition*, May, pp. 85-117.

Chatterjee, B. and Sinha, R.P. (2006); "Intermediation Cost Efficiency: A Tale of two Bank Groups", *The IFAI Journal of Bank Management*, ICFAI University Press, Hyderabad.

Cosimano, F.T. and Hakura, S.D. (2011); "Bank Behaviour in Response to Basel-III: A Cross Country Analysis" *International Monetary Fund Working Paper* WP/11/119, (May).

Das, A. and Ghosh, S. (2004-05); "Examining Excess Capacity in Regional Rural Banks: Some Empirical Insights for India", *Prajnan,* XXXIII (4) 2004-05, NIBM, Pune.

Dash, M. and Pathak, R. (2009); "Canonical Correlation Analysis of Asset-Liability Management of Indian Banks" (June 1). Available at SSRN: http://ssrn.com/abstract=1412739 or http://dx.doi.org/10.2139/ssrn.1412739 (visited on 5/7/11).

Dhaliwal, Kaur, N. and Arora, R.S. (2009); "Profitability of Regional Rural Banks: A Study of Post Liberalization Period. (Report)", *Political Economy Journal of India*, (January).

Frei, B. and Mader, M., (2008), "*The Power of Done*", Retrieved from http://www.smartsheet. com/ productivity/chapter9 (date of visit: 10/7/10).

Frydl, E.J. (1993), "Excess Capacity in the Financial Sector: Causes and Issues", Federal Reserve Bank of New York, Studies on Excess Capacity in the Financial Sector, pp. 1-29.

Ganesh, K. (1979); " Monitoring Profitability in Banks", *The Commerce*, July 1979.

Ghosh, D. and Ghosh, S. (2011);, "Management of Non-Performing Assets in Public Sector Banks: Evidence from India", *International Conference on Management* (ICM 2011) (Proceeding).

Gorton, G. and R. Rosen (1995), "Overcapacity and Exit from Banking", Working Paper No. 36, Board of Governors of the Federal Reserve.

Greenspan, A. (1993), "FDICIA and the Future of Banking Law and Regulation", Federal Reserve Bank of Chicago, *Proceedings of the Annual Conference on Bank Structure and Competition*, May, pp. 1-8.

Haslem, J. (1968); "A Statistical Analysis of the Relative Profitability of Commercial Banks", *Journal of Finance,* Vol. 23, 167-176.

Humphrey, D.B. (1987), "Cost Dispersion and the Measurement of Economies in Banking", Federal Reserve Bank of Richmond, *Economic Review,* 73, 24-38.

Hunter, W.C. and S.G. Timme (1986), "Technical Change, Organisational Form and the Structure of Bank Production", *Journal of Money, Credit, and Banking,* 18, 152-166.

Ibrahim, M.S. (2010); "Performance Evaluation of Regional Rural Banks in India, *International Business Research,* 3(4) (Nov).

Joshi, P.N. (1999), "Banking Sector Reforms: The Other Side of Coin". *Economic and Political Weekly,*: XXXIV (14); 797-798.

Kaushik, A.C. (1999); "Productivity of RRBs Credit in Haryana", *Productivity,* 40(3): (October-December).

Khankhoje, D. and Sathye, M. (2008); "Efficiency of Rural Banks: The Case of India" *International Business Research*, 1(2): 140-149, (April).

Kondle, R. (1986); "Lead Bank Scheme in HP: Progress and Prospectives", Ph.D Thesis, Himachal Pradesh University, Shimla.

Kuchhadiya, D.B. and R.L. Shiyani (1988), "A Retrospection of Overdues of RRBs", *Agricultural Banker*, pp. 5-8.

Kumar, R. and Sharma, M. (2011); "Rural Banking in Himachal Pradesh: A comparative study of Himachal Gramin Bank and Parvatiya Gramin Bank", *Political Economy Journal of India,* (Jan-July).

Kumar, V.A. (2008); "Case for De-amalgamation of Regional Rural Banks" *Economic and Political Weekly*, 43(42):60-68, (October).

Kwast, Myron L. and John T. Rose (1982); "Pricing, Operating Efficiency and Profitability Among Large Commercial Banks", *Journal of Banking and Finance*, Vol. 6.

Leade, R., (2009), *"Productivity and Competitiveness"* Retrieved from http://www.mckinsey com/mgi/ publications/europe/profitability.asp (Date of visit, 12/04/11).

Madhumati, R. and Lakshmi, Kumar (2003), "Multifactor Evaluation and Forecasting of Bank Performance in India, *Prajnan*, XXXII (4): 317-331.

Majumder, N.A. (2001); "The New Architecture of Rural Credit System" Prof. M.L. Dantwala Monograph Series, Department of Economics, University of Mumbai, August 2001.

Malhotra, Rakesh (2002); "Performance of India's Regional Rural Banks (RRBs): Effect of the Umbilical Cord". *URL: http://www.alternativefinance.org. uk/rtf/;7rrbsmalhotra.rtf.*(visited on 23/5/11).

Miller, S. (2010),"*Profitability and Productivity Analysis*", Retrieved from http://ezinearticles.com/? Productivity-and-Productivity-Analysis&id=1033522 (Date of visit: 10.12.10).

Miller, S.M., Noulas, A.G. (1997); 'Portfolio Mix and Large-bank Profitability in the USA", *Applied Economics*, 29 (4), pp. 505-512.

Misra, B.S. (2006); "The Performance of Regional Rural Banks (RRBs) in India: Has Past anything to Suggest for Future?" *RBI Occasional Paper,* 27 (1&2): 89-119.

Molyneux, P., Thornton, J. (1992); "Determinants of European Bank Profitability: A Note", *Journal of Banking and Finance,* Vol. 16, pp. 1173-1178.

Monga, R.C. (1992), "Dynamics of Productivity Management", *Productivity,* National Productivity Council, 33 (1).

Nag, Ashok K. and Amit Mitra (2002), "Analysis of performance trajectory of Public Sector Banks in India using self organizing map", *Prajnan,* XXXI (3): 172-195.

Naidu, M.C. (2001); "Regional Rural Banks: A Review", *Yojana,* 45, -40-50.

Nambiar, P.C.D. (1980); "Banking Policy; Which Direction", *Commerce* (September-20), Vol. 13.

Nitin, Bhatt and Thorat, Y.S.P. (2004); "India's Regional Rural Banks: The Institutional Dimension of Reforms", *National Bank News Review,* NABARD, April-September.

Noor, Basha Abdul and M. Jyoti, (1989); "Viability of Regional Rural Banks with reference to Chaitanya Gramin Bank, Tenali, Andhra Pradesh", *Yojana*, May, pp. 16-31.

Parmar, G.D., R.L. Shiyani and D.B. Kuchhadiya (1988); "Performance of Banaskantha Mehsana Gramin Bank in Gujarat State", *Agricultural Banker*, pp. 24-27.

Pati, A.P. and Shome, D. (2007); "International Commitment and Transformation in Indian Banking", *Business Vision,* Serial Publication, New Delhi, 3(1): 45-61.

Perry, P., (1992); "Do Banks Gain or Lose from Inflation", *Journal of Retail Banking,* 14(2), pp. 25-30.

PNB (1986); *"Profitability and Profit Planning in Banks",* Bank Economists Meet, (Collection of Papers), New Delhi, 1986.

Poongavanam, S. (2011); "Non-Performing Assets: Issues, Causes and Remedial Solution", *Asian Journal of Management Research.* Online Open Access publishing platform for Management Research, 2(1).

Rajkumar, K.P., (2007); "The Earning Performance of Private Sector Banks During 2005-06", *The Journal of Accounting and Finance,* 21(2): 66-77.

Rammohan, T.T. and Roy, S.C. (2004); "Comparing Performances of Public and Private Sector Banks: A Revenue Maximizing Approach", *Economic and Political Weekly*, March-20, pp. 1271-76.

Rangarajan, C, (1996); "The Role of Rural Credit", *RBI Bulletin*, 1(5), May.

Rao, D.S., (2007); "Reforms in Indian Banking Sector: Evaluation Study on the Performance of Commercial Banks", *Finance India,* XXI(2) : 591-597, (June).

Rao, P.K. and S. Thomas (1992), "Performance of the Manipur Rural Bank–An Analytical Study". *Journal of Rural Development,* pp. 443-459.

Raul, R.K. (2004); "NPA Menace and ARCs: An Assessment in Indian Context", *The Management Accountant*, June, pp. 471-476.

Reddy, B. Ramachandra, Sakunthala and S. Vijayulu Reddy (1998), "Growth and Performance of Regional Rural Banks in India", *The Indian Journal of Commerce*, 51(2 & 3) : 71-76.

Reddy, A.A. (2006); "Productivity Growth in Regional Rural Banks", *Economic and Political Weekly*, March, 2006.

Reddy, B.K., Babu, P.P., Mullikarjuna, V and Viswanathan, P. (2006); "Non-Performing Assets of Public Sector Banks: An Investigation", *ICFAI Journal of Financial Economics*, IV(1): 69-79.

Reddy, D.M. and Prasad, K.V.N. (2011)," Evaluating Performance of Regional Rural Banks: An Application of Camel Model", *Research World, Journal of Arts, Science and Commerce*, II (4) Oct. 2011 [61].

Reddy, Y.V. (2001); "Address at the Conference of Indian Society of Agricultural Marketing at Vizag", (A.P) February.

Revell, J. (1979); "Inflation and Financial Institutions", *Financial Times*, London.

Sadakkadulla, J. (2007); "Regional Rural Banks and the Role of Empowered Committees", *Cab-Calling*, (October-December).

Sangwan, S.S. (1989); "Viability of Rural Credit Structure", *Prajnan*, 18(2): 213-23.

Sankariah, T. and B.B. Reddy (1994); "Recovery Performance of Rayalseema Gramin Bank, Guddapah", *Agricultural Banker*, pp. 36-48.

Sarkar, P. and Abraham, Das (1997); "Development of Composite index of banking efficiency: The Indian Case", *The Reserve Bank of India Occasional Papers*, 18(4): 679-709.

Sehgal, M. (1999); "Asset Liability Management of Indian Banks", *Banking Finance*, (Nov.), pp. 12-13.

Shah, S.G. (1979); "Bank Profitability: The Real Issues", *The Journal of the Indian Institute of Business*, July-Sep. (59) 3.

Shajahan, K.M. (1998); "Non-Performing Assets of Banks; Have They Really Declined? And on Whose Account", *Economic and Political Weekly*, (March 21), p. 671.

Shete, N.B. and G.L. Karkal (1989) "Regional Rural Banks: Problems and Perspectives of Rural Credit", *Prajnan*, Vol. 18, No. 2, April-June, pp. 131-161.

Shivappa, H. (2007); "Working of Regional Rural Banks in India," *Indian Journal of Agricultural Economics*, July 1, 2007.

Short, B.K. (1979); "The Relation between Commercial Bank Profit Rates and Banking Concentration in Canada, Western Europe and Japan", *Journal of Banking and Finance*, Vol. 3, pp. 209-219.

Shylendra, H.S (1995), "Lender Viability and Lender Behaviour: A Case Study of RRB in South India" *Saving and Development*, pp. 231-42.

Shylendra, H.S. (1996), "Institutional reform and rural poor: A study on the distributional performance of a regional rural bank", *Indian Journal of Agriculture Economics*, Vol. 51, pp. 301-14.

Sikidar, S. (1997); "Computation of NPA, Income Recognition and Impact on Reporting of Bank Account", *The Management Accountant*, (November), p. 811.

Singh, G.N., J.S. Garg, A.R. Verma and K.N. Pandey (1978), "A Critical Review of Rural Credit by Financing Institutions in Kannauj Block, District Farrukhabad: A Case Study", *Indian Journal of Agricultural Economics*, pp. 33-148.

Singh, R.K.P., Singh, R.P.N. and Singh, B. B. (1987), "Financial Viability of Commercial and Regional Rural Banks in Bihar—A case study", *The Journal of Indian Institute of Bankers*, 58 (2): 83-88.

Singh, N.T and Singh, T.J. (2009); "Recovery Performance of RRBs: A Case Study of Manipur Rural Bank", *Journal of Accounting and Finance*, 23(1): 66-74, October 08 – March 09.

Singh, S.P. (1979); "Cost of Bank Credit and Prices" *The Journal of Indian Institute of Bankers*, October-November.

Sinha, S., Tanmay, C., Orlanda, R. and Pathak, N. (2003); "The Outreach/Viability Conundrum: Can India's Regional Rural Banks Really Serve Low-Income Clients'?" *ODI Working Paper No. 229*, ODI, London.

Sinha, T. (2008); "Operational Risk Management: A Paramount Importance for Banks", *The Management Accountant*, (January).

Tarapore, S.S. (1994); "Rural Banking at Cross Roads", *RBI Bulletin*, September.

Thingalaya, N.K. (1987); "Banking Development in India Since Independence", *Pigmy Economic Review*, (August), 33 (1):1.

Trivedi, J.H. (2012), "A Study of Business Operation of RRBs of Gujarat", *International Journal of Research in Computer Applications and Management*, 2(2): 85-86.

Unny, P.M. (2011), "A Study on the Effectiveness of Remedies Available For Banks in a Debt Recovery Tribunal—A Case Study on Ernakulam DRT", *Centre for Public Policy Research* Kochi, Kerala, 682 020 India.

Uppal, R.K. (2011); "*Profitability and Productivity Analysis of Various Bank Groups in Liberalization Era: Emerging Issues*", APJRBM, Sri Krishna International Research & Educational Consortium, 2(2): (February) http://www.skirec.com (Date of visit: 16/04/11).

Varade, S.D. (1973), "Efficiency of Rural Branches an empirical pilot Study", *Prajnan*, April-June, pp. 187-203.

Yadab, S.M. (2011); "Impact of Non-Performing Assets on Profitability and Productivity of Public Sector Banks In India" *Afbe Journal*, 4 (1) (June).

Reports and Official Publications

Annual Report of Meghalaya Rural Bank, Various Issues.

Bank of International Settlements, (2010a); "Basel-III: A Global Regulatory Framework for More Resilient Banks and Banking Systems." Available at http://www.bis.org/list/basel3/index.htm (Date of visit: 23/3/2011).

GoI, The Estimates Committee (2004-05), Report of the Review of Action taken by Government on the recommendations contained in the Sixteenth Report of Estimates Committee (Thirteenth Lok Sabha), the Ministry of Finance and Company Affairs (Department of Economic Affairs -Banking Division).

Government of India, (June 2002), "Report of the Working Group to Suggest—Amendments in the Regional Rural Banks Act, 1976" (Chalapathy Rao Committee).

Government of India (1975), "Report of the Committee on Rural Banks", New Delhi.

Government of India (1991), "Report of the Committee on Financial System 1991 (Narasimham Committee)", Ministry of Finance, p. 54.

Government of India (1998); "Report on Banking Sector Reforms" (Narasimham Committee - II) Ministry of Finance.

Government of India (2006); Committee on Financial Sector Assessment (CFSA), September 2006.

IBA (2011); Performance Highlight of Banks, Various Issues.

Indian Banks' Association, Indian Banking at a Glance, 2011.

Internal Control Guidelines over Foreign Exchange Business (ICG Retrived from http://www. fedai.org.in/AnnualReports/Annual_Report_2011.pdf (viewed on 23/8/2011).

Khusro Committee (1989) "Report of Agricultural Credit Review Committee", RBI Publication, Mumbai.

NABARD Directives and Circular for All Regional Rural Banks in the country.

NABARD, Annual Report, Various issues.

PEP Committee popularly known as Productivity, Efficiency and Profitability Committee appointed by RBI under the chairmanship of J.C. Lathur, submitted its report on 1977.

RBI (1978): Report of the Committee on Rural Banks (Dantawala Committee, 1978).

RBI (1984); Report of the Working Group on Regional Rural Banks (Kelkar Committee, 1984).

RBI (1995); Report of Expert Group on Foreign Exchange Markets in India (headed by the then Executive Director of RBI, Mr. O.P. Sodhani) (June 1995), popularly known as Sodhani Committee.

RBI (1996) Report of Committee on Revamping of RRBs (Basu Committee).

RBI (2004); "Report of the Advisory Committee on Flow of Credit to Agriculture and Related Activities From the Banking System". (Vyas Committee II) URL: (www.rbi.org. in, date 20/6/2009).

RBI (2004); "Group of CMDs of Select Public Sector Banks", 2004 (Purwar Committee).

RBI (2005); "Report of the Internal Working Group on RRBs", Chairman: A.V. Sardesai, Mumbai. URL: (www.rbi.org.in), visited 24/5/2010.

RBI (2007); "Report of the Technical Group to Review Efficacy of Existing Legislative Framework Governing Money Lending and its Enforcement Machinery".

RBI (2007); "Task Force on Empowering RRB Boards for Operational Efficiency".

RBI, Trend and Progress of Banking in India, Mumbai, Various Issues.

RBI, (1997); "Report of the Expert Group on Regional Rural Banks" (Thingalaya Committee).

RBI, Asset Liability Management (ALM) Guidelines for Regional Rural Banks (RRBs) Retrieved from http://rbidocs.rbi.org.in/rdocs/content/PDFs/78978.pdf (date of visit: 04/7/11).

RBI, Basic Statistical Return of SCBs in India, Various Issues.

RBI, Directive Circular No. POT.SUCB.CIR.9/09.120.00/2001-02 Dated 2nd April 2002, p. 1 to 22.

RBI, Directive, Circular No. DBOD.No.BP.BC.94/21.04.098/98 Dated 10th September 1998.

RBI, Report of the Committee on Restructuring of RRBs (Bhandari Committee, 1994).

Report of the Banking Enquiry Commission, New Delhi, 1972.

Report of the Committee on Financials of RRBs (Chakroborthy Committee), May 2010,http://taxguru.in/rbi/recapitalization-of-regional-rural-banks-rrbs-to-improve-their-capital-to-risk-weighted-assets-ratio-crar.html

Report of the Committee on Man Power Norms in RRBs (Agarwal Committee, 2000).

Reserve Bank of India (1977); "Committee's Report on Financing of Public Sector Banks", RBI (Raj, J. as Chairman).

RRB Monitoring, Key Statistics of RRBs, 2009-10.

The Regional Rural Bank Act, 1976, Act no. 21 of 1976, 9th February, 1976.

Journals and Periodicals

Asia Pacific Journal of Research in Business Management.

Asian Journal of Finance and Accounting.

Asian Journal of Research in Banking and Finance.

Asian Management Review, Asian Association of Management.
Aura, Journal of Indian, Institute of Science and Management, Ranchi.
Banking Finance.
Business Review.
Business Vision, New Delhi.
Decision, Indian Institute of Management, Kolkata.
Economic Affairs, New Delhi Publishers.
Economic Times.
Finance India, Indian Institute of Finance, New Delhi.
Financial Express.
Harvard Business Review.
ICFAI Journal of Financial Economics, ICFAI University.
Indian Economic Panorama.
Indian Journal of Finance, University of Delhi.
Indian Management Studies Journal, Punjabi University, Patiala.
Indian Management, All India Management Association.
International Journal of Business Economics and Management Research.
International Journal of Economics.
International Journal of Financial Management, Publishing India Group.
International Journal of Management.
International Journal of Marketing and Management Research.
Journal of Accounting Research.
Journal of Banking and Finance.
Journal of Banking Financial Services and Insurance Research, Sri Krishna International Research and Educational Consortium.
Journal of Management Research, FMS, Delhi, India.
Journal of North Eastern Council, Shillong.
Journal of Objective Studies, New Delhi.
Management Convergence (An International Journal), Mizoram University.
Metamorphosis: A Journal of Management Research, IIM Lucknow, India.
Nagaland University Research Journal.
Pranjana: The Journal of Management Awareness, Integrated Academy of Management and Technology.
Productivity, National Productivity Council.
Professional Banker, ICFAI University Press.
The Accounting World, ICFAI University Press.
The Alternative, *Journal of Management Studies Research*, BIT, Mesra.
The Banker.
The Hindu.
The Journal of Indian Management and Strategy, Jagannath International Management School.
The Management Accountant, ICWAI, Kolkata.

The NEHU Journal, North Eastern Hill University.
Vikalpa: The Journal for Decision Makers, IIM, Ahmadabad.
Vision: *The Journal of Business Perspective*, MDI-Gurgaon.
Yojana, Ministry of Information and Broadcasting, India.

Index